architectural
drafting

Also by
Herbert F. Bellis and Walter A. Schmidt
"Blueprint Reading for the Construction Trades"

architectural drafting second edition

HERBERT F. BELLIS, M.E.
Professional Engineer
Formerly Director, L.I. Mondell Institute,
   Hempstead, N.Y.
Associate, Manhattan Technical Institute,
   New York, N.Y.

WALTER A. SCHMIDT
Architectural Designer
Chief Draftsman, Brundage, Cohen, Holton, and
   Kroskin, Architects, Norfolk, Va.
Formerly Director, Long Island Drafting School,
   Freeport, N.Y.
Formerly Instructor, Evening Division, State University of New York, Agricultural and Technical Institute, Farmingdale, N.Y.

McGraw-Hill Book Company
New York   St. Louis   San Francisco   Düsseldorf   London   Mexico
Panama   Rio de Janeiro   Singapore   Sydney   Toronto

Architectural Drafting

Library of Congress Catalog Card Number 77-133389
07-004418-X
   4567890BABA79876

*This book was set in Press Roman Medium by Visual Skills,
Inc., and printed on permanent paper and bound by George
Banta Company, Inc. The designer was Visual Skills, Inc. The
editors were Cary F. Baker, Jr., and Margaret LaMacchia.
Robert R. Laffler supervised production.*

We rededicate this book to our wives as a token of our appreciation for their continued support and the assistance given us during its preparation and to our relatives and friends who have cheered and encouraged us in our endeavors.

The Authors

preface
to second edition

From the time it was first published in the spring of 1961, we have used the first edition of "Architectural Drafting" in our course. As a result of the experience gained from this usage, we felt that the text could be improved and expanded: worthwhile material could be added to various chapters and entirely new material included in the book. We found that many students were capable of producing more drawings than the text provided. So that if we added more exercises with new problems their knowledge of drafting procedures could be increased, provided each new drawing involved something different from the previous problems.

Accordingly, new material and exercises have been added to Chaps. 1, 3, 4, 5, 6, 7, 9, 10, 13, and 16, and several figures have been redrawn or improved with the text rewritten to conform. Chapter 17, Curtain Walls and Steel Construction, is entirely new. Related Mathematics and Bibliography are also added units. The Glossary and Abbreviation sections have been enlarged.

Acknowledgment is made to the following companies: Charvoz-Carsen Corporation for the illustrations in Chaps. 1 and 11; Rotolite Sales Corporation for the illustrations in Chap. 10; Long Island Lighting Company for the assistance given us in preparing the specifications in Chap. 16 for the Year-round Comfort System and insulation; and Armco Steel Corporation for the information furnished to the authors, that formed the basis of Chap. 17.

Herbert F. Bellis
Walter A. Schmidt

preface
to first edition

There are many textbooks available for mechanical and architectural drafting written by eminent teachers, engineers, and architects. However, it is frequently found that these texts have been written on an advanced level, with the approach and language not readily comprehended by the student starting at the very beginning of the work.

The text and figures in this book have been arranged in sequence to provide instruction in an orderly and progressive manner, with the assumption that the student has had no previous background or experience in drafting. Only a knowledge of elementary mathematics is necessary.

This book is for students who wish to acquire a sufficient drafting skill to enable them to obtain jobs as beginner or junior draftsmen. Once started in the field, they can advance by further study and by the capabilities they develop.

Herbert F. Bellis
Walter A. Schmidt

contents

introduction

The drawing of lines is older than the pyramids and as new as the latest building whose foundation is being poured. Men have used lines to indicate size, space, and dimension as far back as recorded time and still use them today to design the most modern buildings. Lines are important but more important is the message they convey to the men in the building trades who interpret them. Truly, drafting is the language of the trade and must be performed to bring a complete, understandable message to the men who carry out the information on the drawing. Consequently, drafting is more than just drawing lines; the draftsman must also know why he draws the lines. He must understand that every line indicates a part of the structure to be erected or some portion of building material which has a standard shape, size, and composition. All this is recognized by the contractor when a drawing is prepared using the correct standards. There are no secrets in the building trades to confuse or discourage the beginner; many good reference books are available which cover and explain in detail all the methods of construction. With these books at your command you can draw a detail or a complete structure on which you will be proud to put your initials.

The place to start is at the beginning, where you learn to walk before you run. You cannot draw a complete project until you learn and understand the details. A draftsman cannot draw an elevation of a frame residence until he understands how a building is framed by the carpenter. Therefore, with the reference books as your guide and with this book and the instructor as your guiding light, you are on your way to a new world of education and information. Good luck!

related mathematics

Dimensions for building construction drawings are given in feet, inches, and fractions of an inch except for elevations or levels, which are usually given in feet and decimals of a foot. Dimensions on plot plans are given in feet and decimals of a foot. Therefore, a review of fractions and decimals as used in arithmetic will be an appropriate introduction to architectural drafting.

First study the following definitions of some of the basic arithmetical terms which will be used often during the drafting of architectural drawings.

Integer	A whole number. Examples: 1, 4, 5, 11, 144.
Fraction	Any quantity expressed with a numerator and denominator. Examples: $\frac{2}{3}$, $\frac{7}{8}$, $\frac{4}{3}$.
Denominator	That part of the fraction below the line which indicates the number of parts into which the whole number has been divided. Examples: $\frac{}{2}$, $\frac{}{5}$, $\frac{}{6}$, $\frac{}{12}$
Numerator	That part of the fraction above the line which indicates the number of parts used in the fraction. Examples: $\frac{3}{}$, $\frac{5}{}$, $\frac{7}{}$, $\frac{15}{}$, $\frac{13}{}$.
Proper fraction	A part of a whole number. Examples: $\frac{1}{4}$, $\frac{1}{2}$, $\frac{7}{16}$, $\frac{3}{8}$.
Improper fraction	A fraction equal to or greater than a whole number. Examples: $\frac{4}{4}$, $\frac{9}{8}$, $\frac{7}{2}$.
Mixed Number	An integer and a fraction. Examples: $8\frac{1}{4}$, $5\frac{3}{4}$, $9\frac{1}{2}$, $2\frac{5}{16}$.
Common fraction	Any number of equal parts of an integer expressed with a numerator and denominator. Examples of those used in architectural drawing: $\frac{1}{4}"$, $\frac{1}{8}"$, $\frac{1}{32}"$, $\frac{3}{16}"$, $\frac{1}{2}"$.

The following arithmetical operations can be understood best by reading the brief explanations and carefully examining the illustrating examples.

Common fractions.

Before common fractions can be added or subtracted they must be changed to a common denominator. To reduce $\frac{1}{8}$, $\frac{3}{4}$, and $\frac{3}{16}$ to a common denominator means to change the first two into equivalent numbers of sixteenths. The fractions then become $\frac{2}{16}$, $\frac{12}{16}$, and $\frac{3}{16}$.

Addition

To add a group of fractions and mixed numbers—$\frac{1}{4}$, $2\frac{1}{2}$, $\frac{1}{8}$, and $3\frac{3}{16}$—proceed as follows: Write the numbers down in a vertical column and change the fractions to a common denominator, using the largest given denominator. Add the fractions and the integers separately and then change the improper fraction $\frac{17}{16}$ into a mixed number $1\frac{1}{16}$ and add the two integers 5 and 1.

$$
\begin{array}{ll}
\tfrac{1}{4} & \tfrac{4}{16} \\
2\tfrac{1}{2} & 2\tfrac{8}{16} \\
\tfrac{1}{8} & \tfrac{2}{16} \\
3\tfrac{3}{16} & 3\tfrac{3}{16} \\
\hline
& 5\tfrac{17}{16} \text{ or } 6\tfrac{1}{16}
\end{array}
$$

The plus sign (+) is used to indicate additions, and = is the sign for equals. Thus $\tfrac{3}{4} + \tfrac{1}{4} = \tfrac{4}{4}$ or 1. Figure RM-1 illustrates a problem in addition when encountered in dimensions on drawings.

Thus $1\tfrac{1}{4}'' + 2\tfrac{1}{2}'' + \tfrac{1}{8}'' + 3\tfrac{3}{16}'' = 7\tfrac{1}{16}''$.

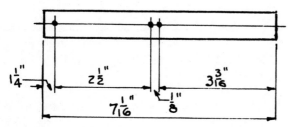

Fig. RM-1. Addition.

Subtraction

To subtract $2\tfrac{3}{32}$ from $13\tfrac{5}{16}$ write the numbers down in a vertical column. Change the $\tfrac{5}{16}$ to $\tfrac{10}{32}$ and proceed to subtract first the fractions and then the integers as shown next:

$$
\begin{array}{cc}
13\tfrac{5}{16} & \tfrac{10}{32} \\
2\tfrac{3}{32} & \tfrac{3}{32} \\
\hline
11 & \tfrac{7}{32}
\end{array}
\qquad \text{Answer is } 11\tfrac{7}{32}
$$

The minus sign (−) is used to indicate subtraction. Thus $\tfrac{5}{16} - \tfrac{1}{16} = \tfrac{4}{16}$ or $\tfrac{1}{4}$. Figure RM-2 illustrates a problem in subtraction which is often found in drafting.

The missing dimension a is equal to $3'' - 2'' = 1''$.

Multiplication

When multiplying or dividing fractions it is not necessary to change them to a common denominator, but the work can be simplified by cancellation as shown in the following example. The times sign (×) is used to indicate multiplication. To multiply $\tfrac{3}{4} \times \tfrac{5}{9} \times \tfrac{8}{15}$ cancel as shown:

$$
\tfrac{3}{4} \times \tfrac{5}{9} \times \tfrac{8}{15} = \tfrac{2}{9}
$$

The 3 above the line in the first term cancels part of the 9 below the line in the second term, leaving 3. The 4 below the line in the first term cancels part of the 8 above the line in the third term, leaving 2. The 5 above the line in the second term cancels part of the 15 be-

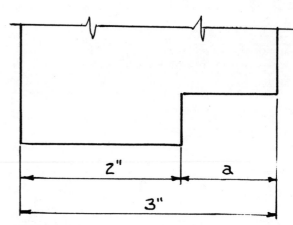

Fig. RM-2. Subtraction.

low the line in the third term, leaving 3. Only 2 is left above the line and 3 × 3 or 9 below the line, making the answer $\tfrac{2}{9}$.

Figure RM-3 illustrates a problem in multiplication often encountered in drafting.

Thus $6 \times 1\tfrac{1}{2} = 9''$ or 6 spaces at $1\tfrac{1}{2}''$ each $= 9''$.

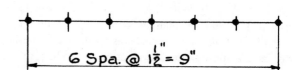

Fig. RM-3. Multiplication and division.

Division

Division is expressed by the term "divided by," or the sign ÷ is used. Thus a problem may be stated: to divide $\tfrac{3}{8}$ by $\tfrac{1}{16}$, or $\tfrac{3}{8} \div \tfrac{1}{16}$. To perform this division it is necessary to change the problem into a form suitable for multiplication. By inverting the second term, in this case $\tfrac{1}{16}$, the problem is then changed to $\tfrac{3}{8} \div \tfrac{16}{1}$. Now we can cancel as explained under Multiplication. The 8 below the line cancels part of the 16 leaving 2 and the result is:

$$
\tfrac{3}{8} \times \overset{2}{\tfrac{16}{1}} = 6
$$

Figure RM-3 may also be used to illustrate division. Thus $9'' \div 1\tfrac{1}{2}'' = 6$ spaces or 6 spaces at $1\tfrac{1}{2}''$ each $= 9''$.

Decimal fractions

Any number of equal parts of a number expressed in tenths, hundredths, thousandths, etc., is a decimal fraction. A period is used to denote the location of the decimal point. Examples: 0.7, 0.78, 0.833.

Addition

To add 0.25, 0.75, 0.475, and 0.0386, write the decimals down in a vertical column and proceed to add them as follows:

```
  0.25
  0.75
  0.475
  0.0386
  1.5136    Answer
```

Subtraction

To subtract 0.347 from 1.679, or to perform the operation 1.679 − 0.347, write the numbers in a vertical column and subtract as follows:

```
  1.679
  0.347
  1.332    Answer
```

Multiplication

To multiply 0.42 by 0.638, or to perform the operation 0.42 × 0.638, place the numbers underneath each other and proceed as in regular multiplication as follows:

```
  0.638
  0.42
  1276
  2552
  0.26796        Answer
```

You will note that the number of places to the right of the decimal point in the answer is five, which is equal to the total number of decimal places in the two numbers multiplied.

Division

To divide 5.6875 by 0.125, or to perform the operation 5.6875 ÷ 0.125, arrange the numbers as follows and proceed as in regular long division.

```
  0.125 | 5.6875
```

The first step, shown above, is to move the decimal point so that it will be correctly located in the answer. The complete operation is shown below:

```
           45.5    Answer
  0.125 | 5.6875
           5 00
           687
           625
           625
           625
           000
```

You will note that the number of decimal places in the dividend (5.6875, the number to be divided) is one more than the number of decimal places in the divisor (0.125). Therefore, to locate the decimal place correctly, point off one place in the answer, thus 45.5. This is accomplished by moving the decimal point as shown in the first step.

Arithmetical applications

Several examples of practical applications of arithmetic are given in the following problems.

1. How many lineal feet of molding will be required to extend around the four walls of a room 9'−6" wide and 14'−6" long? This will be the perimeter of the room.
    (a) Two walls will equal 2 × 9'−6" or 19'−0".
    (b) Two walls will equal 2 × 14'−6" or 29'−0".
    (c) 19'−0" + 29'−0" = 48'−0", the total lineal feet of molding required.
2. How many square yards of linoleum will be required to cover the floor of a room 10'−3" wide and 11'−9" long? This will be the area of the room.
    (a) First change the inches to a decimal part of a foot. That is, 3" to 0.25' and 9" to 0.75'.
    (b) Then 10.25, N 11.75' = 120.4375 square feet (sq ft).
    (c) As 3' = 1 yard (yd), 3' N 3, = 9 sq ft or 1 square yard (sq yd).
    (d) 120.4375 sq ft ÷ 9 sq ft = 13.38 plus sq yd.
3. How many cubic feet in a container 6'−0" long, 5'−0" wide and 4'−0" high?
    (a) 6' × 5' × 4' = 120 cubic feet (cu ft).
    Note: The three dimensions have been multiplied together to obtain the volume or cubical content of the container.
4. How many cubic yards of concrete will be required to build a wall 45'−0" long, 7'−0" high, and 2'−0" thick?
    (a) 45' × 7' × 2' = 630 cu ft.
    (b) 3' × 3' × 3' = 27 cu ft or 1 cubic yard (cu yd).
    (c) 630 cu ft ÷ 27 cu ft = 23 9/27 or 23 1/3 cu yd.

Conversion tables

Linear Measure

12 in.	=	1 ft
3 ft	=	1 yd
5½ yd	=	1 rod (rd)
320 rd	=	1 mile (mi) = 5,280 ft

Square Measure

144 sq in.	=	1 sq ft
9 sq ft	=	1 sq yd
30¼ sq yd	=	1 square rod (sq rd)
160 sq rd	=	1 acre (A) = 43,560 sq ft
640 A	=	1 sq mile (sq mi)

Cubic Measure

1,728 cu in.	=	1 cu ft
27 cu ft	=	1 cu yd

Board measure

Lumber is measured in terms of board feet. A piece of wood having an area of 1 sq ft and a thickness of 1 in. or less is called a board foot of lumber. Therefore, to find the number of board feet in a piece of lumber it is necessary to multiply the length in feet by the width in feet by the thickness in inches, remembering that any thickness less than 1 in. is counted as a full inch. Over 1 in. the nominal sizes run 1¼ in., 1½ in., 1¾ in., 2 in., 2½ in., 3 in., and 4 in. Rough lumber is dressed off on each side. For the dressed dimensions consult the table in Chap. 7. In figuring lumber the full size is used, that is, the rough stock required to make the piece. Building lumber is usually cut in even lengths, as 12 ft, 14 ft, 16 ft, etc. There are some exceptions. In measuring the width of lumber, a fraction of less than ½ in. is disregarded, but ½ in. or more is figured as a full inch. Some examples of how to figure board feet of lumber are given in the following problems.

1. How many board feet are in 10 pieces of lumber $2'' \times 4'' \times 14'-0''$ long? Keep in mind that the width dimension must be reduced to feet to obtain the correct area in square feet. Therefore, $4'' = \frac{4}{12}'$ or $\frac{1}{3}'$.

    $\frac{1}{3} \times 14 \times 2 \times 10 = 93\frac{1}{3}$ board feet measure (fbm)

2. How many board feet are in 6 pieces of lumber $\frac{5}{8}'' \times 8'' \times 12'-0''$ long?

    $1 \times \frac{2}{3} \times 12 \times 6 = 48$ fbm

3. How many board feet are in 9 pieces of lumber $2\frac{1}{4}'' \times 4\frac{1}{4}'' \times 8'-0''$ long?

    $2 \times \frac{5}{12} \times 8 \times 9 = 60$ fbm

1. selection and use of tools

The following list covers the essential tools, instruments, and accessories that the student will need and use.

Drawing board   Protractor
T square   French curves
Triangles, 30—60° and 45°   Scales
Drawing pencils   Drawing paper
Pencil pointers   Tracing paper
Erasing shield   Drafting tape
Pencil eraser   Drawing instruments

We begin instruction with pencil drawings and will therefore postpone any discussion of tools for ink work until a later chapter when ink tracings are discussed. Skill in the use of the above tools can only be acquired by actually working with them, but a few brief words about each will help the student to get started.

Drawing boards

Drawing boards may be of various sizes and styles but should have a smooth surface and true square edges. In drafting rooms where the board is part of the table top, the left-hand side of the board is kept smooth and true for contact with the head of the T square. The reason for this will be explained in the next paragraph.

"Borco" drawing board covering provides an excellent drawing surface. It is made up of laminated inner nondeteriorating rubber and everlasting vinyl outer layers. Compass points and pencil impressions do not leave marks as the resilient material returns to the nor-

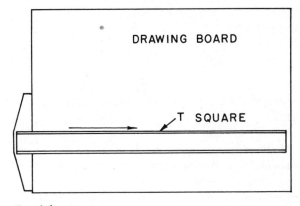

Fig. 1-1

mal surface. The material is reversible, one side green and the other side white. Battleship linoleum, $\frac{1}{8}$-in. thick, also will provide a good board covering.

T square

The T square is used to draw horizontal lines and to hold the triangles in place for vertical and slant lines. The head of the T square is customarily held against the left side of the drawing board as the majority of draftsmen are right-handed (Fig. 1-1). If the student is naturally left-handed, he may find it to his advantage to reverse the position of the T square and triangles. In a drafting room where parallel straightedges or drafting machines are provided, this problem is eliminated. Do not apply drafting tape where it will interfere with the smooth operation of the T square.

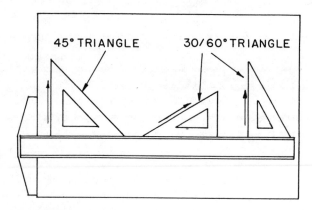

Fig. 1-2

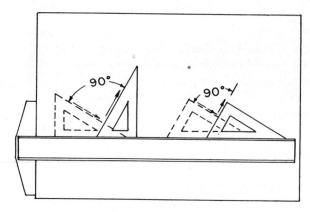

Fig. 1-4

Triangles

30–60° and 45°. Triangles, usually made of transparent plastic, are used in conjunction with the T square to draw vertical and slant lines. Used separately, the two triangles enable the draftsman to draw lines at 30°, 60°, 45°, or 90°. Used together, they allow him to draw lines at 75° and 15° from any other line (Figs. 1-2 to 1-4).

Drawing pencils

The lead in pencils is graded according to the degree of hardness, ranging from very soft up to very hard with markings of B, HB, F, H, 2H, 3H, 4H, 5H, 6H, 7H, 8H, and 9H. As a rule you will find the F, H, 2H, 4H, and 6H most useful. When sharpening wood pencils, remove enough wood with a penknife or a special sharpener in order to prepare a smooth round point or a chisel-shaped point. The kind of point used is generally a matter of personal preference, but some suggestions will be made when we discuss the quality of lines to be drawn.

Leads, without wood covering, graded the same as pencils, may be used in mechanical holders.

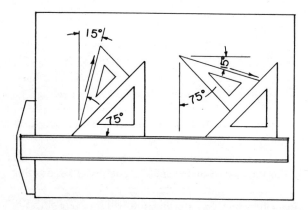

Fig. 1-3

Pencil pointers

Equipment for pointing pencils may be strips of sandpaper or emery paper made into pads, glued to a piece of wood conveniently shaped for holding; a crosscut steel file; or any one of a number of mechanical sharpeners available. The object is to shape the lead to the desired working point.

Erasing shield

A shield may be made of a flat, thin sheet of steel, brass, or plastic with various-shaped holes in it. By placing the shield on the drawing with the hole exposing the part to be erased, the adjacent lines can be preserved. A stainless-steel shield is preferred because the edges do not wear away with repeated rubbing.

Pencil eraser

An eraser of the ruby or pink pearl type especially made for drafting work will give the best results. Learn to erase with firm even pressure in order not to tear the paper or mar its surface. When erasing on tracing paper, it will be found helpful to place a hard surface such as a plastic triangle under the lines which are being erased. Also erase any dirt marks from the reverse side of the tracing paper. This procedure will help to prevent unnecessary lines and markings from appearing on prints made from the tracings. Art gum or a very soft cleaning eraser will be found useful for removing the guide lines and generally cleaning the finished drawing.

Erasers are also made in a stick or pencil form with a twisted paper wrapping which is easy to unwind. Electric erasing machines using a stick eraser are available and can be used to good advantage to save time. Care must be taken to touch the drawing lightly in order not to make a hole in the paper, vellum, or cloth.

Protractor

The protractor is usually made of transparent plastic in the form of a half circle with the circumference divided into degrees, minutes, and sometimes seconds. Use the protractor to mark off angles required in laying out the drawing.

French curves

French or irregular curves are used to draw lines which are not true circles and cannot be drawn with a compass. There are many and varied curves and sets of curves available for all lines of work. One simple French curve will be sufficient for the beginner.

Scales

Scales are the rulers used to measure distances on the drawings. The scale used by the architectural draftsman is usually triangular in shape to accommodate all the scales listed. Flat scales may be used if desired, but they will accommodate fewer different scales.

Architect's Scale

12 in.	=	1 ft (full size)
6 in.	=	1 ft (half size)
3 in.	=	1 ft (quarter size)
1½ in.	=	1 ft ($\frac{1}{8}$ size)
1 in.	=	1 ft ($\frac{1}{12}$ size)
¾ in.	=	1 ft ($\frac{1}{16}$ size)
½ in.	=	1 ft ($\frac{1}{24}$ size)
$\frac{3}{8}$ in.	=	1 ft ($\frac{1}{32}$ size)
¼ in.	=	1 ft ($\frac{1}{48}$ size)
$\frac{3}{16}$ in.	=	1 ft ($\frac{1}{64}$ size)
$\frac{1}{8}$ in.	=	1 ft ($\frac{1}{96}$ size)
$\frac{3}{32}$ in.	=	1 ft ($\frac{1}{128}$ size)

The architect's scale is used to lay out to full size and to reduce large objects or areas to a scale suitable to the size of the drawing paper used. Architectural details are often drawn to the actual or full size. To reduce the drawing to one-quarter size, use the scale 3 in. = 1 ft. It is incorrect to refer to this as ¼ scale because it is then confused with the scale ¼ in. = 1 ft. Always write the scale in terms of 1 ft, or $1'-0''$. For example: Scale $\frac{3}{4}'' = 1'-0''$.

There is another scale which the architectural draftsman uses. This is called a civil engineer's scale and is divided into divisions of 10, 20, 30, 40, 50, and 100 to represent feet, rods, miles, or other linear space units. This scale is used to draw plot plans where the units of measure are given as a surveyor would record them, that is, in feet and decimals of a foot or other units used.

When using a scale, lay it on the drawing along the line to be measured, and mark the distance lightly with a sharp point. Do not use a divider or compass to take measurements directly from the scale. The latter method does not save time and soon ruins the scale. A scale should never be used as a straightedge to draw lines.

It is a *must* for the student to learn the proper use of the scales from the very beginning of his work. Start with the full scale, and then use the fractional scales to reduce large dimensions to a scale suitable to the paper used.

Drawing paper

A good-quality paper, either white or very light cream color, with a good surface for erasing, will be found useful where it is desired to keep drawings or layouts for future use or where ink tracings of the drawings are to be made.

Tracing paper

Most drawings are now made on tracing paper, or vellum as it is called in the trade. There are many grades, the cheaper grades being used for sketching, and a better quality, with a good degree of transparency, for regular drawings. Pencil drawings on vellum with firm black lines can be used to obtain prints or copies without the expense and time delay of making ink tracings.

The size of the paper or vellum for drawing varies from office to office and depends on the kind and type of work to be done. A good size for the student will be about 18 by 24 in. Standard drawing sizes are 8½ by 11 in., 11 by 17 in., 17 by 22 in., and roll-size sheets.

Drafting tape

Drafting tape about ½-in. wide is used to fasten drawing paper or vellum to the drawing board. Thumb tacks may also be used, but using the tape prevents punching holes in the boards.

Drawing instruments

A standard set of instruments consists of a large compass, dividers, bow pencil (small compass), bow dividers, bow pen, pen attachment for large compass, and ruling pen. There are other instruments for special uses which may be purchased after you become more familiar with the work.

The dividers are used to transfer points or measurements. To use them correctly, place your thumb and forefinger on the outside of the legs and near the top. Open or spread the dividers by using your two middle fingers between the legs. Close the dividers by pressing thumb and forefinger together. Use the large dividers for large dimensions, and the bow, or small, dividers for small dimensions.

The large compass and bow compass are used and adjusted in the same manner as the dividers. A sharp, rounded pencil point on the compass will give the best results; learn to rotate the compass by holding the knurled top post between the thumb and forefinger. The steel pin should extend slightly beyond the pencil point. Do not press too hard on the pin in order to avoid making large holes in the drawing paper. When you mark off dimensions, locate centers and set your compass to draw circles. Check back on these measurements as you go along to make sure you are proceeding correctly. This precaution will avoid many erasures.

In general we have mentioned only the basic tools which you should learn to use because it is felt that at first it is essential for you to learn to draw by using the simple basic tools of the trade.

The drawing tables in many drafting rooms are equipped with parallel straightedges which are used in place of T squares. One of these straightedges is illustrated in Fig. 1-5. The parallel straightedge is fitted with pulleys at each end which allow it to be moved on wires attached to the right and left sides of the board. This arrangement facilitates the moving of the straightedge and keeps it in horizontal alignment at all times.

Drafting machines are also available. These are not really machines but are made up of a movable arm which is clamped at the top of the drawing board or table as illustrated in Fig. 1-6. There is an adjustable head mounted on the arm with provision for inserting two scales, the scales being used both for measuring dimensions and for drawing lines. The scales are made of metal and are flat so that our previous advice not to use a scale as a straightedge to draw lines may be disregarded if you are using a drafting machine. By using the machine scales to draw lines less use will be made of the triangles. The movable arm can be swung around to any position on the board, and the head can be adjusted to any angle. Proper use of a drafting machine will save time and eliminate many motions for the draftsman.

Drafting machines and parallel straightedges together with the drafting tables and stools are part of the office furniture provided by the employer.

Experienced draftsmen make use of special plastic templates for circles, architectural and electrical symbols, and other special items that are drawn many times during the course of the work. All of these special aids may be used to cut down on the time to make drawings and thus expedite the work and reduce the drafting expense. However, student draftsmen should learn to draw circles and symbols without templates.

A draftsman should acquire a certain natural skill in handling his tools; in fact, there are a number of things which a novice might be tempted to do which look awkward to a trained draftsman. Therefore, it is best to try not to get into bad drafting habits from the very beginning. The following is a list of some of the *do nots* for a good draftsman. Some of these may have been mentioned before but they will bear repeating, and some are just plain common sense.

Do not use the edges of the T square or triangles as a guide to cut paper with a knife or razor edge.

Fig. 1-5. Parallel straightedge. *(Charvoz-Carsen Corporation, Fairfield, N.J.)*

Fig. 1-6. Drafting machine. *(Charvoz-Carsen Corporation, Fairfield, N.J.)*

Do not use the lower edge of the T square to draw horizontal lines or as a base for a triangle.

Do not use the scale as a ruler to draw lines.

Do not use the head of the T square as a hammer.

Do not wet the point of the drawing pencil in your mouth or any other way.

Do not use a dull pencil, and do not sharpen a pencil over the drawing board.

Do not oil the joints of a compass.

Do not jab the dividers into the drawing board.

Do not use the dividers for extra duties, such as a reamer, pick, or tweezer performs.

Do not begin work until you have dusted the drawing and wiped off your T square and triangles.

Do not clutter up your board with equipment or books not in immediate use.

Do not clean a drawing all over with an eraser as this dulls the lines.

Do not fold drawings or tracings.

Do not eat or drink at the drawing board.

You are now ready to begin your drafting exercises. We recommend that you use a 21- by 30-in. drawing board and the equipment and supplies described in the first part of this chapter. Place the drafting paper on the board and square it up with the T square. Fasten the paper carefully to the board at the four corners with a small piece of drafting tape.

Exercises

Exercise 1. Figure 1-7. Draw a 3-in. square. Divide the top and the left side into six ½-in. divisions. Draw

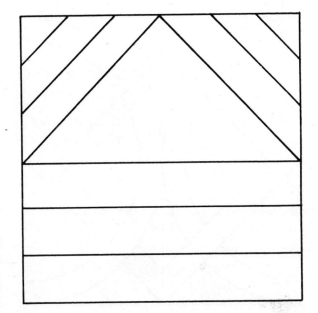

Fig. 1-7

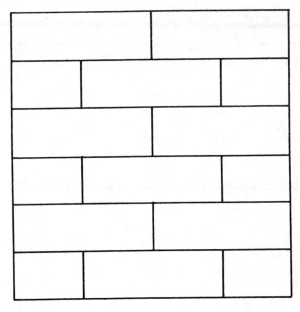

Fig. 1-8

three lines parallel to the base at the ½-in. divisions on the left side. Then draw 45° diagonal lines through the remaining ½-in. marks as indicated in Fig. 1-7.

Exercise 2. Figure 1-8. Draw a 3-in. square. Divide the top into two equal parts and the left side into six equal parts. Complete the figure with vertical lines, dividing the top space into two ½- by 1½-in. blocks; the next space into one ½- by 1½-in. block and two ½- by ¾-in. blocks. Continue alternately as shown in Fig. 1-8.

Exercise 3. Figure 1-9. Draw a 3-in. square. Draw two 45° diagonals. Divide each side in half and connect

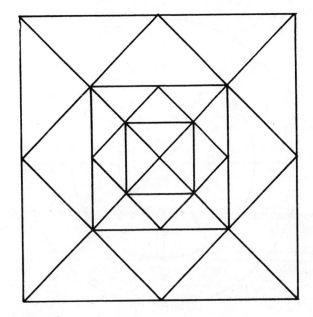

Fig. 1-9

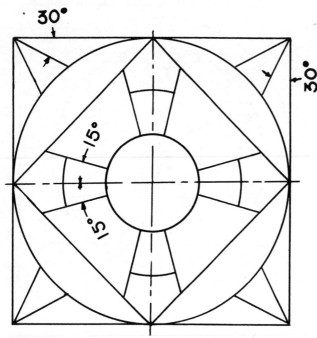

Fig. 1-10

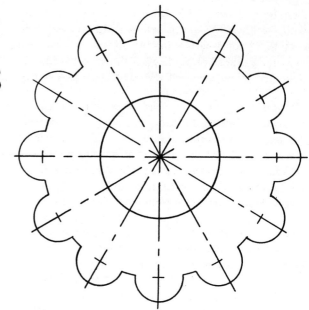

Fig. 1-12

these points with 45° diagonal lines. Draw a second square by connecting the intersecting points of the two sets of diagonals. Again divide the sides of the second square into equal parts, and connect the division points by 45° diagonal lines. Draw a third square by connecting the intersecting points of the last set of diagonal lines and the first diagonal lines drawn.

Exercise 4. Figure 1-10. Draw a 3-in. square with a 3-in.-diameter inscribed circle. From the tangent points draw 45° diagonal lines to form a diamond. Draw a

1-in.-diameter inner circle. Then draw 30° diagonal lines from the corners of the outer square and 15° radial lines from the center outward. Complete by drawing the arcs with a 1-in. radius between the 15° radial lines as shown.

Exercise 5. Figure 1-11. Draw three concentric circles with 1-in., 2-in., and 3-in. diameters. Divide the outer ring into 45° partial sectors. Divide each quarter of the middle ring into three 30° partial sectors. Divide the inner circle into four sectors of 90° each.

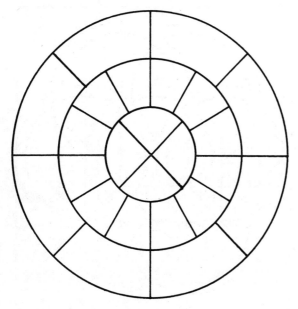

Fig. 1-11

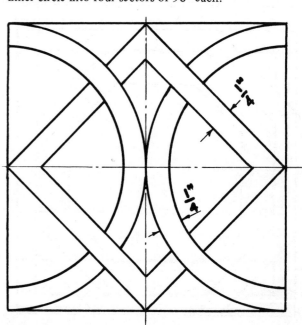

Fig. 1-13

Exercise 6. Figure 1-12. Draw two concentric circles with 1¼-in. and 2½-in. diameters. Divide the outer circle into 12 equal parts using the 30–60° triangle, and draw the 12 radial center lines. With the intersection of the radial center lines and the outer circle as a center, draw semicircles with ½-in. radii.

Exercise 7. Figure 1-13. Draw a 3-in. square with vertical and horizontal center lines. Draw 45° diagonals to these center lines ¼-in. apart as shown. Then draw two concentric semicircles on each side of the vertical center line with 1½-in. and 1¼-in. radii. Intertwine the diagonals and semicircles as shown in Fig. 1-13.

Exercise 8. Figure 1-14. Draw a 3-in. square with vertical and horizontal center lines and 45° diagonal lines. Draw two concentric circles with diameters of 2½ in. and 2 in. Draw an octagon inscribed within the 2-in. circle and a second octagon circumscribed about the 2½-in. circle. Draw the third octagon using the sides of the 3-in. square as part of the octagon. Complete with a ¼-in. border inside the square as shown in Fig. 1-14.

Exercise 9. Figure 1-15. Draw a 3-in. diameter circle with vertical and horizontal center lines and 45° diagonal lines as shown. Using the intersection of each center line and diagonal with the circumference of the 3-in. circle, draw an arc with a radius of 1½ in. as indicated in the figure. To complete, draw a second circle through the intersections of the arcs made with the 1½-in. radius.

Exercise 10. Figure 1-16. This figure is made up of concentric circles with 1½-in. and 1¼-in. diameters.

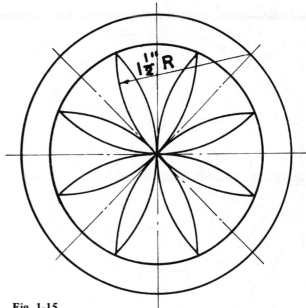

Fig. 1-15

Start with the center of the first pair on the intersection of the vertical and horizontal center lines. Then draw the two concentric circles using as a center the right and left intersections of the first 1½-in.-diameter circle with the horizontal center line. Next draw four sets of the two concentric circles using as centers the four intersections of the 1½-in.-diameter circles previously drawn. As the circles are drawn, intertwine them as shown in the figure.

Exercise 11. Figure 1-17. On the vertical and horizontal center lines draw two triangles with a 2-in. base and a 3-in. altitude, inverting the triangles as shown in the

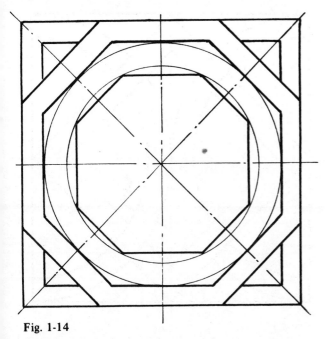

Fig. 1-14

Fig. 1-16

Fig. 1-17

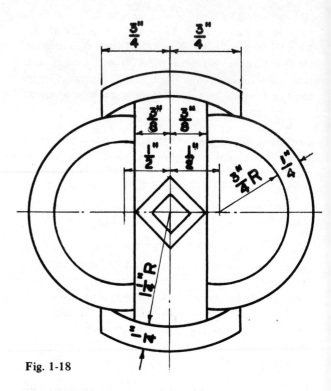

Fig. 1-18

figure. Inside each of the first triangles draw a second triangle so that the sides are parallel and ³⁄₁₆-in. apart. Then draw an outer circle with 1½-in. radius and an inner circle to form a band ³⁄₁₆-in. wide as shown. To complete the figure draw a circle tangent to the sides of the diamond formed by the two inner triangles previously drawn and a final small circle ¼-in. in diameter at the center of the figure.

Exercise 12. Figure 1-18. Draw vertical and horizontal center lines each 3¼-in. long. Proceed to draw the figure as shown using the dimensions given. The larger of the center diamonds made with 45° lines requires no additional dimensions. Draw the smaller diamond with sides ⅛-in. inside the first diamond.

2. lettering, lines, and dimensions

Lettering

Neat, clean drawings are essential as they may be termed the calling cards of the trade. The lettering on a drawing, therefore, should be on a par with the line work and not detract from it. In fact, good lettering can improve the appearance of a drawing. Concentrate first on a plain simple lettering, either inclined or vertical as shown in Figs. 2-1 and 2-2. The inclined letters are usually easier to draw, but the majority of architectural draftsmen use vertical lettering. It is suggested that upper-case (capital) letters be used for the most part and lower-case letters be reserved for general notes on drawings. The letters must be formed carefully, following the form shown in the samples given. Note, for instance, that some letters, such as A, M, and W, are wider than others. Also that the crossbar in the A and 4 is below the middle of the letter and numeral.

It will be found that with practice good lettering skill can be acquired. Speed is not essential at first, but with practice adequate speed will follow. A half hour of lettering practice each day will produce very worthwhile results. It is suggested that an H pencil with a round point, not too sharp, be used for lettering. For the most part $\frac{1}{8}$-in.-high letters and numerals will be used on drawings with $\frac{3}{16}$- or $\frac{1}{4}$-in.-high letters for headings or drawing numbers. Always use light guidelines to obtain letters and numerals of uniform height. An Ames or similar template will be found extremely useful for spacing the guidelines.

The letters shown in Figs. 2-1 and 2-2 are known as single-stroke or one-stroke letters. That is, a single stroke of the pencil determines the width of the letter line, or stem, but it does not mean that the complete letter is made without lifting the pencil from the paper. Hold the pencil comfortably between the thumb and forefinger. If as you draw the letters, you find that you are squeezing the pencil too hard and causing it to jerk, then relax your fingers and pause for a few seconds. Keep a symmetrical point on the pencil by rotating it after several strokes have been made. Make the vertical lines with a downward stroke, and the horizontal lines with a stroke from left to right.

If you draw a horizontal line across the middle of a rectangle, it will give an optical illusion of appearing to be below the middle of the rectangle, making the top section appear larger than the bottom section, or we say the figure appears unstable. In order to avoid this unstable appearance in certain letters and figures, it has been found necessary to make the top portion smaller than the lower portion. This applies to letters B, E, K, S, X, and Z and to numerals 3 and 8. The letter I is the basic single stroke. The letters C, D, G, O, and Q are based on oval shapes. The letters A, M, and W are wider than the other letters. There is no definite rule for spacing of letters and words, but the finished work should result in an even appearance. It will help in the beginning if you block out the letters lightly in the space available in order to obtain good spacing. If a limited space requires that the letters be condensed, try to keep them correctly proportioned. One need not be an artist to learn to letter well, and many draftsmen who do excellent lettering have a very mediocre handwriting.

Either the vertical or the inclined lettering shown in Figs. 2-1 and 2-2 should be mastered first; distinctive

A B C D E F G H I J K L M

N O P Q R S T U V W X Y Z

O I 2 3 4 5 6 7 8 9 & % = "

$\frac{1}{4}$" UPPER CASE VERTICAL

LETTERING FOR TITLE BOXES.

MAY BE INCREASED TO $\frac{1}{2}$" AS

REQUIRED.

ABCDEFGHIJKLMNOPQRSTUVWXYZ   OI23456789 &

$\frac{1}{8}$" UPPER CASE FOR GENERAL NOTES

abcdefghijklmnopqrstuvwxyz   OI23456789 &

$\frac{1}{8}$" lower case for special notes

FR ON T   E LE VA T ION   FRONT ELEVATION
POOR SPACING   GOOD SPACING

A DRAFTSMAN WILL
NEVER LETTER
WITHOUT GUIDELINES

Fig. 2-1. Vertical lettering.

A B C D E F G H I J K L M

N O P Q R S T U V W X Y Z

O I 2 3 4 5 6 7 8 9 & % = "

$\frac{1}{4}$" UPPER CASE INCLINED

LETTERING FOR TITLE BOXES.

MAY BE INCREASED TO $\frac{1}{2}$" AS

REQUIRED.

ABCDEFGHIJKLMNOPQRSTUVWXYZ OI23456789&

$\frac{1}{8}$" UPPER CASE FOR GENERAL NOTES

abcdefghijklmnopqrstuvwxyz OI23456789&

$\frac{1}{8}$" lower case for special notes

FRONT   ELEVATION   FRONT ELEVATION
POOR SPACING   GOOD SPACING

A DRAFTSMAN WILL
NEVER LETTER
WITHOUT GUIDELINES

Fig. 2-2. Inclined lettering.

FREEHAND ARCHITECTURAL LETTERING ⅛" HIGH IS USED ON MOST
DRAWINGS FOR GENERAL NOTES. LETTERING FOR TITLES AND SHEET
NUMBERS ARE USUALLY ¼" TO ⅝" SO THEY CAN BE QUICKLY DISTINGUISHED.
WITH PRACTICE THE BEGINNER WILL GAIN THE FREE STYLE OF THIS TYPE
OF LETTERING. IN THE SPACES BELOW PRACTICE THE ALPHABET AS SHOWN.
AABBCDEEFGHIJKKLMNOPPQRRSTUVWVXYZ 123345
567890 ¢

Fig. 2-3. Informal lettering.

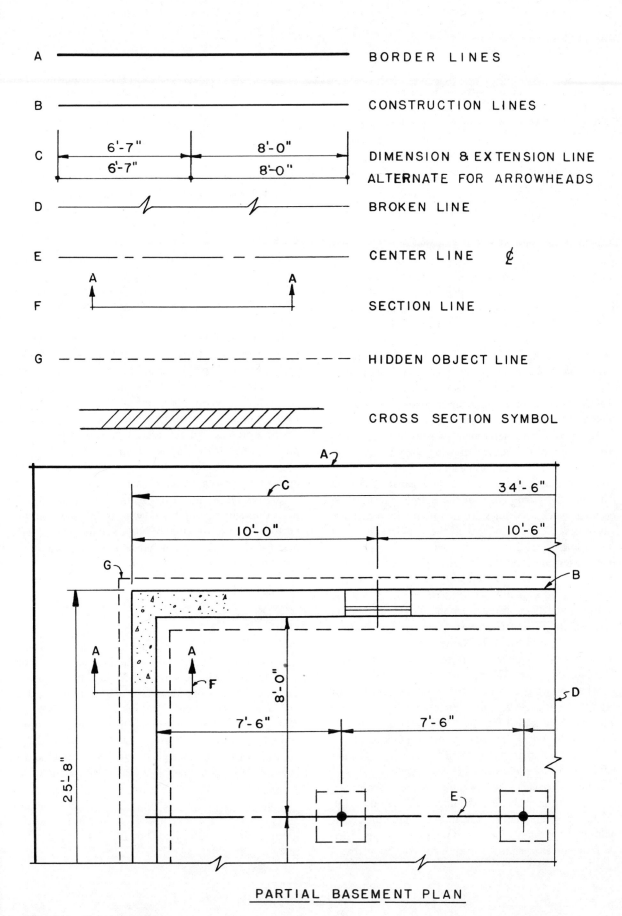

A   BORDER LINES

B   CONSTRUCTION LINES

C   6'-7"   8'-0"   DIMENSION & EXTENSION LINE
     6'-7"   8'-0"   ALTERNATE FOR ARROWHEADS

D   BROKEN LINE

E   CENTER LINE   ℄

F   A   A   SECTION LINE

G   HIDDEN OBJECT LINE

     CROSS SECTION SYMBOL

PARTIAL BASEMENT PLAN

Fig. 2-4. Alphabet of lines.

flourishes of your own should not be added to this lettering. The plain single-stroke lettering is preferred for mechanical drawings.

The lettering shown in Fig. 2-3 is an informal adaptation of the single-stroke or single-line vertical lettering shown in Fig. 2-1 and is also acceptable for architectural drawings.

Lines

The lines on finished pencil drawings should be uniformly black. This is especially true for pencil drawings on vellum, which will be used to obtain blueprints or other types of reproduced copies. However, there must be a distinction between lines representing different aspects of the drawing as noted in the following paragraphs.

When starting a drawing use a 4H or harder pencil with a fine point to make layout or construction lines. These lines should be drawn lightly so that they can be readily erased after the drawing is completed. This applies also to guidelines for lettering.

When you have determined which lines are to remain as part of the finished drawing, then darken these lines with a softer pencil using an H or F, depending on your touch and the surface of the paper. The lines denoting the visible edges of the object drawn should be bold, black solid lines. To denote hidden edges use dash lines, slightly thinner than the solid lines used for the visible edges. Then for the center lines, dimension lines, extension lines, leaders, and cross sectioning, use a very thin black line. Note that all lines on the finished drawing should be of the same blackness but the width of the lines varies to emphasize the distinction between the different representations. A few illustrations are given in Fig. 2-4. The system of three widths for lines has been approved by the American National Standards Institute (ANSI).

When drawing a vertical line hold the pencil point against the triangle and draw upward. For horizontal lines move the pencil from left to right as indicated in Figs. 1-1 to 1-4. This is the general technique of the professional draftsman. As stated in Chap. 1, if you are left-handed, this procedure can be reversed.

When a round or conical point is used, the pencil should be rotated between the fingers to keep the same thickness of line from start to finish. Rolling the pencil will help to retain the point and minimize the necessity of frequent sharpening. A demonstration by your instructor and a little practice will bring proficiency. This does not apply to the use of a chisel-pointed pencil.

Dimensions

When placing dimensions on architectural drawings, give dimensions under 12 in. in inches thus: $6\frac{1}{4}''$ or $11\frac{5}{8}''$. For 12 in. and over, give dimensions in feet and inches, thus: $1'-0''$ or $1'-6''$. Always use foot and inch marks.

Surveyor's dimensions on plot plans are given in feet and decimals of a foot, thus: $92.08'$.

As far as possible give dimensions to center lines and visible edges. Avoid dimensioning to invisible or dash lines.

In Fig. 2-4 note that the dimension lines are drawn about ½-in. away from the object lines. Also note that the extension lines indicating the limits of the dimensions start $\frac{1}{16}$-in. away from the object and extend about $\frac{1}{8}$-in. beyond the dimension line. Attention paid to these details helps to keep the drawing neat and to give it a professional appearance. Note also the appropriate type of arrowheads used in Fig. 2-4.

A dimension shown as $\underline{2'-1''}$ with an underline means that it has not been drawn to scale.

Always place dimensions so that they may be read from the right side of the drawing or looking from the bottom toward the top of the drawing. The general practice is to place the dimension close to and above the dimension line.

Arrowheads

Arrowheads are used to indicate the extent or ends of a dimension line. They should be definite and preferably solid to form a black surface. The size should vary to suit the location but they should be carefully drawn and not too prominent. The drawing outline is of the first consideration, and other lines and arrowheads should be secondary. Arrowheads are also used at the ends of leaders that point out specific items and at the ends of section lines to indicate the direction of the viewing.

Some architectural draftsmen use a small round dot at the ends of the dimension line in place of arrowheads as illustrated in line C of Fig. 2-4. This practice has not been widely adopted.

3. geometric construction

A drafting student will find as he starts to draw lines that he is using his previous knowledge of geometry.

For example, to lay out or draw a straight line between two points demonstrates the theorem: A straight line is the shortest distance between two points. Similarly, he will make use of his knowledge of angles, triangles, circles, and other geometric forms. The accuracy of the drawing depends on the care and skill used in locating the working points and in drawing the necessary lines to complete the work.

Following are examples of the ease with which you can solve simple geometric problems by using the T square, triangles, and compass. The geometric solutions may be reviewed by referring to a plane geometry textbook.

To draw a line between two points

Figure 3-1. Mark off the two points, place the point of the pencil on one of the points, bring the T square or triangle up to the pencil point, and line up the T square or triangle with the other marked point. When the points are in line, draw the line between the two points.

To draw a line parallel to a given line

Figure 3-2. Place the edge of a triangle along the given line, use a second triangle placed in contact with the first triangle as a base along which to slide the first triangle to its new position. Then draw the second line.

To draw a line perpendicular to a given line

Use a T square and triangle as shown in Fig. 3-3, or two triangles as shown in Fig. 3-4.

Tangents

Lines tangent to circles and circle arcs will be drawn many times. A line is tangent to a curve at a definite point. The tangent line is located by first drawing a radius of the circle arc to a given point on the circle

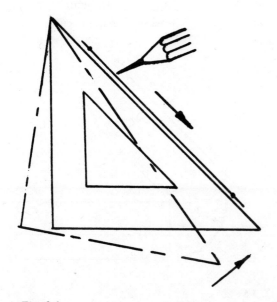

Fig. 3-1

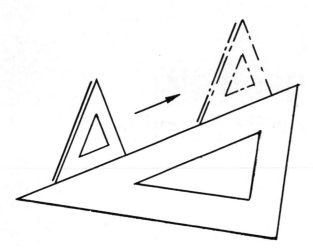

Fig. 3-2

and then drawing the tangent line perpendicular to the radial line through the given point.

To draw an arc tangent to two straight lines

Figure 3-5. Assume two lines AB and CD and the radius of the arc to be r. Then at any two points X and Y draw two arcs with radius r. Next draw two lines parallel to AB and CD through the extremes of the two arcs of radius r. The intersection of the parallel lines at 0 will be the center of the desired arc. Now draw perpendicular lines to AB and CD through 0 to locate the tangent points at t and t'.

To draw a tangent to a circle at a given point on the circle

Figure 3-6. Given a circle with center at 0 and a given point A on the circumference, place a 45° triangle B so that one edge passes through both the center 0 and point A. Then place triangle C against triangle B. Now hold triangle C firmly, and reverse triangle B so that the edge again passes through point A and forms a 90°

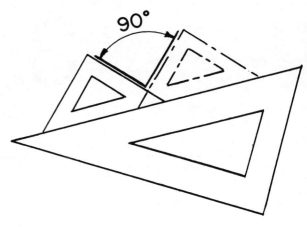

Fig. 3-4

angle, as indicated, with the first position. Draw line XY which will be the required tangent line.

To draw an arc of given radius tangent to a given arc and a straight line

Figure 3-7. Given an arc with radius r' and the straight line XY, draw line AB parallel to line XY at a distance r from XY. From the center at 0, strike an arc with radius r plus r' through line AB. The intersecting point $0'$ will be the center of the required arc with tangent points at t and t'.

To draw an arc of given radius tangent to a given point on a circle of given radius with circle inside arc

Figure 3-8. Through a given point A and the center 0 of the given circle, draw line AB. With 0 as a center, strike an arc, with a radius r' minus r, cutting line AB

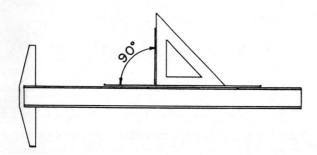

Fig. 3-3

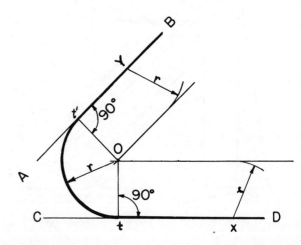

Fig. 3-5

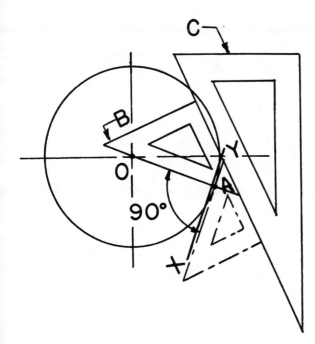

Fig. 3-6

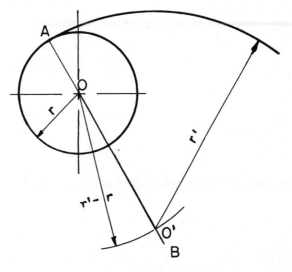

Fig. 3-8

at 0'. The new intersection 0' will be the center of the required arc tangent to the given circle at A.

To draw a reverse or ogee curve through points Z, X, Y

Figure 3-9. Draw parallel lines AB and CD through X and Y, and connect X and Y with a straight line as shown. Erect the perpendicular bisectors of XZ and YZ, and extend the two bisectors to intersect two vertical perpendiculars through X and Y. The intersections 0 and 0' are the centers of the two arcs required to form the ogee curve.

To divide a line into equal parts

Figure 3-10. Assume line XY is to be divided into six equal parts. Draw any line XZ through X. Then place a

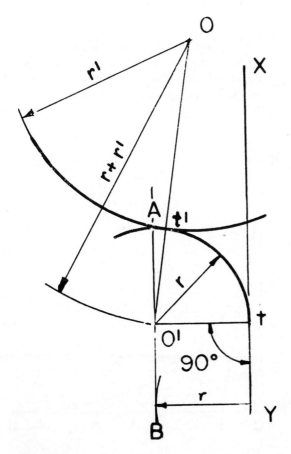

Fig. 3-7

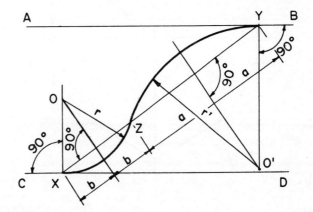

Fig. 3-9

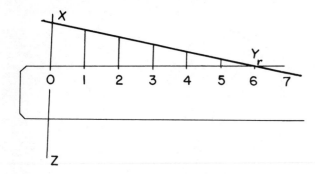

Fig. 3-10

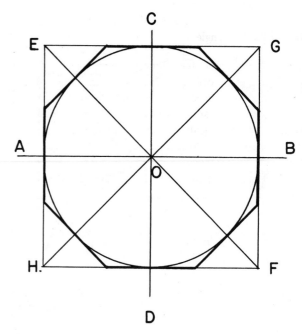

Fig. 3-12

scale on point r at division 6 and rotate until the point 0 is on line XZ. Mark points 0 to 6, then draw lines parallel to XZ through each point to intersect line XY. Line XY will then be divided into six equal parts.

To construct a regular hexagon given the distance across flat sides

Figure 3-11. Draw a circle on center lines AB and CD with radius r equal to one half the distance across the flat sides. Draw six lines tangent to the circle, using the 30–60° triangle as indicated.

To construct a regular octagon given the distance across flat sides

Figure 3-12. Draw a square on center lines AB and CD with sides equal to the given distance across the flat sides. Draw the diagonals EF and GH of the square. Then with center at 0 draw the inscribed circle to the square. At the intersections of the diagonals and the circle, draw tangent lines to the circle to complete the octagon.

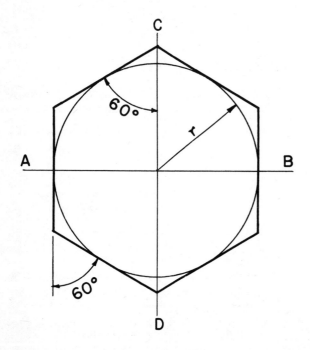

Fig. 3-11

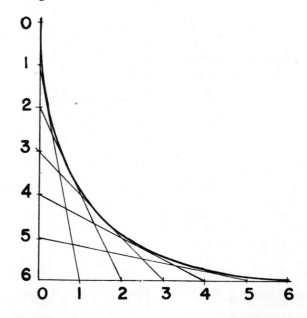

Fig. 3-13

**To draw a parabolic curve to two lines
forming a right angle**

Figure 3-13. Draw two lines at right angles to each other and mark off equal spaces on each line. In the figure six spaces have been used for convenience. Number the points as shown from 0 to 6 horizontally and from 6 to 0 vertically. Then connect like numbered points, as 1 to 1, 2 to 2, and so on. These connecting lines will be the tangents to the curve. Using an irregular curve draw the parabolic curve so that it is tangent to each connecting line as shown in Fig. 3-13.

**To draw a parabolic curve to two lines
forming an acute angle**

Figure 3-14. Draw two lines making an acute angle (less than 90°) with each other and mark off equal spaces on each line. In the figure eight spaces have been used for convenience. Number the points as shown from 0 to 8 on one line and from 8 to 0 on the other line. Then connect like numbered points, as 1 to 1, 2 to 2, and so on. Again these connecting lines will be the tangents to the curve. Using an irregular curve draw the parabolic curve so that it is tangent to each connecting line as shown in Fig. 3-14.

**To draw a parabolic curve to two lines
forming an obtuse angle**

Figure 3-15. Draw two lines making an obtuse angle (greater than 90°) with each other and mark off equal spaces on each line. In the figure six spaces have been used for convenience. Number the points as shown from 0 to 6 on one line and from 6 to 0 on the other line. Then connect like numbered points, as 1 to 1, 2 to 2, and so on. Again these connecting lines will be the tangents to the curve. Using an irregular curve draw the parabolic curve so that it is tangent to each connecting line as shown in Fig. 3-15.

To transpose an angle

Figure 3-16. First draw lines OA and OB to form an assumed angle AOB. The problem is to transpose or construct an angle of this same size in a different location on line PA'. Using a compass draw an arc on angle AOB with a radius OA. Then using the same radius OA with point P as a center describe the arc $A'X$. Adjust the compass to the distance between points A and B on the original angle AOB. Then mark

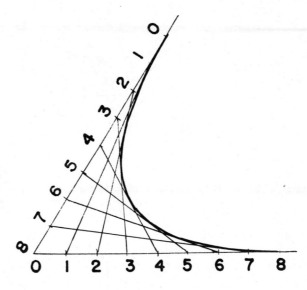

Fig. 3-14

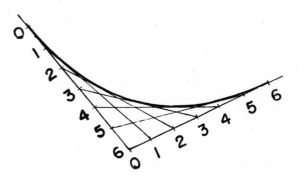

Fig. 3-15

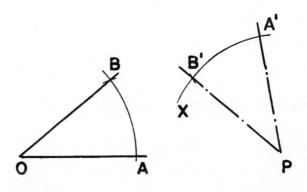

Fig. 3-16

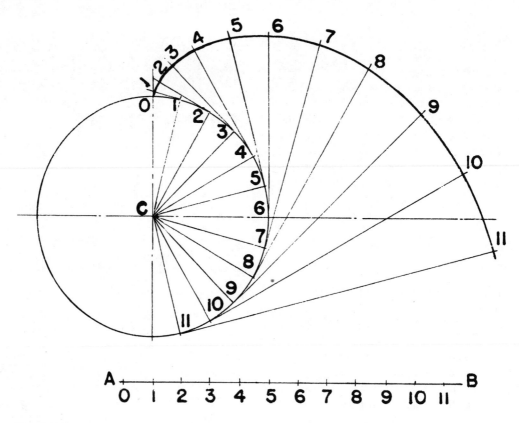

Fig. 3-17

off this distance from A' on arc $A'X$. Mark this last point B'. Draw line PB'. The new angle $A'PB'$ will be equal to the original angle AOB.

To draw a spiral of Archimedes

Figure 3-17. Draw a circle of any convenient diameter. Divide one half the circle into 15° angles. Any number of equal angles may be used depending on the size of the circle drawn. The object will be to draw a curve which will take the same path as a point moving around a fixed point C (the center of the circle) and

away from the center point in a manner measured by the arc of the angle rotated. First carefully measure the length of the arc 0 to 1 and lay off this distance along a straight line AB as shown below the figure. This measurement should be repeated 11 times as the length of each 15° arc is the same. Next erect a tangent perpendicular to each of the 11 radial lines previously drawn in the circle. Now using the measurements on line AB lay off on each tangent line first the length of one 15° arc, then the length of two arcs, three arcs, and so on until the full length of 11 arcs is marked off on the tangent at point 11. With an irregular curve connect the points to form a smooth curve.

4. orthographic projection

Orthographic projection is a system which has been devised to enable us to project various views of an object to a plane surface. These views can then be dimensioned so that the object can be made or built by the craftsman.

In the United States, these orthographic projection drawings, or working drawings, are drawn in what is designated the "third angle." By examining Fig. 4-1, it can be seen what the expression third angle means. Consider the four quadrants formed by a vertical axis and a horizontal axis to be the first, second, third, and fourth angles as marked in Fig. 4-1. You stand in the first angle and place the object to be drawn in the third angle. Now replace the third angle with a transparent box as in Fig. 4-2, and proceed to project each edge of the object directly to the sides of the box as indicated. The next step is to cut the edges of the box and swing the sides into the single plane as shown in Fig. 4-3. This plane becomes the plane of the drawing board. Now it should be readily seen that you can project dimensions from one view to another if the views are kept correctly in line with each other. Or if dimensions cannot be

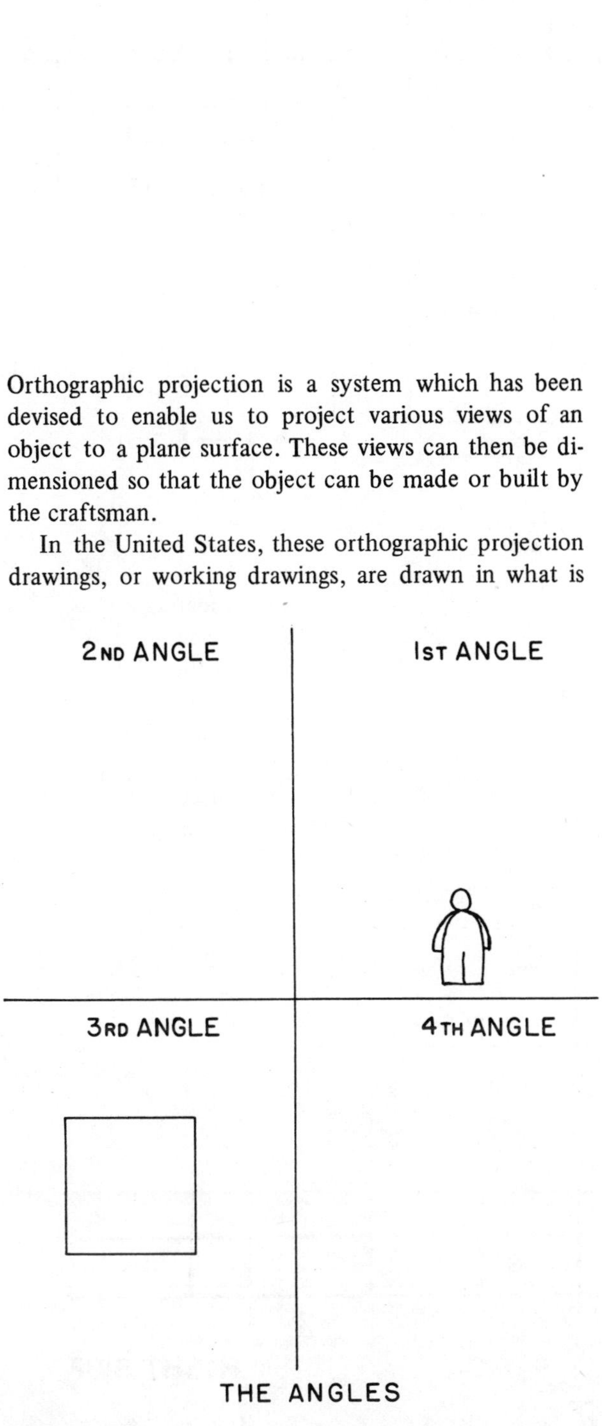

2ND ANGLE | 1ST ANGLE

3RD ANGLE | 4TH ANGLE

THE ANGLES

Fig. 4-1

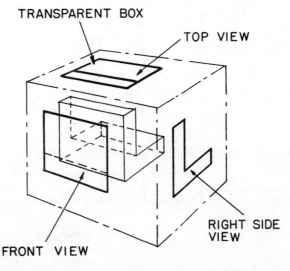

TRANSPARENT BOX

TOP VIEW

FRONT VIEW

RIGHT SIDE VIEW

Fig. 4-2. The box.

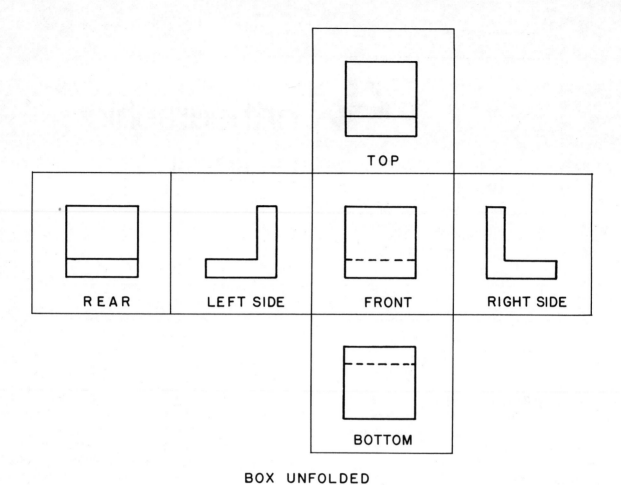

BOX UNFOLDED

Fig. 4-3. Orthographic projection.

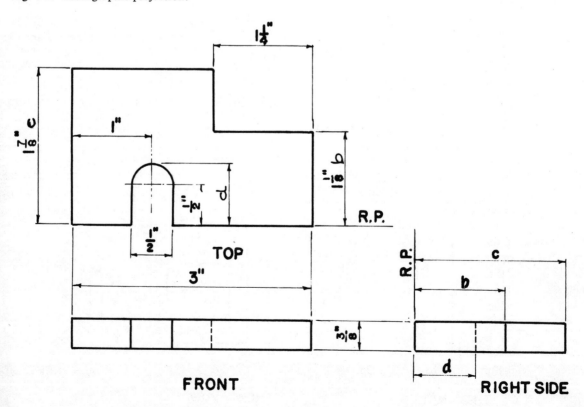

Fig. 4-4. Transferring dimensions.

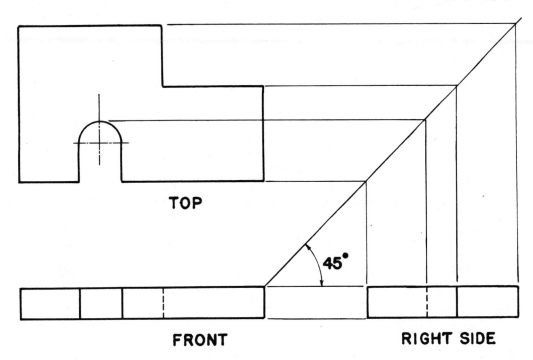

Fig. 4-5. The miter line.

projected directly, they can be transferred by means of a compass, divider, or scale.

In making architectural drawings the top or horizontal view is called the plan view. Thus, you refer to a floor plan or roof plan. But in architectural work the plan views are not always top views, such as a roof plan, but are usually horizontal sectional views cutting through the walls of a structure to show the details of the construction. The vertical front, side, and rear views are called elevations. If the views are small enough to be placed on the same drawing, it is customary to place them in the correct relation to each other as shown in Fig. 4-3. However, it is often necessary to place a plan on one drawing and elevations on different drawings. In this case care must be taken to mark each view clearly to show its proper location with respect to the whole project. Proper cross reference to each of the various drawings must be made.

Further, it is often necessary to draw enlarged sections or parts of the plans and elevations in order to show a part in greater detail with dimensions not possible to show in the full plan. These sections are then given a designation, as section *A-A*, section *B-B*, etc. The location at which the view or section is taken must be indicated on the plan or elevation view, as shown at *F* in Fig. 2-4. The view or section may be drawn at any convenient place on the drawing or even removed to a different drawing if properly cross referenced.

Figure 4-4 shows the front and top views of an ob-

ject, complete with all the dimensions required to draw these two views. To make it possible to draw the right side view of the object, all the dimensions which will be required have been indicated by lowercase letters *b, c,* and *d.* To draw the right side view, first transfer the reference edge or line *RP* shown in the top view to the right side view. Next project the height $\frac{3}{8}$ in. from the front view to the right side view. Then transfer the dimensions *b, c,* and *d* either by using the scale measurements or by means of the dividers. Complete the right side view as shown in the figure.

Another way to draw the third view after the front and top views have been drawn is shown in Fig. 4-5. This is done by projecting the height of $\frac{3}{8}$ in. from the front view as in Fig. 4-4. Then by means of the 45° line shown, transfer points from the top view to the side view using the geometric principle of a 45° isosceles

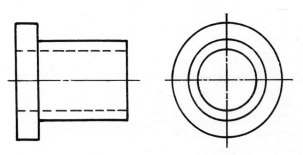

Fig. 4-6. Two views.

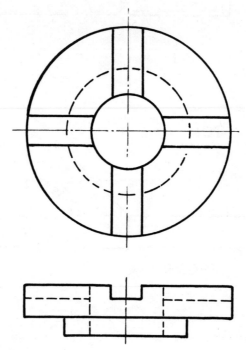

Fig. 4-7. Two views.

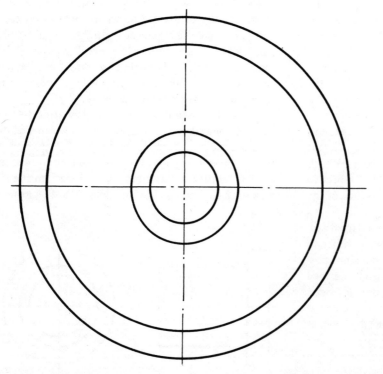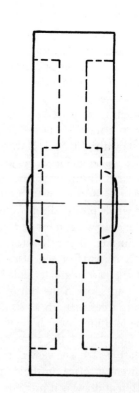

Fig. 4-8. Two views.

right triangle as shown in Fig. 4-5. This 45° line is sometimes called a miter line.

It often happens that some lines in a view cannot be drawn until another view is started and certain points are transferred back to the first view. This means only that it may be necessary to carry along the work on several views at the same time in order to determine the direction and extent of certain lines.

The method of projecting or transferring dimensions for a third view shown in Fig. 4-5 may be used to good advantage by a student at the beginning of his training. However, the student should soon learn to dispense with superfluous guidelines and to use the method of transferring dimensions outlined for Fig. 4-4.

The system of placing the top view directly above the front view and the side views to the right or left of the front view has been adopted by the American National Standards Institute as the standard arrangement of views. It agrees with the system of third-angle orthographic projection. It is sometimes convenient to project a side view to the right or left of the top view as shown in the orthographic projection in Fig. 5-1. This arrangement is called the alternate position for a side view.

It is not always necessary to draw three views of an object. In the case of circular objects like those shown in Figs. 4-6 and 4-7 it will be seen that only two views are required to give a complete picture of the object. Figures 4-8, 4-9, and 4-10 illustrate how other circular objects may be shown in orthographic projection by using only two views. Figure 4-8 shows the front and right side views of a medallion with the hidden edges of the solid web, the hub, and the rim denoted by dash lines. Figure 4-9 shows the value of making the right side view a sectional view through the center of the medallion. The thickness of the different parts is clearly defined by solid lines, and the character of the material is indicated by the nature of the sectioning. By extending the section lines across the web, we show that the web is solid from the hub to the rim. Figure 4-10 shows a similar medallion with openings in the web. The right side view has been drawn as section Y-Y. The web has not been sectioned, to show the conventional way of indicating that a part is not a solid web.

When drawing sectional views there are a few things it will be well to keep in mind. The section lines covering the surface which has been exposed by the imaginary cutting plane should be thin lines of the same thickness as dimension lines. It is customary to draw

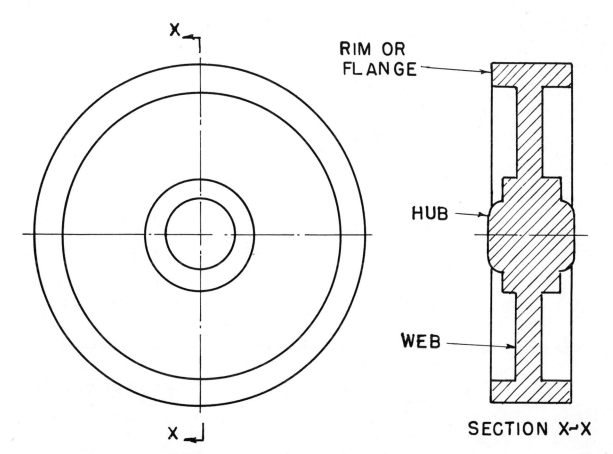

Fig. 4-9. Two views, sectioning.

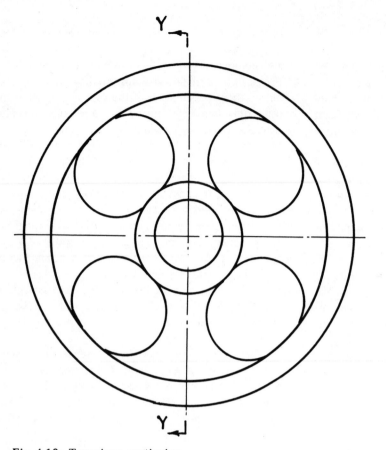

Fig. 4-10. Two views, sectioning.

SECTION Y-Y

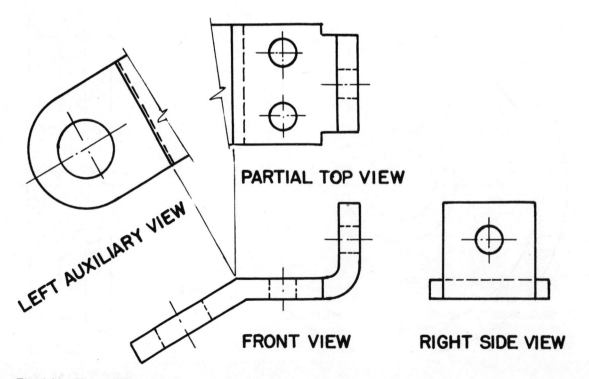

LEFT AUXILIARY VIEW

PARTIAL TOP VIEW

FRONT VIEW

RIGHT SIDE VIEW

Fig. 4-11. Clip, auxiliary view.

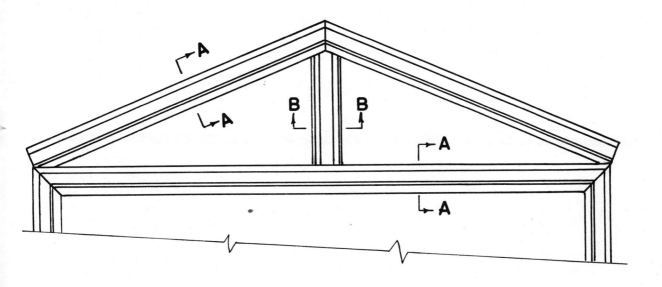

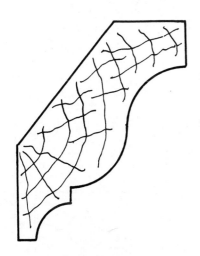

SECTION A-A
ENLARGED

SECTION B-B
ENLARGED

Fig. 4-12. Sectional views, enlarged.

Fig. 4-13. Orthographic projection. Exercises.

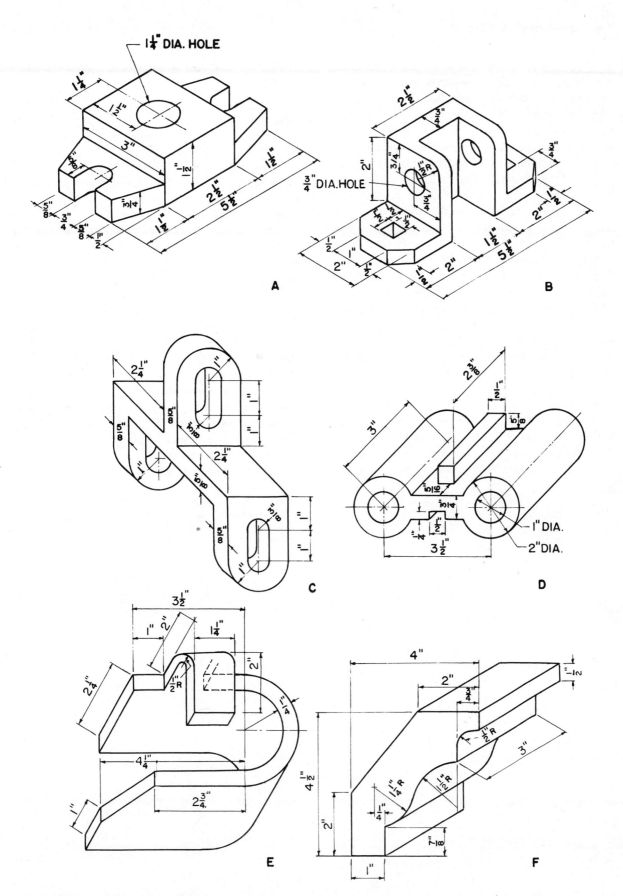

Fig. 4-14. Orthographic projection. Exercises.

33

them at an angle of 45° with the horizontal object lines. Hidden edges are not required to be shown in the sectional view unless they are needed to clearly define certain dimensions which are necessary but cannot be shown otherwise. However, solid lines never appear in the sectioning lines. If in an assembly of separate parts, two or more surfaces are contiguous, it is good practice to reverse the section lines on each side of the parting lines where possible. Standard symbols have been adopted by the ANSI to denote different materials, and the proper symbols should be used. It is good practice to draw the section lines after the object lines and the dimensions have been completed.

Figure 4-11 shows how a bent clip should be drawn, using a partial top view and a partial left auxiliary view. The auxiliary view is a true view obtained by projecting at right angles to the inclined portion of the front edge view. When partial views are drawn, the surfaces shown depict the true form. In this manner we are able to simplify the drawing and avoid foreshortened or distorted views.

Figure 4-12 shows a portion of a door frame made of molding. The true shape of the moldings is shown in sections *A-A* and *B-B*, which have been enlarged to facilitate dimensioning. Use of partial enlarged sectional views may be advantageous in showing clearly and defi-nitely how the various parts of the work should be executed.

Exercises

Draw full-scale orthographic projection drawings, or shop drawings, of the objects shown in Fig. 4-13, using the T square, triangles, instruments, and scale. The objects have been drawn half size or to a scale of 6″ = 1′–0″. Using the correct scale, measure the dimensions for each view to the nearest ⅛ in. Then draw three views of each object, that is, a front view, a top view, and a side view. Be sure to place the views in the correct relation to each other as shown in Fig. 4-3. These views may be drawn without dimensioning, but each object should be given a title such as Fig. 4-13*A* or Fig. 4-13*B*.

In a similar manner draw the full-scale orthographic projection drawings, or shop drawings, of the objects shown in Fig. 4-14, using the T square, triangles, instruments, and scale. Draw three views of each object, full-scale, using the dimensions shown in Fig. 4-14. Dimension each object completely and locate the dimensions where they will best identify the information intended. Some dimensions should be placed on each view, but do not repeat dimensions. Give each object a title such as Fig. 4-14*A* or Fig. 4-14*B*.

5. pictorial representation

Isometric drawing

The system most commonly employed to draw a picture of an object so that it can be easily dimensioned is known as isometric drawing, or pictorial representation.

Figure 5-1 shows three views of a simple object using the method of orthographic projection. Just below the orthographic representation is shown the isometric picture. Note that the horizontal lines of the front view and side view have each been drawn to an angle of 30° to the horizontal, using the dimensions given in the orthographic drawing. The vertical lines are shown vertically, using the dimensions on the original views. The vertical lines and the 30° lines are known as the isometric lines. Isometric means characterized by equal measurements or, in this instance, equal angles. Measurements can be laid out only along the isometric lines. For a nonisometric line it is necessary to obtain the locations of the ends of the line and then connect the two end points. It is customary to use the 30° angles as this gives the least distortion to the picture, and the 30–60° triangle may be conveniently employed.

A circle and an arc of a circle will become an ellipse in an isometric drawing. Any curve can be redrawn in the isometric picture by plotting points along the curve, but circles and arcs of circles are commonly drawn by using an approximate four-point method.

Figure 5-2 shows the isometric square of D diameter in three views. Note the diagonal lines connecting the center points of each side of the square with the corner of the square. The intersections of the diagonal lines are used for the center of radius r for the small ends of the ellipse. The two corners indicated are used for the center of radius r' for the long sides of the ellipse. Note that the diagonal lines are perpendicular to the side of the isometric square.

Exercises

Draw the full-scale pictorial representation or isometric picture of the objects shown in Fig. 5-3, using the T square, triangles, instruments, and scale. Figure 5-3 shows the objects drawn in regular orthographic projection with the front, top, and side views of each object. The views have been drawn half size, or to a scale of $6'' = 1'-0''$. Using the correct scale, measure the dimensions of each view to the nearest $\frac{1}{8}$ in. Draw the isometric picture of each object in accordance with the explanation given in Chap. 5 for Figs. 5-1 and 5-2.

Oblique drawing

Another form of pictorial representation, called oblique drawing, uses the parallel planes of the drawing to depict an object. In Fig. 5-4a the front and right side views of an object are shown in orthographic projection. To the right of these two views in Fig. 5-4b, the same object is shown in an oblique drawing. The student will note that we start with the front view drawn just as it was drawn in the orthographic view. Next we project the center of the semicircle to the right at an angle as indicated. In this case an angle of 30° was used, but a 45° angle or another angle could be used,

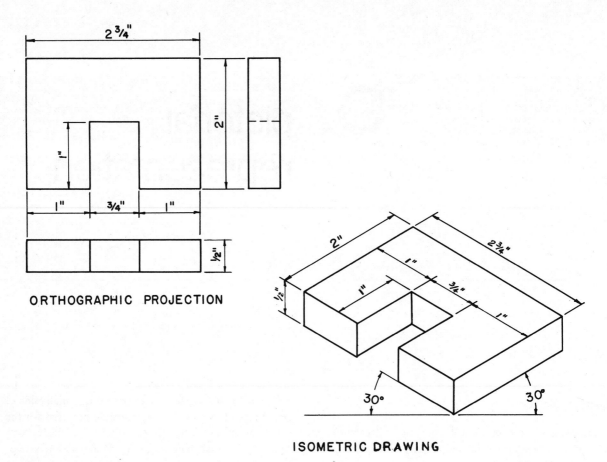

ORTHOGRAPHIC PROJECTION

ISOMETRIC DRAWING

Fig. 5-1. Pictorial Representation.

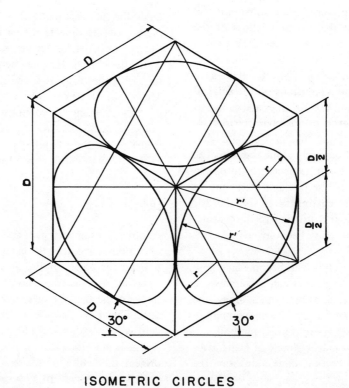

ISOMETRIC CIRCLES

Fig. 5-2

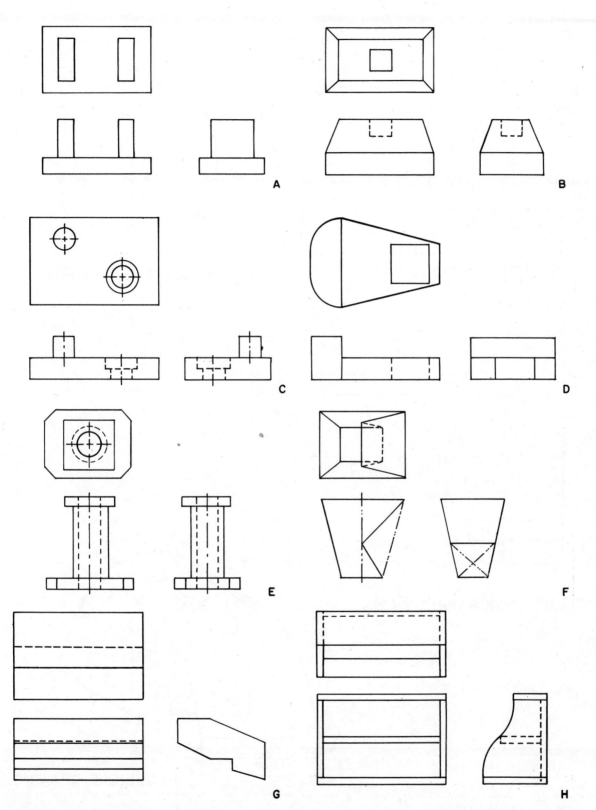

Fig. 5-3. Isometric drawing. Exercises.

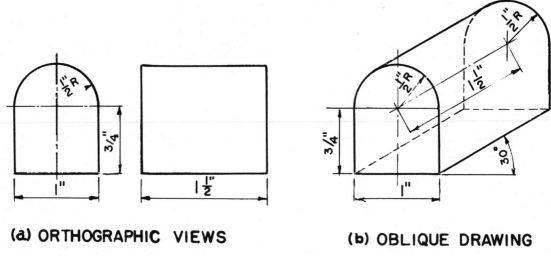

(a) ORTHOGRAPHIC VIEWS

(b) OBLIQUE DRAWING

Fig. 5-4. Oblique drawing.

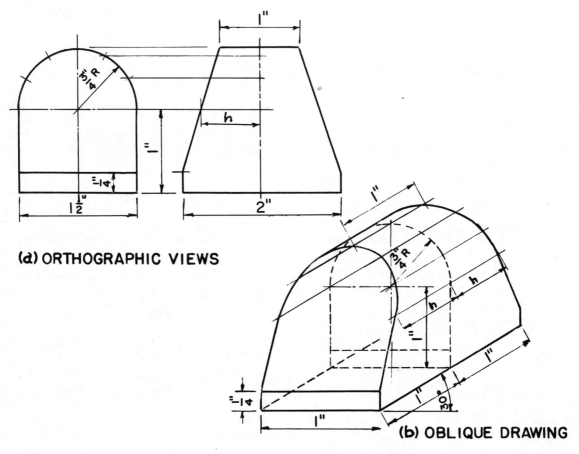

(d) ORTHOGRAPHIC VIEWS

(b) OBLIQUE DRAWING

Fig. 5-5. Oblique drawing.

38

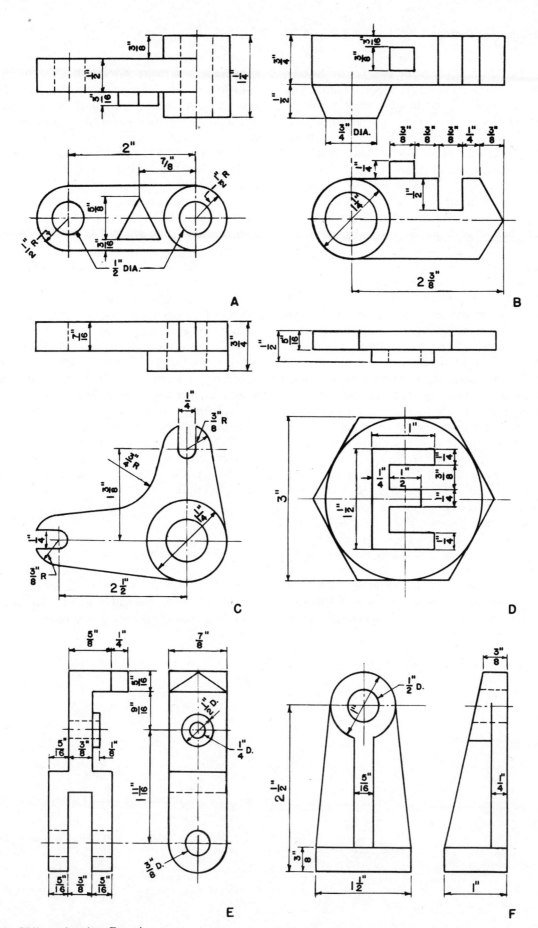

Fig. 5-6. Oblique drawing. Exercises.

39

depending on the final picture desired. Locate the center of the rear view 1½ in. from the center of the front view, along the 30° line and draw the rear view parallel to the front view. Connect the two lower right-hand corners with a 30° line and draw a line tangent to the left side of the semicircle, both as shown. The dash lines denoting the hidden edges of the object were drawn to bring out the idea of the use of parallel planes, but as in isometric drawing the hidden edges are not usually drawn in oblique pictorial representation. From this illustration it will be noted that the semicircles remain semicircles in the parallel planes, and we avoid drawing an elliptical semicircle.

If an object has surfaces which are parallel we can avoid drawing ellipses for curved surfaces by using the method of oblique drawing. But if the curved surfaces are not parallel, as shown in Fig. 5-5a, then they must be plotted somewhat in the same manner as that used to draw nonisometric lines. Figure 5-5b illustrates nonparallel surfaces drawn in an oblique representation. First divide the semicircle in the front view of the orthographic projection into a number of equal parts—in this case six equal parts. Project these points to the right side view in order to obtain distances such as h from the center reference line. Next start the oblique picture by drawing the vertical portion of the front view ¼ in. high and the base line of the side view at 30° to the horizontal line. Draw the base line 2 in. long, and in the center draw the front orthographic view with phantom lines. This will serve as a parallel reference plane corresponding to the center reference line in the right side view of Fig. 5-5a. Divide the semicircle in the phantom view into six equal parts and extend lines forward and backward through these points as shown. Next transfer distances similar to h from the right side

view in Fig. 5-5a to the corresponding lines in Fig. 5-5b both forward and backward from the phantom reference plane. An irregular curve may be used to connect the points of the semicircle, which has become elliptical in the oblique picture. Complete the picture by drawing straight lines from the elliptical semicircles down to the parallel vertical faces. Draw a line tangent to the left side of the elliptical faces.

There are several other methods of pictorial representation. Dimetric and trimetric drawings are variations of isometric drawing. Both isometric and dimetric methods are used for pictorial representation of structural work and single-line piping drawings. The isometric projection is most often used and satisfies more cases. In describing the method of making oblique picture drawings it was stated that angles other than 30° could be used. By changing the angle and the length of the receding lines different results will be obtained. When the angle is 45° and the receding lines perpendicular to the plane of projection are drawn in full length, the resulting picture is called cavalier projection. If the receding lines perpendicular to the plane of projection are one-half scale, then the resulting picture is called cabinet projection.

The systems of pictorial representation other than isometric and oblique, which have been described in this chapter, are more likely to be used in technical illustration work.

Exercises

Draw full-scale oblique pictures of the objects shown in Fig. 5-6, using: the T square, triangles, instruments, and scale. Figure 5-6 shows the objects drawn in regular orthographic projection with a front and top or a front and side view and all necessary dimensions.

6. perspective drawing

Assume that you are employed as a draftsman. For your firm's client you have made the plans, elevations, and sectional views of a house, that is, orthographic projection drawings. The client, not being familiar with this type of drawing, is not able to picture how this house will look from the outside. Therefore, you must prepare a drawing of the house as it will appear to the client when standing at some distance from the house or at a viewing spot which will be called the *station point*. Such a drawing, called a perspective drawing, will change flat surface drawings to a picture drawing showing the house as an object seen by the eye. It is necessary for the draftsman to learn how to make a perspective drawing and to learn the meanings of the various terms which will be used.

If you will look out the window at any building, you will observe that the parallel horizontal lines of the building appear to approach each other at a distant point. This point is termed the *vanishing point*, and the line on which this meeting occurs is called the line of the horizon. Looking across a large body of water, the sky and water seem to meet in the distance. This meeting line provides a good example of a continuous *horizon line* and must be considered as always present even when hidden by intervening objects such as ships or islands. Imagine yourself standing between the rails of a railroad track looking down at them. Now raise your eyes and look along the tracks in the distance where the rails appear to meet at a point, which is called the vanishing point because the distance between the rails seems to disappear. The vanishing point is on the horizon line and is also at *eye level*. If you sit down and look toward the horizon line it will still be at eye

level but lower than when you were standing up. Keep in mind that we have established that the vanishing point is on the line of the horizon and that the horizon line is at eye level.

The term *picture plane* is used frequently in perspective drawing; hence an explanation of the meaning of the term is in order before we proceed. Stand in front of a window looking out at a building, and use your finger to trace on the windowpane the outline of the building as you see it through the glass. Imagine the glass to be a sheet of paper on which you have just made a perspective drawing. The windowpane is the picture plane. If we could remove the glass and lay it flat on the drafting table, the drawing would look like any perspective drawing made on paper. Our vision brought the actual lines of the building up to the picture plane, which became the plane of the drawing paper.

Two-point perspective

Study the rectangular object shown in Fig. 6-1. Note that it rests on a supporting plane indicated by the *ground line* and that the length and width lines of the object when extended meet at two points on the horizon line, which in this example has been placed near the vertical center of the object. Thus, having established a right and a left vanishing point, we are drawing a two-point perspective.

The following steps will describe the proper procedure for the two-point perspective drawing. Following Fig. 6-1, first draw the horizontal line marked picture plane. This line represents the top or plan view of the imaginary vertical plane on which you will project

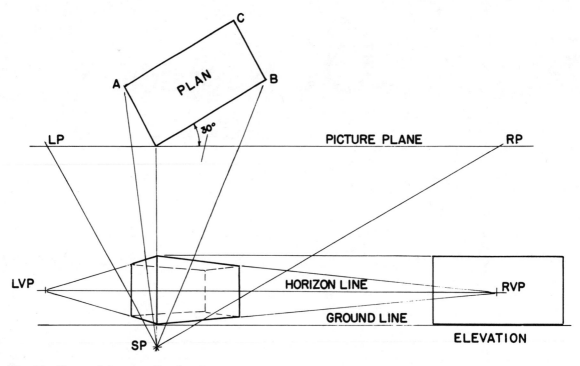

Fig. 6-1. Two-point perspective drawing.

the perspective representation of the object. Next draw the top or orthographic view of the object at 30 to 60° to the picture plane with one corner of the object on the picture-plane line. In the lower right-hand corner on the ground line, draw the orthographic right side view of the object. Draw the horizon line above and parallel to the ground line and at about the center of the object. The next step is to determine the right and left vanishing points for the drawing. From the station point *SP*, draw two lines parallel to the sides of the plan view of the object until they intersect the picture plane line at points *LP* and *RP*. Then project these last two points vertically downward until they meet the horizon line. Mark the two intersecting points *RVP* and *LVP*, that is, right and left vanishing points.

Since the corner edge of the object is on the picture plane, it can be projected vertically downward to the ground line, and the true height of this edge can be projected over from the orthographic right side view of the object. Since this corner edge is on the picture plane it will be seen in its true height in the perspective drawing. In the same manner any other edge extended to the picture plane will be seen in its true height when brought down to the perspective view. Now from the upper and lower ends of this corner edge, draw lines to the right and left vanishing points to establish the boundary lines of the side views of the object. From the station point *SP* draw two lines to points *A* and *B* on the plan view of the object, and from the point where these lines intersect the picture plane, project vertically downward to the boundary lines previously

established for the side views in the perspective drawing. The vertical corner lines and the upper and lower boundary lines between the vertical lines should be firm black lines to delineate the perspective picture of the object. If the ends of the corner lines *A* and *B* in the perspective view are extended to *RVP* and *LVP* as indicated by the dash lines, it will be seen that they lie within the first two boundary lines and are therefore invisible. The vertical corner line at *C* will also be invisible in the perspective drawing. Recall that the horizon line is at the eye level and since we placed the horizon line below the top of the object, the top of the object is not visible in the perspective drawing. The vertical or height lines are drawn parallel in the perspective drawing, and the vanishing point is not considered. This is because we see only a small portion of the lines at a time unless we are viewing a very tall structure. They could be compared to the vertical lines on a window.

In Fig. 6-2 we have drawn a perspective view of the same object used in Fig. 6-1, but in this case the horizon line (eye level) has been raised above the top of the object. If you will proceed in the same manner as described for Fig. 6-1 you will finish the perspective drawing of the object shown in Fig. 6-2. However, note that the top of the object is now visible because the horizon line has been elevated above the object.

Figure 6-3 shows a two-point perspective drawing of a house that has very simple lines but is more complicated than the object in Figs. 6-1 and 6-2. In order to review the method of drawing and familiarize you with

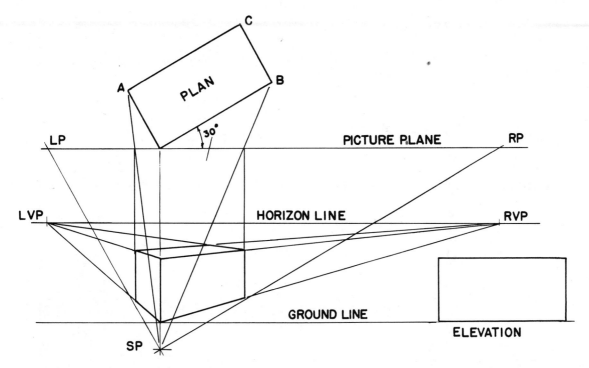

Fig. 6-2. Two-point perspective drawing.

the procedure, we will again note in detail the required steps in their correct order.

First draw the horizontal line marked picture plane. This line represents the top or plan view of the imaginary vertical plane on which you will project the perspective representation of the object. Next draw the top view or plan of the object (outline of the house) at 30–60° to the picture plane with one corner of the object on the picture plane line. Use a suitable scale so that the drawing can be contained within the limits of the drawing paper. Now select the station point marked *SP*, and draw a horizontal line marked ground line. Draw the horizon line parallel to and about 5 to 6 ft above the ground line, that is, about eye level. In the lower right-hand corner on the ground line, draw the orthographic right side view or elevation of the object, and in the lower left-hand corner on the ground line, draw the orthographic front view or elevation of the object.

The next step is to determine the right and left vanishing points for the drawing. From the station point *SP*, draw two lines parallel to the sides of the plan view of the object until they intersect the picture plane line at points *LP* and *RP*. Then project these last two points vertically downward to the horizon line and mark the points *RVP*, right vanishing point, and *LVP*, left vanishing point.

In order to project a point from the plan view to the perspective picture, the point must be brought to the picture plane by drawing a line from the station point to the given point in the plan view. The lines *SP* to points *B*, *C*, and *D* with intersecting points *X*, *Y*, and *Z*

on the picture plane line are examples of this procedure. Point *A* in the plan view lies on the picture plane line and can therefore be projected vertically downward to the ground line. To obtain the height of line *A* above the ground line, project directly across from the side or front elevation to form the line *AA'*, and from the top and bottom of line *AA'*, draw lines to *RVP* and *LVP*. These four lines will define the direction of the main horizontal lines of the object. Now project points *Y* and *Z* on the picture plane line vertically downward, and draw the vertical lines between the defining horizontal lines marking the ends of the object.

In order to determine the height of the ridge, the ridge line in the plan view must be extended to the picture plane line intersecting at *P*, and this point must be projected vertically downward. Now project the true height of the ridge over from the side elevation to point *E'*. Then draw a line from *E'* to *RVP* to obtain the directional line for the ridge. To find the extent of the ridge line, project its extremities in the plan view through the picture plane line to *SP*, and then project the intersecting points on the picture plane line vertically downward to the directional line previously obtained from the ridge. All other points in the plan and elevations must be projected to the perspective picture in a similar manner to complete the perspective picture of the object.

The 30–60° angles used in drawing the plan view of the subject were chosen for convenience in drawing, but other angles may be used if a different view of the subject is desired. A line drawn perpendicular to the

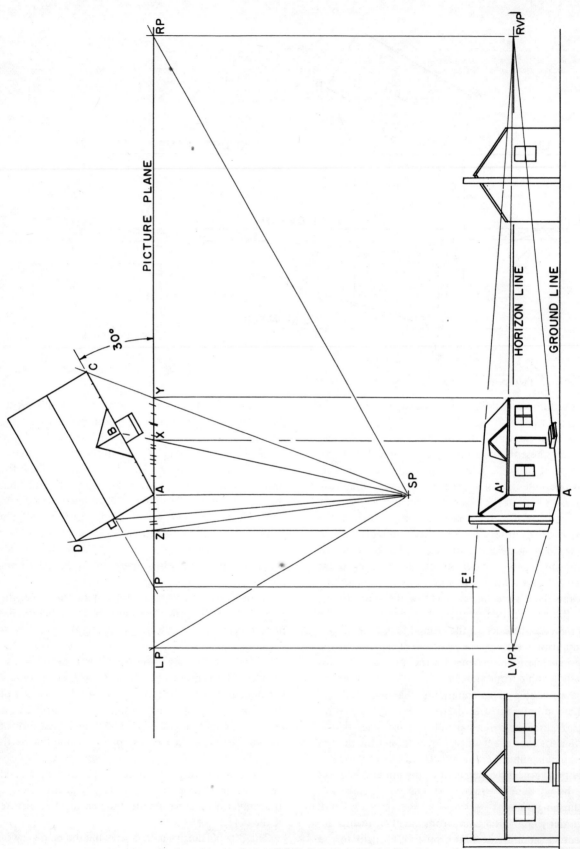

Fig. 6-3. Two-point perspective drawing.

44

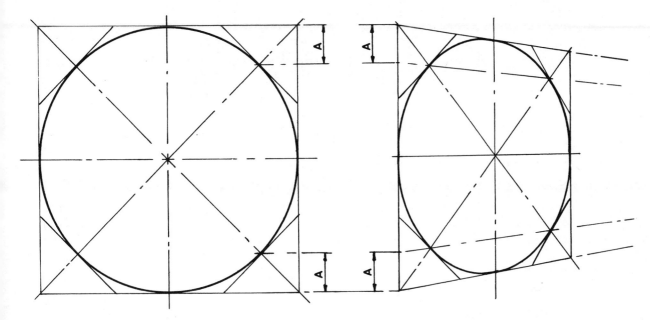

Fig. 6-4. Perspective circles.

picture plane line and passing through the station point intersects the picture plane line at a point called the center of vision. It is the usual practice in architectural perspective drawings to keep the center of vision near the center of interest of the subject. The station point may also be located in various positions to the right or left, nearer or farther from the subject, and even above or below it, all depending on the resulting picture desired by the viewer.

When a circle is on a plane parallel to the picture plane, it is drawn as a circle in the perspective drawing. But when the circle is in a plane not parallel to the picture plane, the circle must be projected to the perspective picture as an ellipse. A simple method of drawing an ellipse in the perspective picture is shown in Fig. 6-4.

First, draw the circle in orthographic projection and enclose it in a square, drawing the vertical and horizontal center lines and 45° diagonal lines as shown. Complete the octagon by drawing the tangent lines perpendicular to the 45° diagonals. Then mark the distance A. Now draw the enclosing square in perspective with its center lines and diagonals. Next transfer distance A in the orthographic view to the perspective square as indicated in Fig. 6-4. You will note that the center lines and the diagonals do not intersect in the center of the perspective square.

The next step is to extend points A to the vanishing point obtaining four intersecting points on the diagonals. With the four points obtained by the intersections of the center lines with the four sides of the perspective square, we now have eight points plotted for the

perspective ellipse. Complete the octagonal boundary lines and draw in the ellipse with an irregular curve. The ellipse must be tangent to the eight boundary lines.

The preceding paragraphs explain a simple method of making a perspective drawing which may be used when the dimensions of the subject can be reduced to fit the size of the drawing paper available. For cases not readily adaptable to the two-point method as outlined, it will be necessary for you to study more advanced texts which have been written on the art of making perspective drawings. There you will find methods for bringing the vanishing points within the range of the drawing when they appear to be located somewhere beyond the confines of the drawing paper. Such texts will also contain more detailed discussions concerning the picture plane, the horizon line, the location of the station point, methods for reducing various forms for perspective delineation, for shading, and for rendering.

Exercises

Draw the perspective delineation or picture of the objects shown in Fig. 6-5, using the T square, triangles, instruments and scales. Figure 6-5 shows objects drawn in regular orthographic projection with the front, top, and side views of each object. Using the scale $6'' = 1'-0''$, measure the dimensions of each view, and proceed to make the perspective drawing of the object by using the two-point method described in Chap. 6 and illustrated in Fig. 6-3.

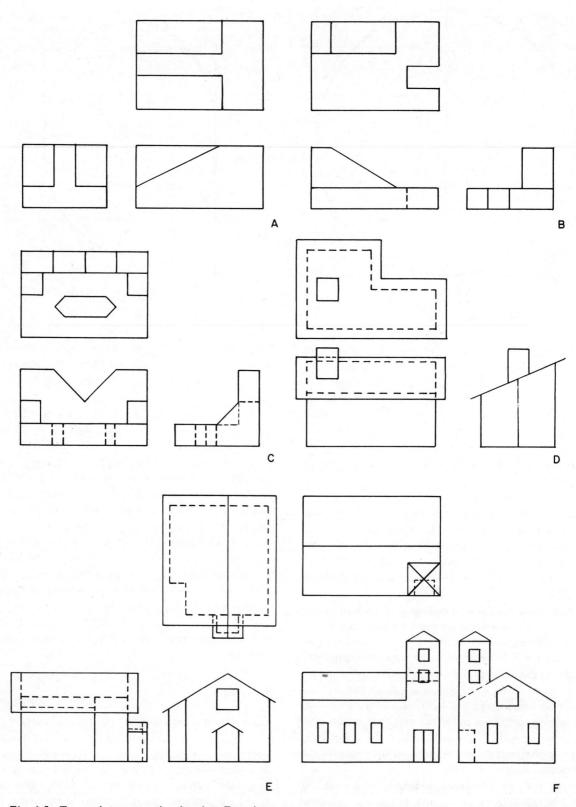

Fig. 6-5. Two-point perspective drawing. Exercises.

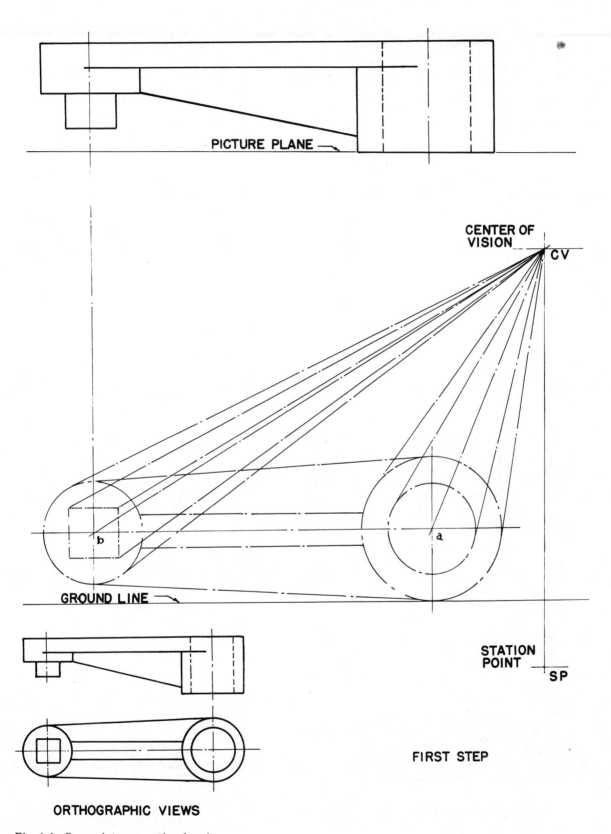

PICTURE PLANE

CENTER OF VISION — CV

GROUND LINE

b   a

STATION POINT — SP

FIRST STEP

ORTHOGRAPHIC VIEWS

Fig. 6-6. One-point perspective drawing.

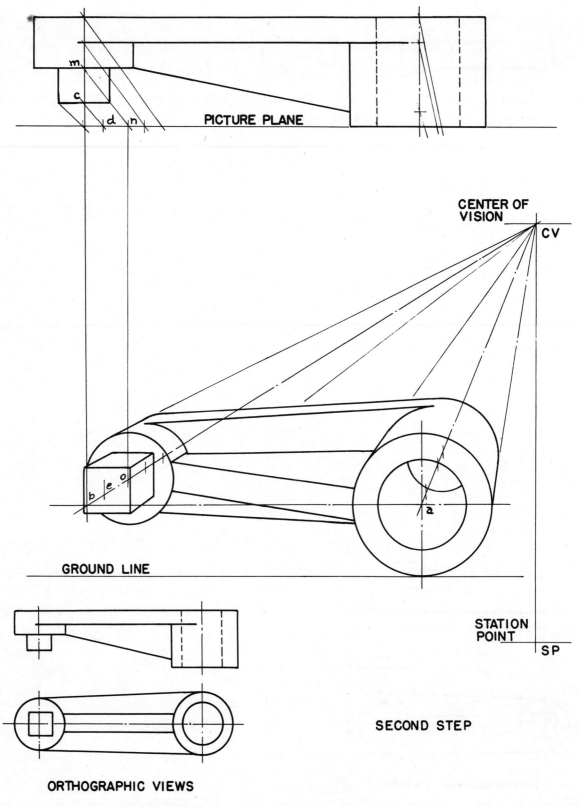

PICTURE PLANE

CENTER OF
VISION

CV

GROUND LINE

STATION
POINT

SP

SECOND STEP

ORTHOGRAPHIC VIEWS

Fig. 6-7. One-point perspective drawing.

One-point perspective

One-point or single-point perspective drawing is also called parallel or oblique perspective. This method is illustrated in Figs. 6-6 and 6-7 and is useful for depicting objects with circular faces. You will note that if the surfaces of the object are parallel to the picture plane, circles remain circles and the drawing of perspective ellipses is avoided.

In order to present a clearer picture of the procedure required in drawing a one-point perspective, the procedure is illustrated in two steps. Figure 6-6 covers the first step and in the lower left-hand corner the front and top views of an object are shown in orthographic projection. Above these two views, the object is drawn using the one-point perspective method. An enlarged scale is used in making the perspective drawing in order to clarify the construction. Begin with the picture plane line and draw the orthographic top view of the object. One of the parallel faces may be placed on the picture plane or off the picture plane, but the parallel faces must be drawn parallel to the picture plane line. Below the picture plane select a convenient ground line or base line. Next select a point called the *center of vision*, which corresponds to the horizon line used in two-point perspective. But in place of two vanishing points, all lines converge to a single point at the center of vision. The station point is placed below and directly in line with the center of vision. The center of vision and the station point may be located at the center of the object or to the right or left of the center, but the two points are always in line. Imagine that you are standing at the station point and looking toward the center of vision. Having drawn the top view parallel to the picture plane and selected the ground line, center of vision, and station point, you are ready to start the one-point perspective drawing. Draw the front view of the object on the ground line in thin dot-and-dash lines as indicated. Connect the centers at *a* and *b* to CV, center of vision, and draw tangent lines from *CV* to the circumference of the circles to establish boundary lines for the diminishing circles on the receding parallel surfaces. The corners of the square at *b* are also connected to the center of vision in a similar manner. All these lines should be very thin or light lines as they are used only as construction lines and can be erased when the picture has been completed.

The final lines of the one-point perspective picture and the method by which they are shown can be followed in the second step shown in Fig. 6-7. To find the location of each surface located behind the picture plane, proceed as in two-point perspective. For example, connect point *c* with *SP*, station point, and where this line crosses the picture plane at *d*, project

vertically downward to *e* on the center line which has been vanished from *b* to *CV*. Point *e* is the center of a new square which must be drawn within the boundary lines previously drawn to *CV* in the first step. In a like manner connect point *m* to *CV*, and where the connecting line intersects the picture plane line at *n*, project vertically downward to *o* for the new center of the first circular face.

Complete the one-point perspective by first establishing the location of the center of each parallel surface and draw the new circles within the boundary lines set up in the first step, Fig. 6-6. Note that the circles and squares become smaller as they recede from the picture plane.

Exercises

Draw the figures shown in Fig. 6-8 in one-point perspective, full scale, using the dimensions shown. Select a suitable center of vision and a suitable station point. Also mark the picture-plane line and the ground line. Do not dimension the final picture.

Interior perspective

Figure 6-9 illustrates a perspective drawing of one end of a room. Note the plan view at the top with the picture plane established and the *line of sight* located 6'–6" from the left side of the room. The station point is located twice the distance or 13'–0" from the picture plane and is on the line of sight. Next draw line *EF* at 45° to the picture plane and lines *G'G* and *H'H* also at 45° to the picture plane.

Now project the line of sight vertically downward and directly below the plan view, and draw the eye-level or horizon line 5'–6" above the floor line. The eye-level line can be raised or lowered if desired, assuming a tall or short observer. Locate the right and left vanishing points on the eye-level line 13'–0" from the line of sight. Note that the station point is also 13'–0" from the picture plane. Next draw the outline of the room *ABCD* at the picture plane with true dimensions. Extend the line of sight downward to intersect the eye-level line at *O*. Draw the four corner lines *AO*, *BO*, *CO*, and *DO*. Project points *F*, *G*, and *H* from the picture plane in the plan down to the floor line. Draw lines from *F* to the left *VP* and from *G* and *H* to the right *VP*. From the intersection of line *FVP* with line *AO*, the boundary lines of the rear wall in the perspective view may be drawn. From the intersection of lines *GVP* and *HVP* with line *DO* locate the door opening in the right wall. The true height of the door opening can be marked off in the picture plane and joined with the

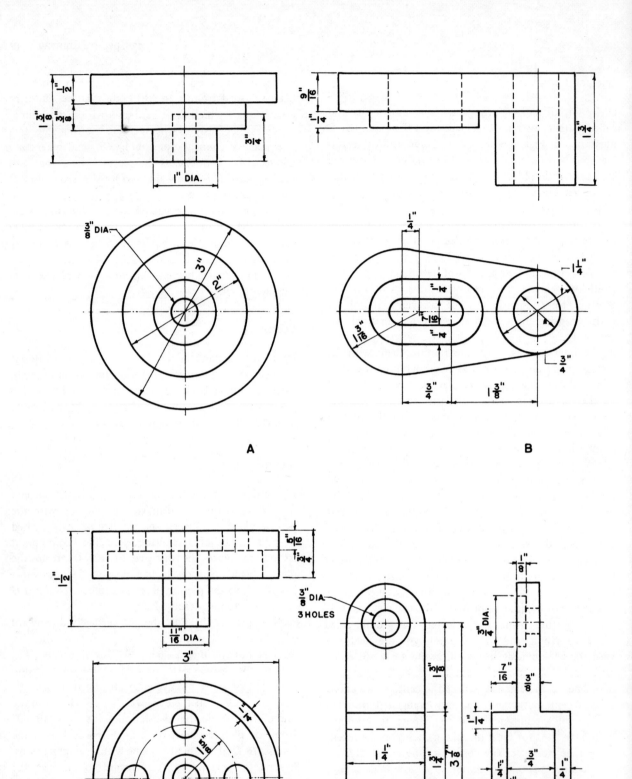

Fig. 6-8. One-point perspective drawing. Exercises.

50

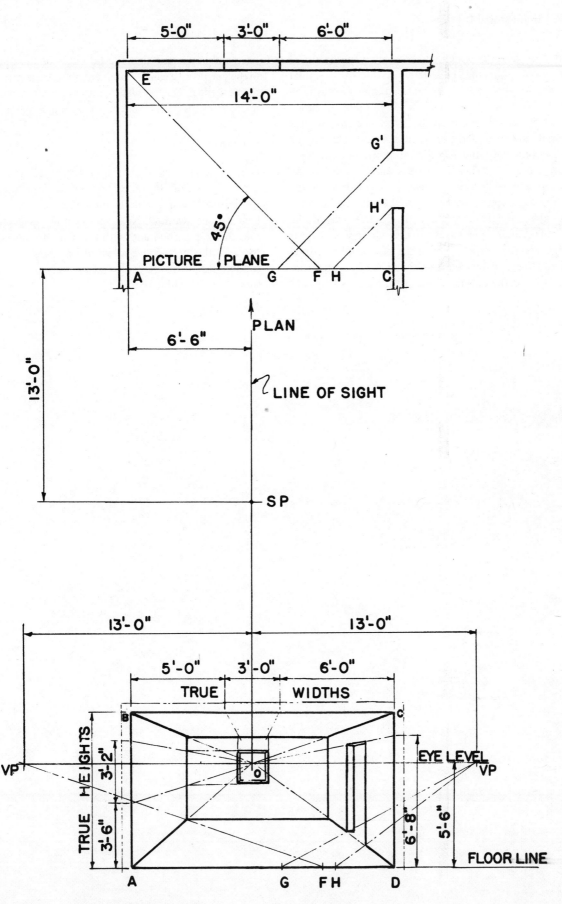

5'-0"   3'-0"   6'-0"

E

14'-0"

G'

H'

45°

PICTURE   PLANE

A   G   F H   C

PLAN

6'-6"

LINE OF SIGHT

13'-0"

SP

13'-0"   13'-0"

5'-0"   3'-0"   6'-0"

TRUE   WIDTHS

B   C

TRUE HEIGHTS

3'-2"

3'-6"   O   EYE LEVEL

VP   VP

6'-8"

5'-6"

FLOOR LINE

A   G   F H   D

Fig. 6-9. Interior perspective drawing.

51

center of vision O which will determine the height of the opening in the perspective view. In a similar manner the opening in the rear can be drawn as indicated. Project the window $3'-0''$ from the plane down to the picture plane outline in the perspective, connect these points to O, and project straight down from the intersection with the top line of the rear wall. Next mark off the true height of the window as shown on the left side of the perspective. Connect these points with O and project the height of the window horizontally from the intersection with the left side of the wall. To obtain the edges of the window and door which are farthest away from the picture plane, draw the thickness of the walls as shown by the phantom lines around the outline at the picture plane. It should

be readily apparent that the far edges of the openings in the perspective can be obtained in the same manner as the near edges. Objects placed in the room may be transferred from the plan to the perspective in a like manner.

Exercise

Draw the plan as shown in Fig. 6-9 to a scale of $3/8'' = 1'-0''$, adding a cabinet or bookshelves along the left wall and a table in the center of the room or beneath the window. Next redraw the perspective as previously described and with the help of your instructor add the perspective view of the new objects. A suitable height for the table and cabinet or bookshelves should be determined.

7. construction details

This chapter will deal with the details most commonly required for light, or frame, construction.

Use of scales

Figure 7-1. In Chap. 1 the architect's scale was listed as one of the draftsman's tools. It is a most important tool, and you must endeavor to use it properly from the very beginning of your work. In previous chapters we have mentioned making drawings to full- or half-size scale, but nearly all architectural drawings are made to even smaller scale. Except when drawing comparatively small details, it is not practical to draw plans of structures or even parts of them to full scale. The drawings would be too cumbersome to work on, and handling, filing, and storing them would be impossible, not to mention obtaining the necessary copies for distribution to all parties concerned.

Therefore, reduce the drawing to a workable scale to fit the size of drawing paper. For instance, if you had to draw a building which was 80 ft long, you would represent each foot by $\frac{1}{8}$ or $\frac{1}{4}$ in. to reduce the size of the drawing. Thus we would use as the scale either $\frac{1}{8}'' = 1'-0''$ or $\frac{1}{4}'' = 1'-0''$. If the entire drawing is made to one scale, the scale is noted in the space usually provided for it in the title box. When several different scales are used on one drawing, the correct scale should be placed directly under the portion of the drawing which was made to that particular scale as shown in Fig. 7-1. The several scales used may be listed in the title box as Scale—$\frac{1}{8}''$, $\frac{3}{16}''$, $\frac{1}{4}''$, and $\frac{3}{4}'' = 1'-0''$, or Scale—as noted.

All drawings should be made to scale and fully dimensioned. If dimensions are missing on finished drawings or copies of them, the drawing should not be scaled to obtain the missing dimensions. Written specifications covering buildings or other structures usually contain a clause stating that drawings must not be scaled. Any missing information should be obtained from the architect's representative in charge or from the construction superintendent. Blueprints of tracings are made by a wet process and then dried and ironed, hence are subject to shrinkage. There are dry methods of making prints or reproductions of tracings, but even with the greatest of care a small detail or part of a drawing may quite often be out of scale, either deliberately or because it was too late to make the necessary corrections. For the contractor or workman to scale a drawing often leads to inaccuracies which would cause serious trouble or disputes at a later stage of the work.

If a missing dimension can be obtained by subtracting the total of the subdimensions from the overall total or in any other mathematical manner which allows for definite checking, then the dimension obtained may be used, but do not depend on dimensions obtained by scaling a drawing.

Foundation and footings

Figure 7-2. Every structure requires a foundation. If there is no basement, the foundation walls should be carried below the average frost line to comply with the local building code. When the plans include a basement, the ground should be excavated to the depth required by the local building department. The ground should be solid and firm; in case of marshy ground,

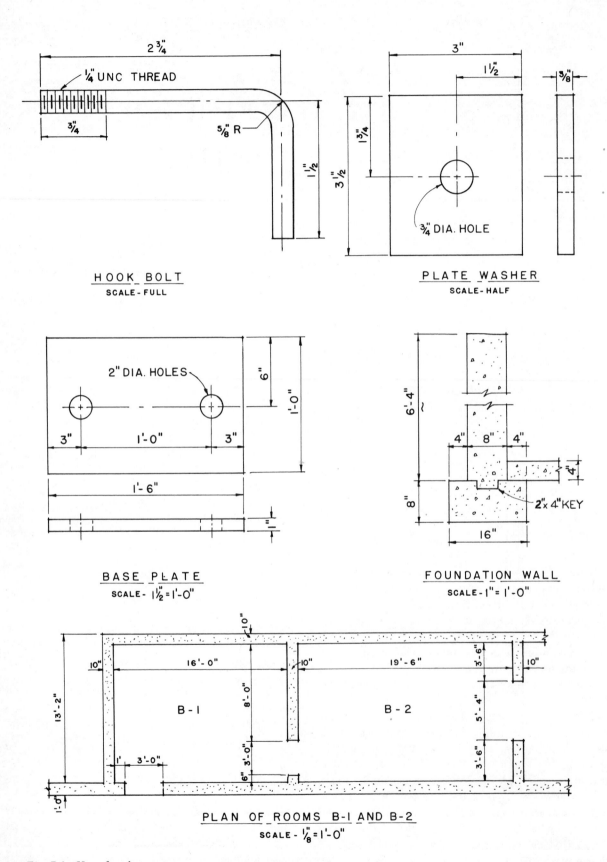

HOOK BOLT
SCALE - FULL

PLATE WASHER
SCALE - HALF

BASE PLATE
SCALE - $1\frac{1}{2}$" = 1'-0"

FOUNDATION WALL
SCALE - 1" = 1'-0"

PLAN OF ROOMS B-1 AND B-2
SCALE - $\frac{1}{8}$" = 1'-0"

Fig. 7-1. Use of scales.

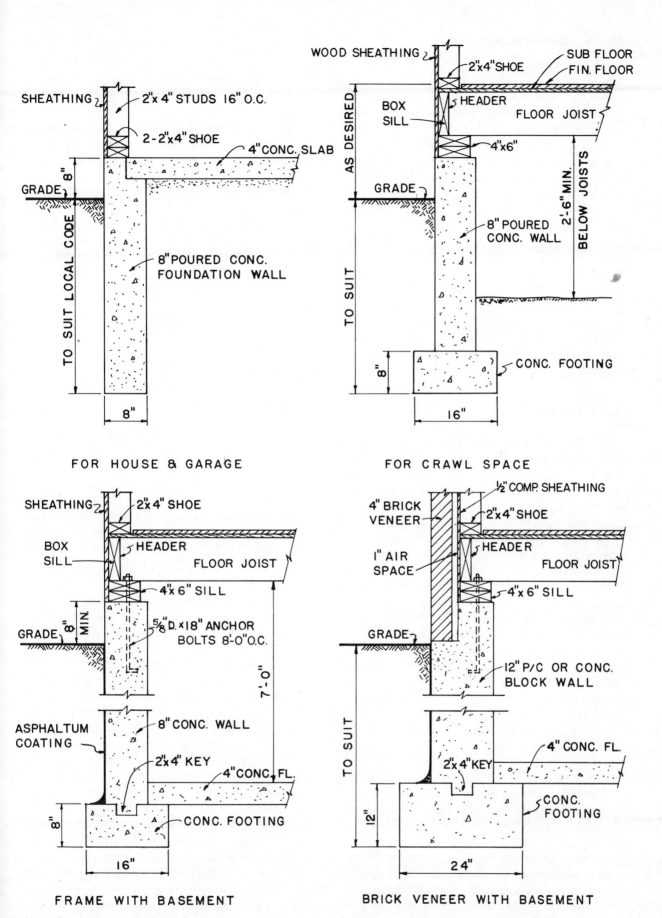

SHEATHING — 2"x 4" STUDS 16" O.C.

2-2"x4" SHOE

4" CONC. SLAB

8"

GRADE

TO SUIT LOCAL CODE

8" POURED CONC. FOUNDATION WALL

8"

FOR HOUSE & GARAGE

WOOD SHEATHING — 2"x4" SHOE — SUB FLOOR / FIN. FLOOR

BOX SILL — HEADER

FLOOR JOIST

AS DESIRED

4"x 6"

GRADE

2'-6" MIN. BELOW JOISTS

8" POURED CONC. WALL

TO SUIT

8"

CONC. FOOTING

16"

FOR CRAWL SPACE

SHEATHING — 2"x 4" SHOE

BOX SILL — HEADER

FLOOR JOIST

4"x 6" SILL

8" MIN.

GRADE

⅝"D. x18" ANCHOR BOLTS 8'-0" O.C.

7'-0"

ASPHALTUM COATING

8" CONC. WALL

2"x 4" KEY

4" CONC. FL.

8"

CONC. FOOTING

16"

FRAME WITH BASEMENT

½" COMP. SHEATHING

4" BRICK VENEER — 2"x 4" SHOE

I" AIR SPACE — HEADER

FLOOR JOIST

4"x 6" SILL

GRADE

12" P/C OR CONC. BLOCK WALL

TO SUIT

4" CONC. FL.

2"x 4" KEY

12"

CONC. FOOTING

24"

BRICK VENEER WITH BASEMENT

Fig. 7-2. Footings, foundations, and sills.

long wood or concrete piles are often suitably spaced under the foundation. Wood piling should be used only where the ground is always moist so that the piles will not dry out and rot.

It is good practice to place a footing under the foundation walls; the width of the footing depends on the bearing value of the soil, but it is usually twice the width of the foundation wall and as deep as the width of the wall. Where the soil is of poor bearing quality, the footing must be spread out adequately to carry the estimated load. Piers under single columns are treated in a similar manner. Footings are usually made of concrete poured into forms. In most cases the earth is tamped down firmly, and wood forms are used only for the sides of the footing. The foundation walls may be made of poured concrete or concrete block. Where additional strength is required, steel reinforcing rods may be added in the footings and walls as specified by the architect or engineer.

Box and solid sills

Figure 7-2. With a modern frame construction either the box sill or the solid sill can be used. For the box sill the studs are nailed to a shoe or sole which has been nailed to the subflooring. The box sill is used with the western platform framing. In the solid-sill, or balloon-framing, construction the studs extend down to the sill plate which has been bolted to the foundation wall, and the studs are nailed directly to the floor joists. In solid-sill construction the header is placed between the joists, while in box-sill construction the header is a continuous member. Sills are anchored to the foundation with bolts $\frac{5}{8}$ in. in diameter by 18 in. long and spaced 6 to 8 ft apart. Less shrinkage and settling may be expected with the solid-sill than with the box-sill construction. Excessive shrinking and settling will cause floors to become uneven, plaster to crack, and doors and windows to jam because they are twisted out of alignment.

The sizes of lumber shown on the figures are commonly used for small homes but may be varied to suit larger units or special cases as determined by the architect or designer.

Lumber is stocked by the lumberyard in rough (nominal) and dressed sizes and is classified by size, nominal, as follows:

1. *Boards*. Lumber less than 2 in. in nominal thickness and 2 in. or more in nominal width. Boards less than 6 in. in nominal width may be classified as strips.
2. *Dimension*. Lumber from 2 in. to, but not including, 5 in. in nominal thickness, and 2 in. or more in nominal width. Dimension may be classified as framing, joists, planks, rafters, studs, small timbers, etc.
3. *Timbers*. Lumber 5 in. or more nominally in least dimensions. Timber may be classified as beams, stringers, posts, caps, sills, girders, purlins, etc.

The dressed or smooth lumber is made from the rough sizes and is therefore smaller than the rough lumber. However, the dimensions of the rough lumber are always used to figure the board measure and the cost of the lumber. The following table gives a list of the more common framing lumber sizes. Dimensions are given in inches for dry lumber.

	Rough, nominal	Dressed, minimum
Boards	1 × 2	¾ × 1½
	1 × 3	¾ × 2½
	1 × 4	¾ × 3½
	1 × 6	¾ × 5½
	1 × 8	¾ × 7¼
	1 × 10	¾ × 9¼
	1 × 12	¾ × 11¼
Dimension	2 × 3	1½ × 2½
	2 × 4	1½ × 3½
	2 × 6	1½ × 5½
	2 × 8	1½ × 7¼
	2 × 10	1½ × 9¼
	2 × 12	1½ × 11¼

Source: A Recommended Revision of Simplified Practice Recommendation 16-53, American Lumber Standards for Softwood Lumber, May 1969. U.S. Department of Commerce, National Bureau of Standards.

Wood-frame construction

Figure 7-3. The vertical wall members, called studs, are 2 by 4 in. and are usually spaced 16 in. center to center (in some cases 12 in. center to center). They are nailed to the shoe and held together at the top by a double 2 by 4-in. plate. For exterior walls the studs are covered with wood or composition-board sheathing, then with a layer of building paper to seal all cracks, over which the shingles or siding is applied. A stucco or cement finish may be used in place of shingles, in which case expanded wire lath is applied over the building paper to provide a bond for the stucco. Wood sheathing provides a stronger structure when laid diagonally than when laid horizontally, but it is somewhat more expensive because of excessive cutting. When horizontally laid sheathing is used, the diagonal corner braces are let into the studs to make the frame rigid. As a substitute for 1- × 8-in. wood sheathing and let-in corner bracing, ½-in. plywood or nailable gypsum sheathing 4 × 8 ft provides equal or greater rigidity and has greater insu-

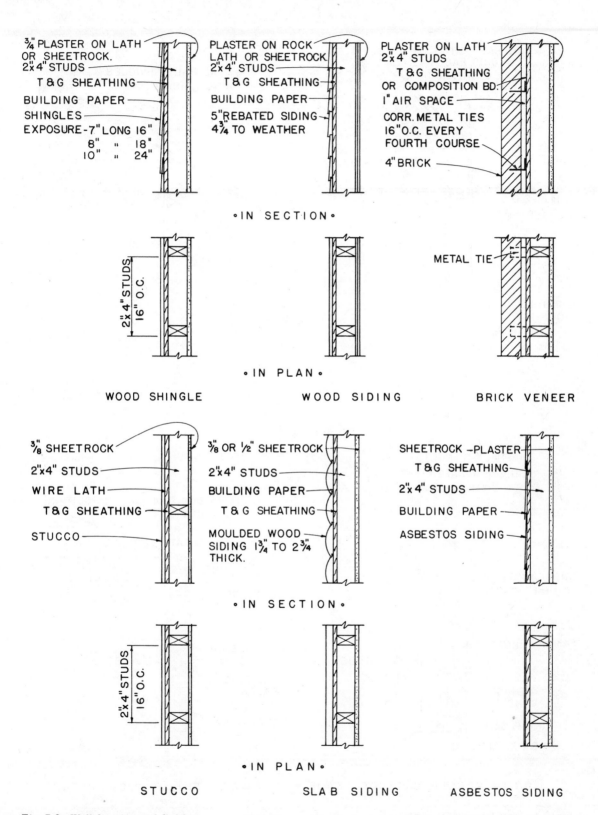

¾" PLASTER ON LATH OR SHEETROCK.
2"x 4" STUDS
T & G SHEATHING
BUILDING PAPER
SHINGLES
EXPOSURE - 7" LONG 16"
8"   "   18"
10"   "   24"

PLASTER ON ROCK LATH OR SHEETROCK.
2"x 4" STUDS
T & G SHEATHING
BUILDING PAPER
5" REBATED SIDING
4¾" TO WEATHER

PLASTER ON LATH
2"x 4" STUDS
T & G SHEATHING OR COMPOSITION BD.
1" AIR SPACE
CORR. METAL TIES 16" O.C. EVERY FOURTH COURSE
4" BRICK

• IN SECTION •

2"x 4" STUDS 16" O.C.

METAL TIE

• IN PLAN •

WOOD SHINGLE   **WOOD SIDING**   **BRICK VENEER**

⅜" SHEETROCK
2"x 4" STUDS
WIRE LATH
T & G SHEATHING
STUCCO

⅜" OR ½" SHEETROCK
2"x 4" STUDS
BUILDING PAPER
T & G SHEATHING
MOULDED WOOD SIDING 1¾" TO 2¾" THICK.

SHEETROCK - PLASTER
T & G SHEATHING
2"x 4" STUDS
BUILDING PAPER
ASBESTOS SIDING

• IN SECTION •

2"x 4" STUDS 16" O.C.

• IN PLAN •

STUCCO   **SLAB SIDING**   **ASBESTOS SIDING**

Fig. 7-3. Wall framing and finishes.

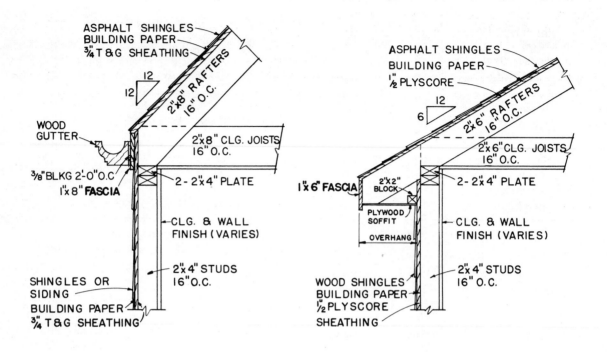

ASPHALT SHINGLES
BUILDING PAPER
¾ T & G SHEATHING

2"x8" RAFTERS 16" O.C.

12 / 12

WOOD GUTTER

2"x8" CLG. JOISTS 16" O.C.

⅜" BLKG 2'-0" O.C
1"x8" **FASCIA**

2-2"x4" PLATE

CLG. & WALL FINISH (VARIES)

SHINGLES OR SIDING
BUILDING PAPER
¾ T & G SHEATHING

2"x4" STUDS 16" O.C.

• WOOD FRAME WITHOUT OVERHANG •

ASPHALT SHINGLES
BUILDING PAPER
½" PLYSCORE

2"x6" RAFTERS 16" O.C.

6 / 12

2"x6" CLG. JOISTS 16" O.C.

1"x6" FASCIA

2"x2" BLOCK

2-2"x4" PLATE

PLYWOOD SOFFIT

OVERHANG

CLG. & WALL FINISH (VARIES)

WOOD SHINGLES
BUILDING PAPER
½" PLYSCORE
SHEATHING

2"x4" STUDS 16" O.C.

• WOOD FRAME WITH OVERHANG •

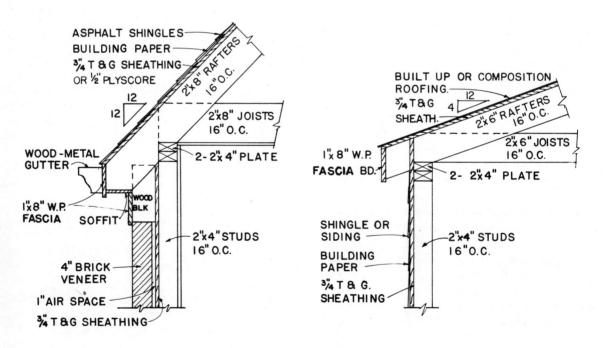

ASPHALT SHINGLES
BUILDING PAPER
¾" T & G SHEATHING
OR ½" PLYSCORE

2"x8" RAFTERS 16" O.C.

12 / 12

2"x8" JOISTS 16" O.C.

WOOD-METAL GUTTER

2-2"x4" PLATE

WOOD BLK

1"x8" W.P. FASCIA

SOFFIT

2"x4" STUDS 16" O.C.

4" BRICK VENEER

1" AIR SPACE

¾" T & G SHEATHING

BRICK VENEER ON WOOD FRAME •

BUILT UP OR COMPOSITION ROOFING.
¾ T & G SHEATH.

4 / 12

2"x6" RAFTERS 16" O.C.

2"x6" JOISTS 16" O.C.

1"x8" W.P. FASCIA BD.

2- 2"x4" PLATE

SHINGLE OR SIDING
BUILDING PAPER
¾ T & G. SHEATHING

2"x4" STUDS 16" O.C.

• WOOD FRAME - LOW PITCH •

Fig. 7-4. Roof framing.

lating value against heat or cold than wood sheathing. The plywood or gypsum may cost more than the wood sheathing, but the time and labor saving for installation will compensate for the additional cost of material. Regular gypsum sheathing nailed to studs is used with brick veneer, and nailable gypsum sheathing is used under wood siding or shingles. The use of cement-coated nails is recommended. Building paper over the sheathing is used in either case.

There are numerous varieties of shingles and siding material on the market. It should always be noted on the drawings or in the written specifications that the manufacturer's instructions for their installation must be followed carefully.

Interior walls may be finished with lath and plaster or gypsum board. The use of wood lath has become obsolete because of the high labor cost involved; in place of the wood lath an expanded wire lath is fastened to the studs. The rough or scratch coat of plaster is then applied to the wire lath, which provides a bonding surface. A third method replaces the expanded wire lath with a gypsum or rock lath perforated with holes into which the scratch coat of plaster is forced to provide the necessary bond. This board is $\frac{3}{8}$ or $\frac{1}{2}$ in. thick. Many houses are now erected using large sheets of gypsum board, also called sheet rock, which is fire-resistant. The sheet rock is nailed directly to the studs in place of the lath and plaster. The joints are then spackled, taped, and sanded, and the walls are painted or covered with various wall coverings. This is called dry-wall construction.

Brick-veneer walls

Figure 7-2. Box-sill construction can also be used with 4-in. brick or stone veneer. In this case the foundation is increased in thickness to carry the brick veneer. Building paper is nailed to the sheathing, as in the construction previously described, before the brick veneer is started. An air space is left between the sheathing and the veneer to dry any moisture which may seep in. In order to anchor the veneer to the sheathing, corrugated metal ties spaced approximately 16 in. on center (oc) vertically are placed between courses, about 32 in. oc horizontally as shown in Fig. 7-12. The brick veneer is used only as an exterior finish and is not designed to carry any of the building load. Other types of veneer material, such as cut stone and fabricated stone or tile, may be used, and it is well to follow the manufacturer's directions for their proper installation. In new structures, hollow-tile, cinder-block, or concrete-block backing can be used in place of the wood-frame construction.

Solid-brick walls

In solid-brick construction the floor joists or beams are enclosed in the brickwork, and the ends of the beams are fire-cut on an angle toward the inside of the wall as required by building codes. This is done to allow the floor joists to fall, in case of fire, without toppling the walls above. The beams must have at least 4-in. bearing in the wall. The wall thickness must conform to the requirements of the local building code.

The mortar joints from $\frac{3}{8}$ to $\frac{1}{2}$ in. thick are staggered for bonding and to minimize water seepage and air infiltration. Also in certain rows or courses bricks are laid at right angles to the bricks in the adjacent courses above and below in order to form a bond between the face and the backup course. Various arrangements of the brick have been devised to form different wall patterns. However, the simplest arrangement, known as American or running bond, is ordinarily used. This arrangement has a header or bonding course every sixth row, and the row is started with a three-quarter brick to maintain the staggered joints.

Bricks are laid with well-filled mortar joints to avoid water seepage. Masonry walls are often porous, and some seepage may occur. To avoid damage to the interior, either the inside of the walls is furred or a coating of hot pitch is applied. Furring usually consists of wood strips, $\frac{3}{4}$ by $1\frac{1}{2}$ in., nailed both vertically and horizontally to the wall and spaced 24 in. apart to hold the metal lathing, rock lath, or sheet rock previously mentioned. The rough flooring, called subflooring and usually $\frac{3}{4}$ in. thick, is nailed directly to the floor beams and is laid tight against the wall. The grounds for the baseboard are nailed to the furring strips just above the subflooring.

Exercises

To become thoroughly familiar with the construction details discussed so far, redraw the illustrations shown in Figs. 7-2 and 7-3 to a scale of $1\frac{1}{2}'' = 1'-0''$. Show all dimensions and designations given in the figures. For an original exercise make a similar drawing of a solid-brick-wall construction with basement wall as described in the preceding paragraph. The brick should be laid in American bond with mortar joints approximately $\frac{1}{2}$ in. Make this drawing to a scale of $1\frac{1}{2}'' = 1'-0''$. Give dimensions and notes similar to the examples in Fig. 7-2.

Roof framing

The roof members which provide a support for the sheathing or roofing materials do the same job for the roof as the joists do for the floors. These members are called the rafters, or common rafters. They should have a minimum bearing of 4 in. on the plate and should extend from the plate to the ridge. The ridge is the member at the upper end of the rafters. It holds them together and keeps them properly aligned. When two sloping roof surfaces meet to form an exterior angle, the angle is known as a valley. The rafter in the angle is called a valley rafter, and the shorter rafters extending from the valley rafter up to the ridge are called valley jacks.

Figure 7-4 shows four examples of wall framing carried up to the roof. Note in each case the plate is formed of 2- by 4-in. lumber at the top of the studs. The ceiling joists and the rafters rest directly on the plate. In the first case, without overhang, the rafters are not notched on the plate; but in the examples with an overhang, the rafters are notched to seat securely on the plate. The size of the joists and rafters and the slope or pitch of the rafters vary with the general design of the structure. The top corners of the joists are cut to match the line of the rafters. The ends of the rafters are cut vertically to receive the fascia board and horizontally to accommodate the soffit, sometimes called the plancher.

Gutters to carry off rainwater may be made of wood, copper, or aluminum and should be of ample size. Wood gutters, if properly made and frequently painted, or if lined with metal, will last for many years. The gutter should be hung or secured at the proper height so that snow will naturally pass over it as the snow slides off the roof.

There are many kinds of roof covering, but generally ¾-in.-thick tongue-and-groove sheathing is laid over the rafters, then covered with roofing paper and asphalt or composition shingles. Formerly slate shingles were often used, and in some sections ceramic tiles are used. For roofs with a low pitch, a built-up or composition construction is used. This consists of several layers of building paper and hot pitch with fine slag scattered over the top coat of pitch. Such a roof, if installed by a reliable contractor, will be given a 20-year guarantee and is called a bonded roof.

Exercises

Draw the four examples of roof framing shown in Fig. 7-4 to a scale of 1½″ = 1′–0″. When making the drawing of the wall with the brick veneer, draw the brick courses with the mortar joints and a metal tie inserted in the joint every fourth or fifth course. Show all dimensions and designations given in the figure.

Wall sections

We have now discussed the foundation, wall framing, and roof framing. Figure 7-5 shows two examples of complete wall sections, each with these three elements assembled in one picture. An exterior wall rests on the foundation and constitutes a bearing unit for the upper floors and the roof. The exterior wall also forms the outer framework for the inner construction. There are three main parts to the wall, namely, the framework, the weatherside finish, and the interior or roomside finish. The exterior walls serve to tie or hold the structure together. The exterior or outer bearing walls may be built up of wood timbers, steel shapes, stone, brick, concrete, hollow tile, or concrete blocks, to mention the materials most commonly used. The finishes previously described and shown in Fig. 7-3 are in use, and newer materials, such as aluminum and magnesium sheets and steel sheets with baked-on enamel finishes, are continually appearing on the market. Full instructions for the installation of different materials will be supplied by the manufacturers or trade associations marketing them.

You will note that reference has been made in Fig. 7-5 to asphaltum waterproofing for the exterior of the foundation wall. It is difficult to make a concrete mixture that will be impervious to water after it has hardened. However, there are chemical compounds on the market which can be added to the concrete mix to make it impervious or nearly so. Another way to keep water from seeping through the concrete is to coat the outer side of the foundation wall with hot asphaltum, or tarry substance, which if properly applied, will seal the surface against water seepage. There are other methods more complicated, such as membrane waterproofing, which can be investigated for cellar or sub-basement installations on sandy beaches or swampy areas.

Exercise

Draw the wall sections shown in Fig. 7-5 to a scale of 1½″ = 1′–0″. Show brick with ½-in. mortar joints. Take note of the ledge in the foundation wall to hold the brick for the veneer. Also note, in each case, the box-sill construction using the sill, the sill header, and the shoe or sole resting on the subflooring.

Western framing

The western, or platform, framing shown in Fig. 7-6 is a variation of the braced frame and provides a rigid

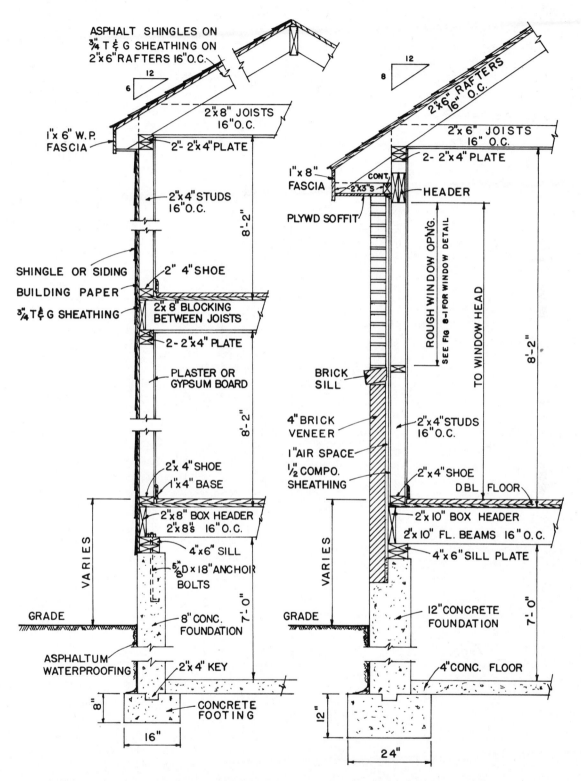

ASPHALT SHINGLES ON
¾ T & G SHEATHING ON
2"x 6" RAFTERS 16"O.C.

12
6

2"X 8" JOISTS
16" O.C.

1"x 6" W.P.
FASCIA

2- 2"x 4" PLATE

2"x 4" STUDS
16" O.C.

8'-2"

SHINGLE OR SIDING

2" 4" SHOE

BUILDING PAPER

¾ T & G SHEATHING

2"x 8" BLOCKING
BETWEEN JOISTS

2- 2"x 4" PLATE

PLASTER OR
GYPSUM BOARD

8'-2"

2"x 4" SHOE

1"x 4" BASE

2"x 8" BOX HEADER
2"x 8's 16" O.C.

4"x 6" SILL

⅝ "D x 18" ANCHOR
BOLTS

GRADE

8" CONC.
FOUNDATION

7'-0"

VARIES

ASPHALTUM
WATERPROOFING

2"x 4" KEY

8"

CONCRETE
FOOTING

16"

• TWO STORY WESTERN FRAME CONSTRUCTION •

12
8

2"x 6" RAFTERS
16" O.C.

2"x 6" JOISTS
16" O.C.

2- 2"x 4" PLATE

1"x 8"
FASCIA

CONT.
2"x3's

HEADER

PLYWD SOFFIT

ROUGH WINDOW OPN'G.
SEE FIG 8-1 FOR WINDOW DETAIL

TO WINDOW HEAD

8'-2"

BRICK
SILL

4" BRICK
VENEER

1" AIR SPACE

½" COMPO.
SHEATHING

2"x 4" STUDS
16" O.C.

2"x 4" SHOE

DBL FLOOR

2"x 10" BOX HEADER

2"x 10" FL. BEAMS 16" O.C.

4"x 6" SILL PLATE

GRADE

VARIES

12" CONCRETE
FOUNDATION

7'-0"

4" CONC. FLOOR

12"

24"

• ONE STORY BRICK VENEER CONST. •

Fig. 7-5. Wall sections.

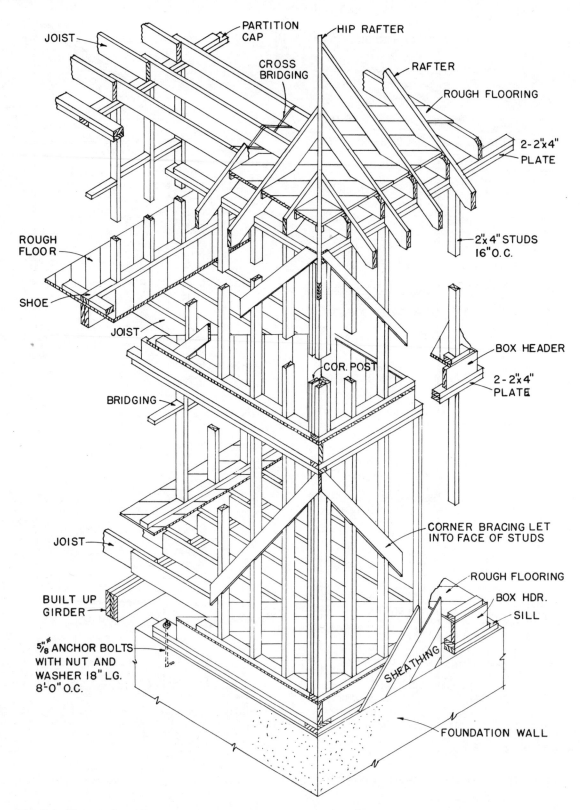

JOIST

PARTITION CAP

HIP RAFTER

CROSS BRIDGING

RAFTER

ROUGH FLOORING

2-2"x4" PLATE

ROUGH FLOOR

2"x 4" STUDS 16"O.C.

SHOE

JOIST

BOX HEADER

COR. POST

2-2"x4" PLATE

BRIDGING

JOIST

CORNER BRACING LET INTO FACE OF STUDS

ROUGH FLOORING

BUILT UP GIRDER

BOX HDR.

SILL

5"⌀ ANCHOR BOLTS WITH NUT AND WASHER 18" LG. 8¹O" O.C.

SHEATHING

FOUNDATION WALL

Fig. 7-6. Western framing.

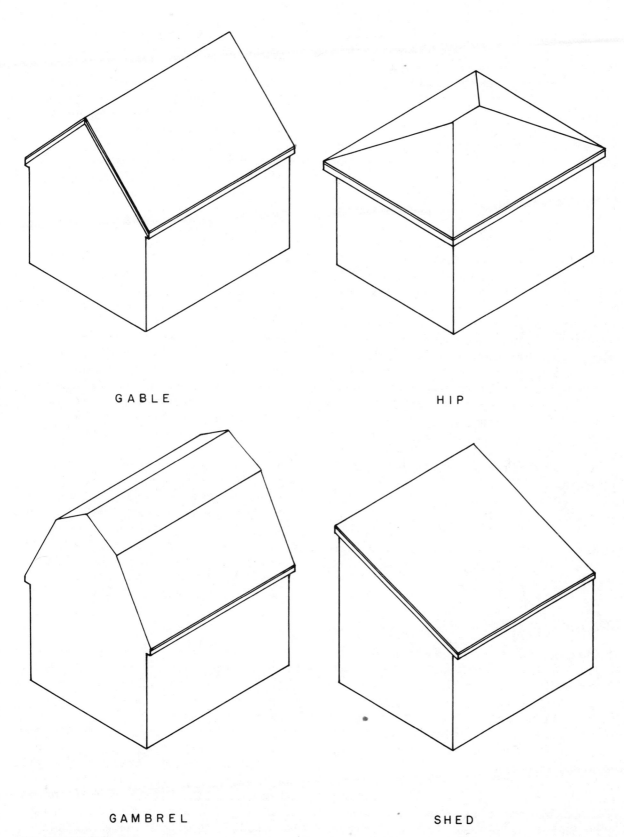

GABLE

HIP

GAMBREL

SHED

Fig. 7-7. Roof types.

structure. It also allows for the use of smaller lumber sizes and does not require the structural members to be mortised. Because of the simplicity of its erection, the western framing has gained in popularity throughout the country.

The framing is formed on the box sill with the standard spacing for the studs and joists 16 in. center to center. The subflooring is laid diagonally to give additional strength, but if it is laid at right angles to the joists, there is some saving in the cutting. Diagonal sheathing also provides extra strength but may be installed horizontally if extra precautions are taken to brace the corners securely with diagonal corner bracing. Using large sheets of plywood instead of sheathing boards will give added rigidity to the framing.

The cross bridging between the floor joists is installed about 8 ft apart longitudinally and is usually made of ¾- by 2½-in. lumber or special metal strapping. The diagonal bridging reinforces the joists and increases their resistance to buckling and turning sideways. The runs of bridging should be in straight lines along the floor in order that each bridging strut will be directly opposite the strut opposing it. Metal bridging which will fit between standard joist spacing is also available and may be installed economically. Horizontal wall bridging is also used between the studs about halfway from floor to ceiling and is required by local building codes to serve as a fire stop. It also stiffens bearing walls.

Exercise

Draw the western framing shown in Fig. 7-6 to a scale of ¾″ = 1′–0″, and include all the items shown with the correct designations.

Roof types

The language of the engineering and architectural field has many words and names which are more or less descriptive in nature. When the architect or designer creates a new device or form he gives it a name which fits either its appearance or its function. For the roof types shown in Fig. 7-7, we will consult the dictionary for definitions of the words and see if these definitions in any way describe the forms shown.

Gable. "A vertical triangular portion of the end of a building from the cornice or eaves to the ridge of the building." Hence a gable roof is one forming a gable at each end of the roof. This roof slopes up from two walls of the house.

Hip. "The external angle formed by the meeting of two sloping sides of a roof." Therefore a hip roof is a roof having sloping ends and sloping sides. In other words, a hipped roof is one sloping up from four walls of the building.

Gambrel. "The hock of an animal, especially a horse." In a horse's hock there is an offset or we might say a curb or double-slope effect. Thus we arrive at a curb roof or a roof having a double slope. A curb roof is also called a gambrel roof.

Shed. "A structure for shelter or storage, especially a light one for wagons or wood." We usually think of a shed in terms of a lean-to alongside another building or even a separate light structure with a single sloping roof. Hence the term "shed roof," or a roof sloping in one direction only.

Roof pitch. Roof pitches are selected to suit various conditions. Sometimes the height desired for the upper story will be a factor, and again a steeper roof may be deemed advisable in northern climates to allow snow to slide off. But these factors must still be fitted into the general scheme or proportions of the structure in order that the appearance will be balanced and pleasing. The pitch finally selected is expressed as a ratio of the rise to the total span and is shown on the drawing as the slope or rake, or the rise in each 12 in. of the run. The run equals one half the total span, that is, 6 in 12 for ¼ pitch or 8 in 12 for ⅓ pitch, as shown in Fig. 7-8. When drawing the roof rafters, first draw the pitch line at the given slope from the outside corner or face of the top plate to the center of the span. Then draw the rafter parallel to the pitch line with the lower edge of the rafter starting at the inside of the top plate. Draw the ridge, usually a 2-in.-thick piece of lumber; the intersection of the sides of the ridge with the top line of the rafter will determine the total rise of the roof above the top of the plate.

Brick details

The United States Bureau of Standards recommends that common brick and rough-faced brick be made 8 in. by 3¾ in. wide and 2¼ in. high. Bricks are usually laid with the largest face horizontal in courses 2¼ in. high, not counting the thickness of the mortar joints. Bricks laid thus with the 8- by 2¼-in. face exposed on the face of the wall are called *stretchers*, and bricks laid with the 3¾- by 2¼-in. end exposed on the face of the wall are called *headers*. When bricks are arranged with the 8-in. edge vertical and the 2¼-in. edge horizontal, they are called *soldiers*. Bricks arranged with the 3¾-in. edge vertical and the 2¼-in. edge horizontal are called *rowlocks*.

Bricks are also made in various other sizes and shapes for special purposes. Manufacturer's catalogs or

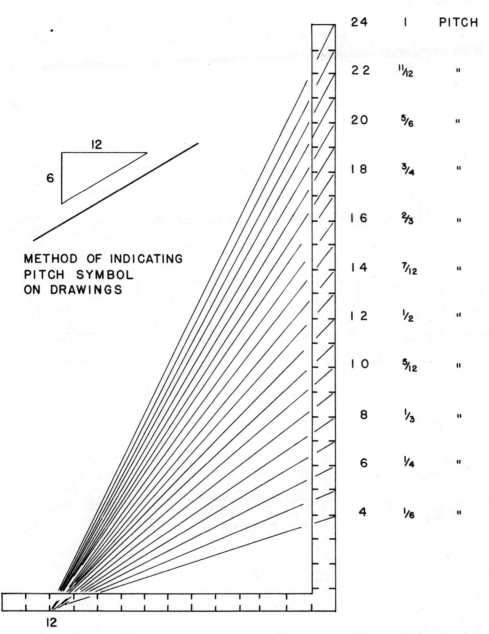

METHOD OF INDICATING
PITCH SYMBOL
ON DRAWINGS

24	1	PITCH
22	$^{11}/_{12}$	"
20	$^5/_6$	"
18	$^3/_4$	"
16	$^2/_3$	"
14	$^7/_{12}$	"
12	$^1/_2$	"
10	$^5/_{12}$	"
8	$^1/_3$	"
6	$^1/_4$	"
4	$^1/_6$	"

FINDING THE ROOF PITCH USING A CARPENTER'S STEEL SQUARE

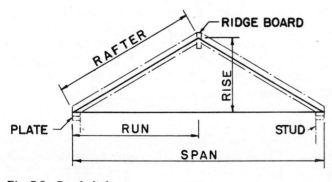

TO FIND THE PITCH OF A ROOF
DIVIDE THE SPAN BY THE RISE.
6 GOES INTO 24 FOUR TIMES,
MAKING A $^1/_4$ PITCH. DIVIDING
THE RISE BY THE SPAN, 6
DIVIDED BY 24 EQUALS $^1/_4$.
THEREFORE THE PITCH IS $^1/_4$.

Fig. 7-8. Roof pitch.

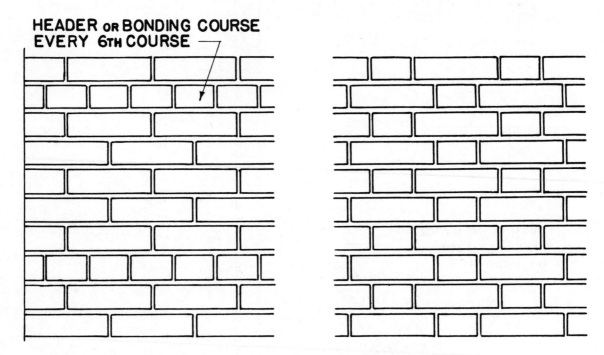

Fig. 7-9. Common bond.

Fig. 7-10. Flemish bond.

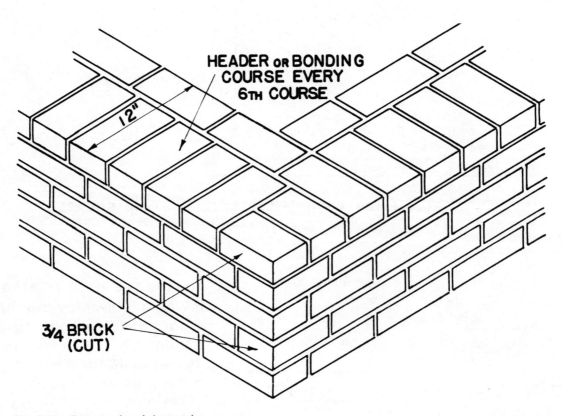

Fig. 7-11. Common bond, isometric.

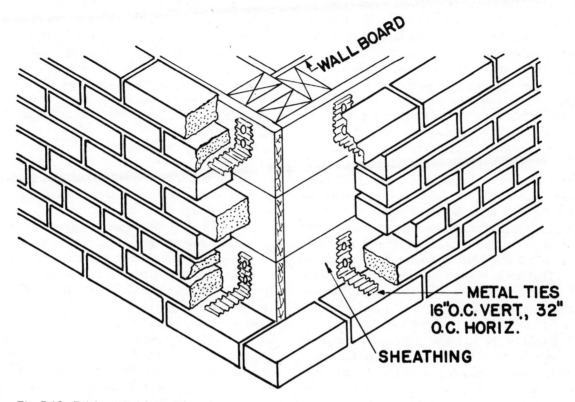

Fig. 7-12. Brick veneer, isometric.

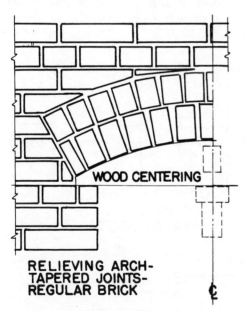

RELIEVING ARCH-
TAPERED JOINTS-
REGULAR BRICK

Fig. 7-13. Relieving arch.

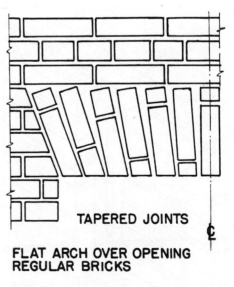

FLAT ARCH OVER OPENING
REGULAR BRICKS

Fig. 7-14. Flat arch.

reference books will provide details of the shapes and information about their proper uses.

The term *bond* is used to indicate two different things. In one case it means that the bonding course provides overlapping brick in order to tie the masonry units together and give the wall greater strength. In the other use of the word, the pattern bond provides a variety of appearances for the face of the wall. When the wall is laid up in common or running bond, also called *American bond*, as shown in Figs. 7-9 and 7-11, a full header should be provided every sixth row or course. Figure 7-10 illustrates a wall laid up in Flemish bond with alternate headers and stretchers in every course. Such a wall with full headers throughout requires one-third more face brick, which adds to the cost of the wall. Full headers may be used only in alternate courses in Flemish bond in order to provide structural bonding equal to a wall laid up in common bond. The Flemish bond pattern is maintained by using half bricks in the other course. The standard bonding usually required by city building codes is the one described for brick laid up in common bond.

It should be noted that in all brick walls the joints are staggered and the joints should be well filled with mortar in order to provide sealed joints. A careful procedure along these lines will make a tight wall and prevent leakage from either side of the wall.

Figure 7-12 illustrates a brick-veneer wall covering a wood frame. The bricks are laid up with staggered joints and any standard type of bonding pattern may be used. However, since the veneer wall is only the thickness of one brick, all the headers are half bricks and are sometimes called *blind headers*. They do not add to the structural bonding of the wall as in the case of full headers. Therefore the brick-veneer wall must be tied to the building frame with wall ties fastened through the sheathing to the studs every fourth or fifth course. These metal ties should be spaced about 32 in. apart.

It should be noted that the information and explanations in the text pertain chiefly to drafting requirements. The precise method and manner of actual bricklaying procedures may be studied in books especially written to describe the bricklaying trade.

Arches may be built of special wedge-shaped bricks or by using common brick. Common bricks are more often used as they are less expensive and can be fitted to the curve of the arch by making the joints slightly thinner at the inner edge and thicker at the outer edge of the course. Figures 7-13 and 7-14 illustrate two types of arches, both formed by using common brick size 8 in. long, 3¾ in. wide, and 2¼ in. high. The wood centering, shown in Fig. 7-13, is made by the carpenter, and the bricklayer helps the carpenter set the centering in place. The ends of the centering rest on the side walls as shown. Both the relieving arch and the flat arch shown are laid with tapered joints.

There are times when it is necessary or desirable to provide a chase or recess in a wall to accommodate pipes or ducts so that they will not protrude beyond the face of the wall. An example of this arrangement is shown in Fig. 7-15.

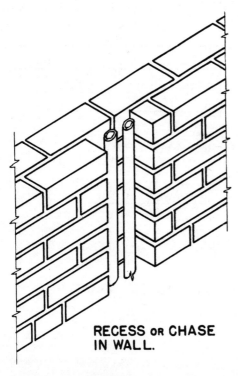

RECESS or CHASE IN WALL.

Fig. 7-15. Pipe chase.

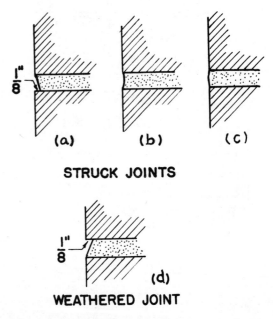

STRUCK JOINTS

WEATHERED JOINT

Fig. 7-16. Brick joints.

Mortar joints may vary in thickness from ⅛ in. to ⅞ in. The very narrow joints are used for smooth-pressed brick and the thicker joints for rough-textured brick. Common bricks are laid with joints ⅜ to ½ in. thick. The struck joints in Fig. 7-16a and 7-16b are used in nearly all exposed walls made of common brick. The indentation is made with the point of the bricklayer's trowel. The struck joint is usually made when the bricklayer works from an inside scaffold, and the weathered joint shown in Fig. 7-16d is made when an outside scaffold is used. The struck joint shown in Fig.

7-16a is not favored because water can collect on the small ledge that is formed. Another type of joint shown in Fig. 7-16c has a slight outward bulge and can be used to form a very effective pattern.

Exercises

Draw the brickwork illustrated in Figs. 7-9 to 7-13 inclusive using common brick dimensions and a scale of 1½" = 1'−0". Include all items and all notations shown in the figures.

8. more construction details

Windows

In tropical countries we often find native houses with openings in the walls to admit air and light to the interior. However, in many houses, especially in non-tropical countries, the openings are fitted with frames and sash to hold glass in order to keep out cold or rain, and the next step is to make the sash movable to permit varying degrees of adjustment.

Generally, many sizes of windows of various types are carried in stock by manufacturers. These sizes are listed in catalogs and reference books as stock items; the architect or draftsman will try to use stock sizes to avoid excessive costs and to expedite delivery. In unusual cases where odd sizes or designs are used, detail drawings or specifications and often both will be required in order to obtain quotations from the manufacturer.

The windows in a house not only serve a useful purpose but also must be arranged to enhance the building architecturally. That is, consideration must be given to the location, size, and type with regard to the inside of each room, and also their arrangement and proportions must enhance the outside appearance of the structure. In these days of air conditioning where windows are sometimes omitted entirely, the architect must take into consideration the effect of a blank wall and must design so that this wall will appear to be part of the natural lines or intent of the work.

Probably wood has been the most common material for windows, but steel and aluminum are also being used in increasing amounts. Metal windows are made up of formed metal shapes, but the names of the different parts are the same as for wood windows and the functions of the windows are the same in any material. Two of the more common types of windows are the double hung and the casement, which are shown in Figs. 8-1 and 8-2, respectively. The sliding window and the awning, or projected, window are shown in Fig. 8-3.

When we use the term "window" we mean the frame which is fixed and fits into the rough wall opening and the movable part or sash which holds the glass. The lower horizontal side of the frame is called the sill, the vertical sides the jambs, and the horizontal top side the head section. The frame is set into a suitable rough opening which has been provided in the wall at the desired location. The frame should be constructed so that the joints between the wall and the frame can be sealed by building paper and caulking compound to keep out dust and prevent air leakage.

In wood-frame construction, it will be necessary to cut some of the studs to provide the opening for the window frame. The ends of the cut studs are framed into headers which will extend horizontally between the adjacent uncut studs. These headers are made up of two wood members with a $\frac{3}{8}$-in. spacer between and are designed to span the window opening. The spacer may be a $\frac{3}{8}$-in. continuous piece of plywood or shorter strips of $\frac{3}{8}$-in. plywood serving as spacers. Double studs are framed vertically under the header at each side to support the header and complete the opening for the

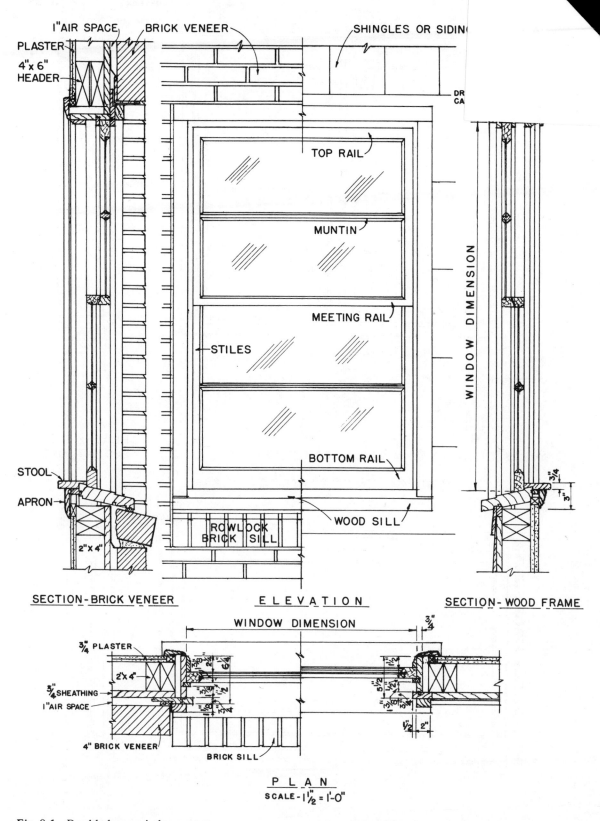

I" AIR SPACE   BRICK VENEER
SHINGLES OR SIDING
PLASTER
4"x 6"
HEADER
DR
CA
TOP RAIL
MUNTIN
MEETING RAIL
STILES
WINDOW DIMENSION
BOTTOM RAIL
STOOL
APRON
3/4"
3"
2" X 4"
ROWLOCK
BRICK SILL
WOOD SILL

SECTION-BRICK VENEER   E L E V A T I O N   SECTION-WOOD FRAME

WINDOW DIMENSION   3/4"

3/4" PLASTER
2"x 4"
3/4" SHEATHING
I" AIR SPACE
4" BRICK VENEER   BRICK SILL

P L A N
SCALE- 1 1/2" = 1'-0"

Fig. 8-1. Double-hung window.

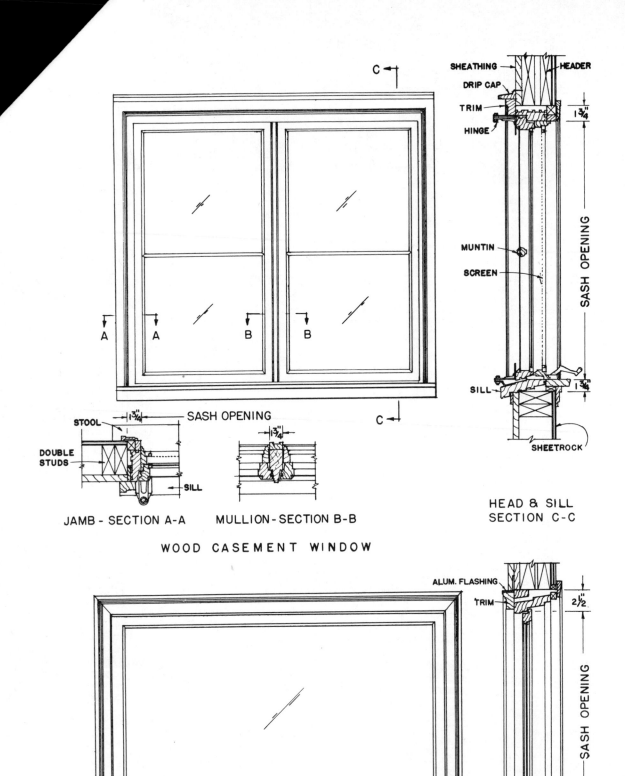

Fig. 8-2. Casement windows.

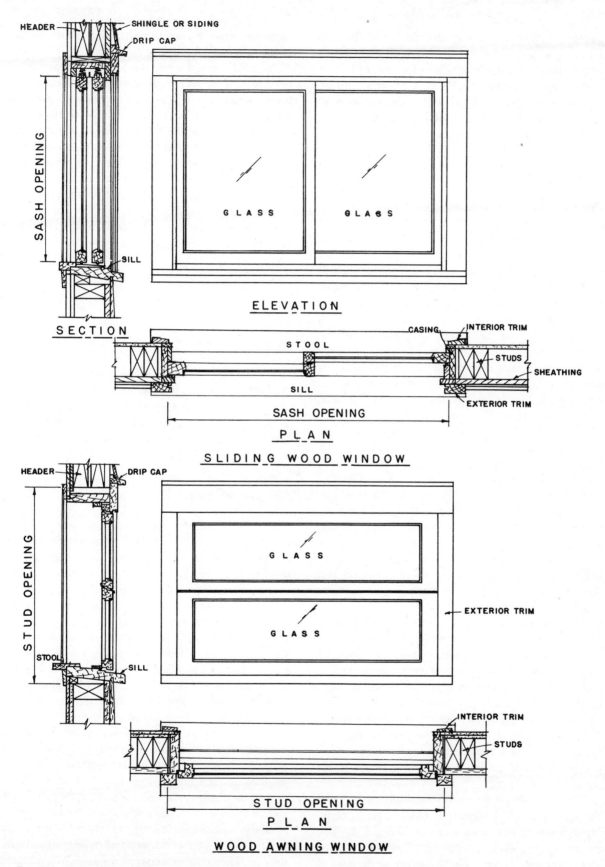

Fig. 8-3. Sliding and awning windows.

73

window frame. In this way the weight of the wall above the window opening is carried down on each side of the window and the framing is not weakened.

In masonry construction, the same effect is achieved by providing a lintel made of steel angles, channels, or beams which are extended out beyond the window opening to bear and support the load over the window.

Double-hung windows

Figure 8-1 shows a typical wood double-hung window in a wood frame and a brick-veneer construction. The frame is made up of the window box, or inside casing; the stool, or lower horizontal part of the casing; and the parting strip. Around the inside casing you will note the trim and apron which finish off the frame. The parting strips are fitted into the head and jamb sections to separate the upper and lower sash which may be moved up and down and which give the window its name of double-hung. Cast-iron weights, which were formerly used to balance the weight of the sash, allowing for easy raising and lowering, and which were hung inside the window box jambs on each side, have been replaced by a spring-balance arrangement which is furnished as part of the complete window frame and sash. The necessary hardware required for a window has not been shown as this is best covered in the detailed specifications by description or manufacturers' catalogue numbers. The right-hand side of Fig. 8-1 shows a wood double-hung window and frame set in frame construction. Note the wood sill and drip cap. The left-hand side of Fig. 8-1 shows the same window set in frame construction with a brick veneer. The bricks are laid on edge to form a rowlock brick sill, and there is a steel-angle lintel to carry the brick veneer above the window opening.

The window sash consists of the top and bottom rails, the sides, or stiles; the center, or meeting, rails; and the muntins, or strips, which separate the panes of glass. The muntins may extend vertically as well as horizontally. Stock sizes of sash with various arrangements and combinations of standard glass sizes are carried by the mills which manufacture window frames and sash. Therefore, it is best to refer to manufacturers' stock lists when selecting windows. The stock lists give the sash size and the rough, or stud, opening required for the frame.

While care should be taken to seal all joints around the window frames by means of building paper, caulking compounds, and in some cases flashing, it may also be found necessary to provide weather stripping around the sash. The weather stripping may be made of felt, copper, or aluminum strips fastened to the frame at the sides, top, and bottom of the sash. Some manufacturers design the weather stripping so that it is part of the sash and is applied at the factory.

In some locations it is considered good practice to provide houses with extra storm sash which may be hung outside the regular window sash to give extra protection against air leakage in cold weather. Such sash are usually hinged at the top and are installed for winter use only. A newer development is an aluminum storm sash with a removable glass section which can be replaced by a screened section for summer use. This type of storm sash can be left in place the year round.

The use of steel lintels over window openings has been noted. A lintel can also be formed in a brick or stone wall by arranging the brick or stone to form an arch over the opening. In a brick wall the arch is formed by using the brick as headers or stretchers.

Exercise

In order to become familiar with the details of the double-hung window construction, draw the sill, jamb, and header section of a stock-size window to a scale of $1\frac{1}{2}'' = 1'-0''$, showing the elevation and plan similar to the window in Fig. 8-1. Select the stock window size from a manufacturer's stock list, and show the window set in a frame construction and in a brick-veneer construction.

Casement windows

Figure 8-2 shows two types of wood casement windows. A casement window has a frame similar to the double-hung window and a single sash hinged on one side or two sash hinged on opposite sides. The sash may be installed to swing inward or outward. Since it is difficult to make a casement window tight against the weather, it is often provided with a drip molding along the bottom rail to keep out water at the window sill. When a casement window swings out, a separate screen may be installed on the inside as indicated in Fig. 8-2. If the window swings in, the screen is installed on the outside of the window. In either case, the screens may be hung in place at the top so that they may be swung upward or even hinged at the side to swing the same as the sash. Steel or aluminum casement windows can be set in a mastic cement and made tight against the weather. Metal window frames may be used with wood sash or matching metal sash. In most cases metal casement windows are arranged to swing outward.

Single casement windows are often hinged at the top to open inward or outward; when opening outward they are known as awning-type windows. When hinged at the bottom to open in a downward direction, the casement windows are known as hopper-type windows.

Single casement windows hinged at the top are frequently used in basements that are all or partly below the ground level. In basements where the windows are below ground level an areaway is provided to clear the windows and admit light. Casement sash may be secured with factory-applied weather stripping.

When an expensive hardwood is used for the inside trim of a room, the parts of a wood window frame which show in the room should be made of matching hardwood. The outer parts of the frame which are to be painted can be made of softer lumber. It is not necessary to use hardwoods for the heavy parts of the frames.

Stock sizes of glass and windows noted for double-hung windows apply equally to all other types of windows.

Exercise

Select a stock window size from a manufacturer's stock list for a double-sash wood casement window and a single-sash casement window. Draw the two windows with the head, sill, jamb, and mullion sections as shown in Fig. 8-2, using a scale $1\frac{1}{2}'' = 1'-0''$.

Sliding windows

The sliding windows shown in Fig. 8-3 are also called gliding window units by some manufacturers and are made with all the sash movable or with a combination of fixed and movable sash. Sliding windows are often used for picture windows where a large expanse of glass is desired, or in an arrangement of three sash with the center sash fixed and the two side sash movable. The sash are designed to slide past each other in grooves or tracks which are part of the window frame and are located at the top and bottom of the frame. Some sliding sash are fitted with a spring arrangement at the top which allows the sash to be removed from the frame by pressing upward on the top rail of the sash. The easy removal of the sash allows for window cleaning or painting at a convenient location. The head and sill tracks are usually made of aluminum; some manufacturers use a plastic sill track with a plastic-faced head track. Weather stripping is also provided as part of the sash. With sliding windows, screens can be installed on the outside of the windows.

Awning windows

Awning windows, shown in Fig. 8-3 and also called projected windows, are made of one or more single sash mounted in a vertical or horizontal line and hinged

at the top to swing outward. The awning-type arrangement provides maximum ventilation and also protects against adverse weather conditions. An arrangement of single narrow sash in a horizontal line is called a ribbon window and may have fixed or movable sash.

Exercise

Select a stock window size from a manufacturer's stock list for each of the window types shown in Fig. 8-3, and make a drawing to scale showing all the views similar to those in Fig. 8-3. Use a scale of $1\frac{1}{2}'' = 1'-0''$.

Louvers

Used in window openings where a glazed sash is not required to close the opening. An example of this use would be in an attic or tower. However, some arrangement is required to protect the opening against the weather and still provide for ventilation. This is accomplished by placing slats of wood or metal in the opening and sloping them to keep out the rain or snow. These slats are known as louvers. They may be fixed, or they may be movable so that the angle of the slope can be adjusted as desired. In place of the slats movable narrow glazed frames or sash have been fitted into the window frame to form the louvered window or jalousie.

Jalousie windows allow fresh-air ventilation from top to bottom and at the same time keep out rain. Both sides of the louvers can be cleaned from the inside of the room. The louvers deflect the air, thus avoiding drafts, but admit the light. Jalousie windows provide a safety feature because they avoid the hazard of an open window. They give extra protection as they cannot be opened from outside.

Doors

A door is a movable barrier which may be opened or closed to provide entrance or exit from one space to another space. Generally exterior and interior doors are hinged on one side to swing either in or out, and exterior doors are usually wider than interior doors. We will discuss wood doors and frames first and later take up other materials and types of doors in common use. The mills which make doors and door frames list many stock sizes in their catalogues, and it is best to select the doors required from stock lists. Every door is set in a frame, and a rough opening must be provided in the studding to accommodate the frame. The opening should be about 2 in. larger than the frame. Depending on the width of the door, the studs are cut out, and a

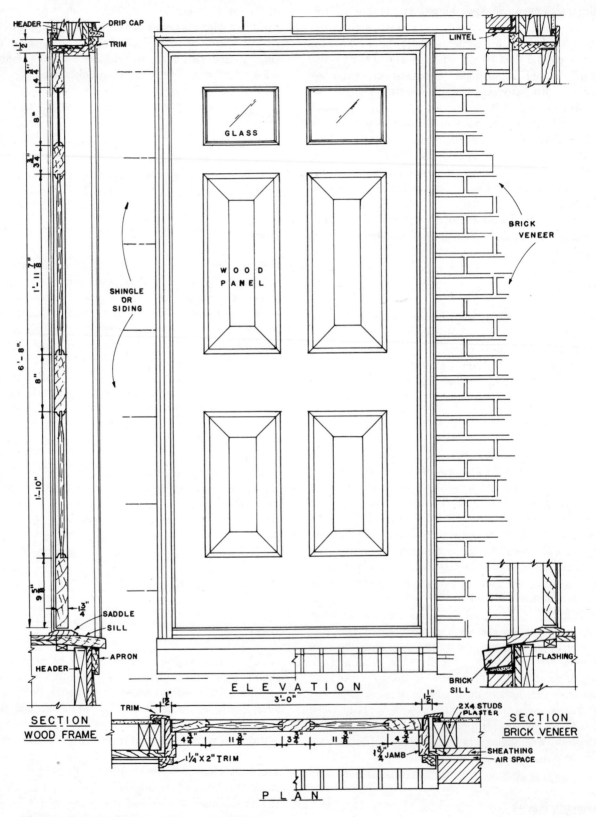

HEADER
DRIP CAP
TRIM
$\frac{1}{2}$"
$4\frac{3}{4}$"
8"
$3\frac{3}{4}$"
1'-11$\frac{7}{8}$"
6'-8"
SHINGLE OR SIDING
8"
1'-10"
9$\frac{5}{8}$"
1$\frac{3}{4}$"
SADDLE
SILL
APRON
HEADER

SECTION
WOOD FRAME

ELEVATION

GLASS

WOOD PANEL

3'-0"

LINTEL

BRICK VENEER

SECTION
BRICK VENEER

BRICK SILL

FLASHING

2X4 STUDS
PLASTER

SHEATHING
AIR SPACE

TRIM

$\frac{1}{2}$"

$\frac{1}{2}$"

$4\frac{3}{4}$" 11$\frac{3}{8}$" 3$\frac{3}{4}$" 11$\frac{3}{8}$" 4$\frac{3}{4}$"

1$\frac{1}{4}$"x 2" TRIM

1$\frac{3}{4}$" JAMB

PLAN

Fig. 8-4. Exterior door.

double header is framed horizontally over the top of the door opening. The full-length studs on each side of the opening are reinforced by adding a short stud framed under the lintel and extending down to the floor.

Exterior doors

An exterior door or doorway is the entrance to a house and should present a pleasing and inviting appearance. The entrance must at the same time fit in with the general architectural style of the house. Manufacturers' catalogues show designs of exterior entrances for all types of dwellings and other structures and list a great variety of stock sizes from which a suitable selection may be made. A well-chosen exterior entrance will give added charm and character to a house. Good proportions and simple lines make for economical construction. The side and rear, or service, doors may be simpler, but still both material and workmanship should be of good quality. Exterior doors are usually made of No. 1 ponderosa pine 1¾ in. thick with solid wood panels or various combinations of wood and glazed panels. A typical paneled door as shown in Fig. 8-4 consists of the top and bottom rails, the stiles or vertical sides, the lock rail, and the mullion, or vertical center section. The wood panels may be flat or raised, and either style may be flush or ovolo mounted. All first-class wood doors should be made with hardwood dowels and good moisture-resistant glue. Details of the construction should be checked in the manufacturer's catalog.

Exterior door frames are set on a masonry or wood sill and should have a threshold saddle under the door extending from jamb to jamb to cover the joint between the sill and the inside flooring. The door frame, consisting of the outside casing and the jambs, is fitted into a rough opening which has been provided in the studs and sheathing. The doorstop and the inside casing in turn are applied after the door is hung. Frames made of metal are called door bucks.

Exterior entrances are also made with sidelights, that is, with a fixed narrow glazed section on one or both sides of the door. This arrangement is decorative as well as useful for admitting light to the interior vestibule or entry. The main exterior door should be at least 3'–0" wide. Other exterior doors are preferably 2'–8" or 2'–10" wide.

A good height for a door is 7'–0", but in stock lists doors vary from 6'–6" to 7'–0".

Interior doors

Doors for the interior of a house are usually simpler than the main exterior door but are often made of the same woods and 1⅜ in. thick with solid panels. The frame for an interior door is not mill-assembled as a unit but is fitted by the carpenter into the rough stud opening. The doorstop and casing, or trim, are applied after the door is hung. The threshold saddle is sometimes omitted between rooms. Manufacturers also make flush-panel doors for interior use as shown in Fig. 8-5. A flush-panel door is made up of an interior framework or honeycomb on each side of which is glued a single large panel of plywood. Interior doors are usually 2'–6" wide. A good height for convenient passage is 6'–8" to 7'–0". Manufacturers' stock lists for interior doors also include smaller widths which may be used to shut closets and cupboards.

In addition to the swinging door which is hinged on the side, there are many other types of doors which we will mention briefly.

Sliding doors which overlap and therefore do not require extra wall space for their operation are used for closets. See section in Fig. 8-5. Valuable room space is saved as the doors do not swing out into the room.

Other doors

French doors, which are rather decorative, are a type of casement door in which wood panels have been replaced by glass. They are used where a room opens out onto a terrace or balcony. They are also useful to separate rooms in the living area of a house or to close off a dining room from a hall or foyer, that is, in an area where complete privacy is not desired.

A dutch door is divided in half horizontally so that the lower portion can remain closed while the upper half is open. This style of door adds charm to certain types of country homes.

Combination exterior doors that have a removable glazed section which can be replaced by a screened section are available. Storm doors are extra doors that are hung outside the regular doors for added protection in severe winter weather. There are also aluminum storm doors which have a removable screen section for summer use that can be replaced by a glazed section for winter use. The aluminum storm door can be left in place all year round. This type of door is more practical than a separate screen door installed in spring and removed at the end of the summer.

Garage doors may be made in two sections to swing outward; their use depends on the size of the garage. There are also overhead garage doors, some of which are operated manually, sliding upward and overhead on tracks. Others are operated by an electric motor which is started by an electrically operated switch as the car approaches the garage door.

Metal trim and doors are seldom used for homes but are used extensively for all other types of buildings and

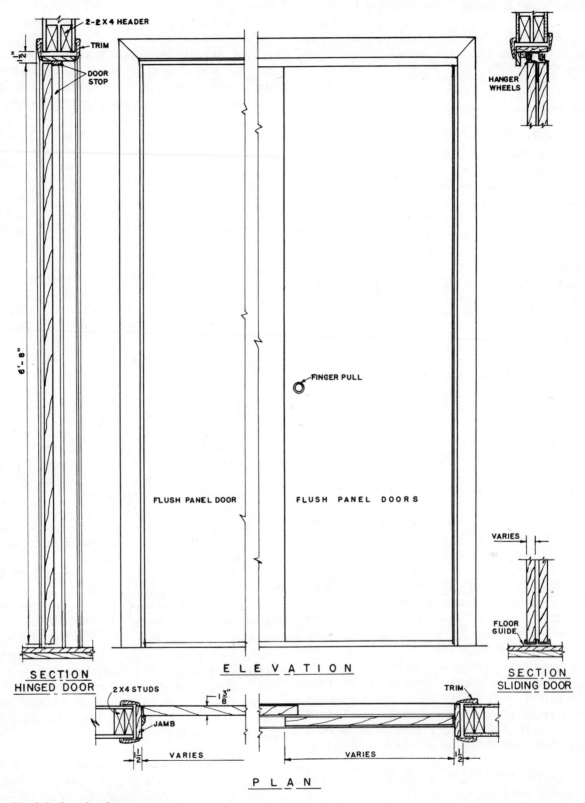

2-2 X 4 HEADER

TRIM

$1\frac{1}{2}"$

DOOR
STOP

HANGER
WHEELS

$6'-8"$

FINGER PULL

FLUSH PANEL DOOR

FLUSH PANEL DOORS

VARIES

ELEVATION

FLOOR
GUIDE

SECTION
HINGED DOOR

2 X 4 STUDS

$1\frac{3}{8}"$

TRIM

SECTION
SLIDING DOOR

JAMB

$\frac{1}{2}$

VARIES

VARIES

$\frac{1}{2}$

PLAN

Fig. 8-5. Interior doors.

are effective for fireproof construction. The trim and doors are similar to wood types but are made of special formed-metal shapes and flat-metal sheets welded together at the joints. The term "hollow metal" applies to a door and trim which do not have an interior core of wood. The term *kalamein* is commonly applied to all metal-covered trim and doors, but originally kalamein referred to a special form of galvanized iron. Metal-covered doors are generally used where fire doors are required.

The entrance doors for banks and public buildings are sometimes made of bronze or aluminum, and such doors would be made from detail drawings prepared by the manufacturer to meet the architect's specifications.

Hardware

Windows and doors require certain items of hardware which are not shown in detail on architectural drawings except when an enlarged view or section is required in order to show a special detail desired by the architect. The hardware items are mechanical details which are designed and manufactured by firms that specialize in the production of these articles. In most specifications, all items of hardware are described and listed by manufacturer's name and catalogue number. In the case of some structures, the window and door schedules are enlarged to list the hardware required for each item included in the schedule. The following list covers some of the hardware items usually required for windows and doors.

For windows:

Operating hardware for raising and lowering sash for double-hung windows
Sash locks to suit each type of window
Hinges and sash operators for casement windows
Head and sill tracks for sliding windows
Hinge adjuster for projected windows

Some manufacturers include the hardware items with the window, in which case all the items included should be listed in the specifications with the description of windows.

For doors:

Hinges or door butts
Locks (right-hand or left-hand)
Lock sets with knobs and escutcheon plate
Door closers
Screen-door pulls, latches, and closing device
Cupboard-door turning sets and friction catches

If a door opens away from the user and swings to the right, it is called a right-hand door. A door opening away from one and swinging to the left is called a left-hand door. It is important to specify whether doors are right-hand (RH) or left-hand (LH) as this will affect some of the hardware items.

Exercises

Select a stock-size exterior and interior door from a manufacturer's stock list. Draw the elevation, plan, and sections for each type of door as shown in Figs. 8-4 and 8-5. Use a scale of $1\frac{1}{2}'' = 1'-0''$.

Stairs

Stairs consist primarily of the treads, or the part on which one steps, and the vertical part, or riser. The total rise is the sum of all the risers from floor to floor and the sum of all the treads; that is, the horizontal distance from the face of the bottom riser to the face of the top riser is referred to as the run of the stairs. Certain rules have been developed for proportioning stairs in order to make them safe and comfortable for ascending and descending by the average person. One rule is to make the sum of two risers and one tread equal to a figure between 24 and 25 in. Another rule is to make the sum of a riser and a tread equal to a figure between 17 and 18 in. A good average riser height should be between 7 and 8 in., and the width of the tread not less than 9 in., and preferably 10 in. The nosing, or overhanging part, of the tread is about 1 in. wide and is not included in the width of the tread when laying out the stairs. All risers must be the same height and all treads the same width in a stairway.

Having determined the total rise or height from floor to floor, assume a trial riser height of 7½ in., and divide the total rise by the height of the single riser. If the result is not an exact whole number of risers, then use the nearest whole number as the number of risers, and refigure to obtain the exact height of a single riser. The risers and treads may be laid out on the drawing by the method shown in Fig. 8-6 in the following manner.

On a strip of paper mark off a number of equal spaces to represent the number of risers. In this example we have assumed fourteen risers. Now place the strip of paper diagonally so that the point marked 14 is on the second-floor line at a point representing the beginning of the stairs and the zero is on the first-floor line. The width of the spaces marked does not matter as long as they are equal, and the spaces on the architect's scale may be used in place of a strip of paper if desired. With the paper or scale in the diagonal position, mark the height of each riser and draw the horizontal lines which will be used for the treads. The number of treads will be one less than the number of

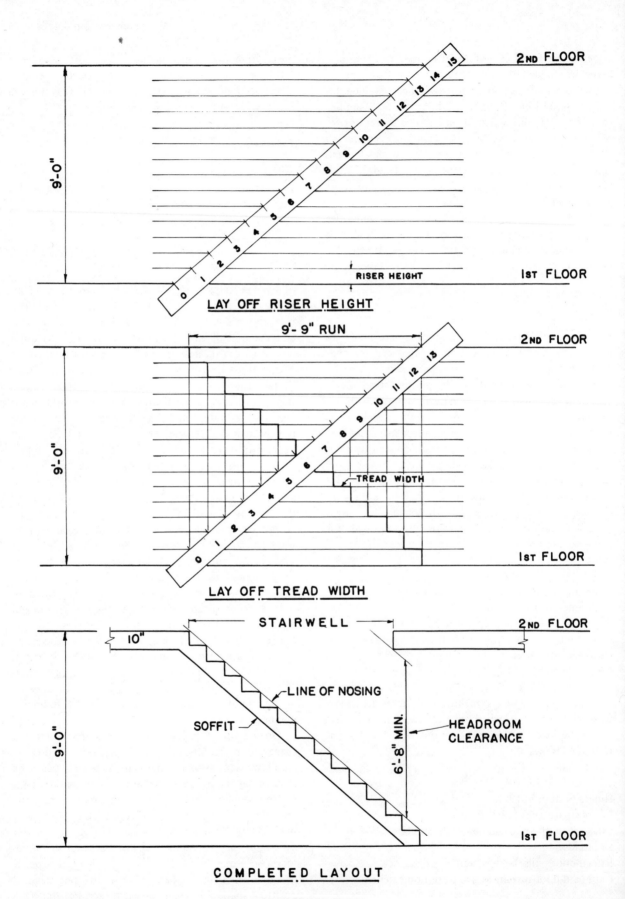

Fig. 8-6. Stair layout.

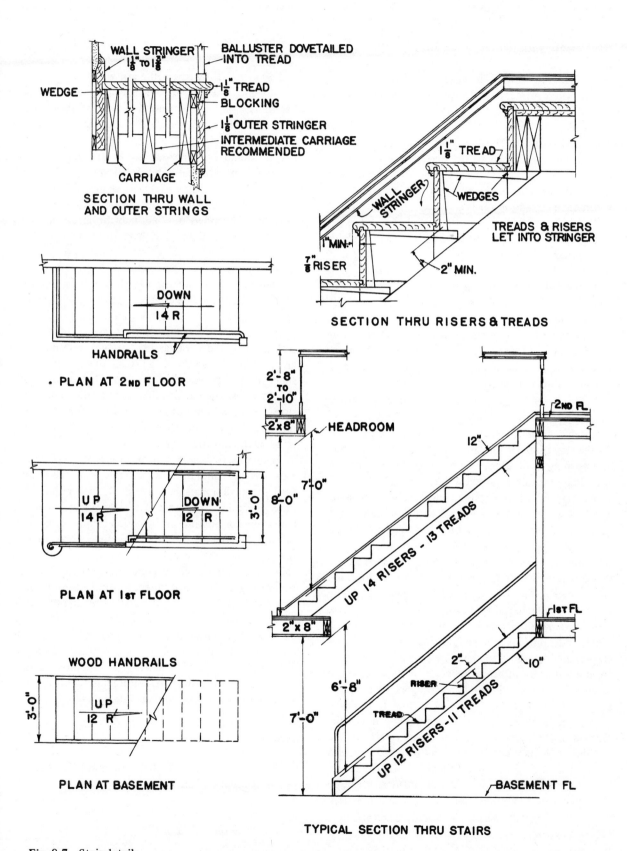

WALL STRINGER
$1\frac{1}{8}"$ TO $1\frac{5}{8}"$
BALUSTER DOVETAILED INTO TREAD
WEDGE
$1\frac{1}{8}"$ TREAD
BLOCKING
$1\frac{1}{8}"$ OUTER STRINGER
INTERMEDIATE CARRIAGE RECOMMENDED
CARRIAGE

SECTION THRU WALL AND OUTER STRINGS

$1\frac{1}{8}"$ TREAD
WALL STRINGER
WEDGES
1" MIN.
$\frac{7}{8}"$ RISER
2" MIN.
TREADS & RISERS LET INTO STRINGER

SECTION THRU RISERS & TREADS

DOWN
14 R
HANDRAILS

• PLAN AT 2ND FLOOR

UP 14 R
DOWN 12 R
3'-0"

PLAN AT 1st FLOOR

WOOD HANDRAILS
3'-0"
UP 12 R

PLAN AT BASEMENT

2'-8" TO 2'-10"
2"x8"
HEADROOM
8'-0"
7'-0"
2ND FL.
12"
UP 14 RISERS - 13 TREADS
2"x8"
1st FL.
2"
10"
RISER
6'-8"
7'-0"
TREAD
UP 12 RISERS - 11 TREADS
BASEMENT FL

TYPICAL SECTION THRU STAIRS

Fig. 8-7. Stair details.

risers, hence with fourteen risers we will have thirteen treads.

In Fig. 8-6 we have assumed a total run of 9'–9", which will provide treads 9 in. wide. Next, on the second diagram in Fig. 8-6, mark off the run of 9'–9". Then take a fresh strip of paper or the scale, and lay it diagonally from the starting point of the stairs on the second-floor line down to the end of the run on the first-tread line. Now at the intersection of the tread lines with the edge of the paper or scale, mark off the width of the treads on the tread lines.

For interior stairs, treads 10 in. wide and risers 7½ in. high are desirable, but because of the space available for the stairs the figures for the risers or the treads may be changed slightly from these figures. Outside stairs and especially stone steps are often made with treads wider than 10 in. and risers less than 7½ in. high. Where conditions necessitate very steep stairs, as in confined quarters or aboard ships, the stairs are more in the nature of ladders. It is not expected that anyone would ascend or descend without grasping the handrails which must be provided on both sides.

In Fig. 8-6 in the lower diagram, the headroom clearance is shown as 6'–8" minimum. This figure is acceptable in the basement, but a clearance of 7'–0" for the stairs in the main part of the house is preferable. The opening in the floor necessary to obtain the clearance desired is called the stairwell opening.

We have talked of the risers and treads of the stairs and how they are determined. Mention has also been made of the nosing part of the tread. The treads and risers must be supported by or framed into the two side timbers or stair stringers (sometimes called strings or stair horses) which extend from floor to floor and are secured to the floor joists at the upper end. Figure 8-7 shows a number of typical stair details. In the *open type of stairs*, the stringers are cut out to support the treads and risers, and the ends of the treads and risers are exposed to view. In the *closed type*, the stringers are not cut out, but grooves are cut in the stringers to receive the treads and risers. The stringers then conceal the ends of the treads and risers from view. In this type of construction the treads and risers are glued into the grooves in the stringers. Not too many years ago the building of stairs was a special form of carpentry, and the stair builder was considered a highly skilled artisan. Now the stairs are laid out and assembled in the shop and shipped to the job as a unit ready for installation.

A very fine example of stair building in colonial times may be seen in the Governor's Mansion at Williamsburg, Virginia. Here all the nails or pegs used to fasten the risers and treads were recessed into the wood, and the holes were carefully fitted with plugs in

the shapes of spades, hearts, diamonds, and clubs to form inlays.

Figure 8-7 shows how the arrows should be placed to indicate whether the stairs lead up or down. The handrails along stair stringers should be about 2'–6" high vertically from the tread to the top of the railing, but on the horizontal runs around the stairwell, this height should be increased to 2'–10" high. A good width for interior stairs in residences is 3'–0" as indicated in Fig. 8-7. Here again, space available and usage may cause variations in this figure. Stairs not often used or in cramped quarters may be made narrower. Stairs in public places may have to be made wider to accommodate more people and also to comply with local building codes. There is no hard-and-fast rule that stairs must be laid out for a single run from one floor to the next. It may be convenient and advantageous to break up the run or after the first landing to turn the second part of the run at right angles to the first section. The width of landings should be equal to or greater than the width of the stairs. In curving or spiral stairs the treads are called winders. The use of winders should be avoided if possible because they are expensive to build and not as safe as straight stairs. It is good practice to make all stairs in the house with the same tread width and riser height.

Handrails for stairs may be made of various materials. Wood handrails are probably most commonly used for small homes, but ornamental iron railings with brass trimmings are used. With the increased use of aluminum for building construction purposes, handrails of this material are available. We find stone used for handrails in public buildings, and for other construction outside, handrails of concrete are used. Stairs are often designed by the architect to form a central theme in a room, and the form of the stairway and the design of the handrailing are worked out in great detail to achieve very harmonious and beautiful effects. The main post at the foot of the stairs or a secondary post at a landing is called a newel post. Manufacturers of stairs are able to furnish beautiful railing posts and rails from the stock designs in their catalogues.

Exercises

Draw the stairs shown in Figs. 8-6 and 8-7, using the following specifications:

Basement floor to first floor	7'–11"
First floor to second floor	8'–11"
Second floor to third	8'–11"
Floor joists	10" deep
Risers	7½" high (approx)

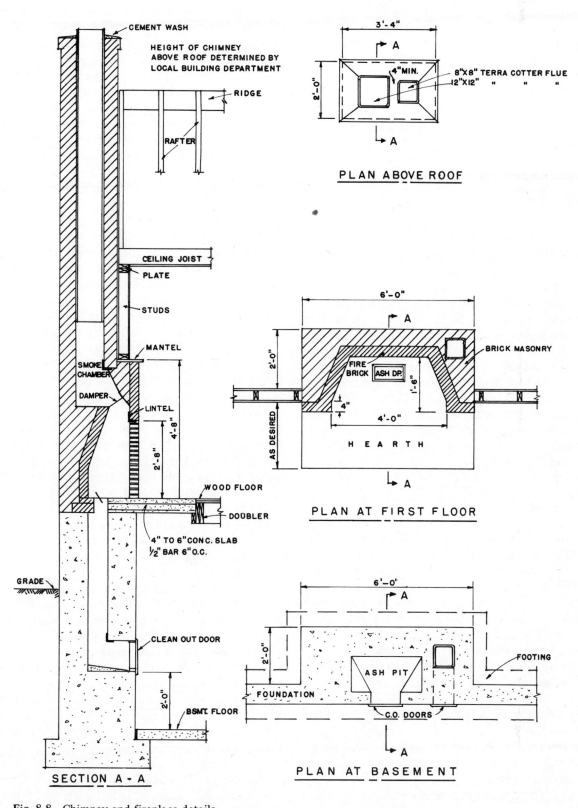

CEMENT WASH

HEIGHT OF CHIMNEY
ABOVE ROOF DETERMINED BY
LOCAL BUILDING DEPARTMENT

RIDGE

RAFTER

CEILING JOIST

PLATE

STUDS

MANTEL

SMOKE
CHAMBER

DAMPER

LINTEL

4'-8"

2'-8"

WOOD FLOOR

DOUBLER

4" TO 6" CONC. SLAB
½" BAR 6" O.C.

GRADE

CLEAN OUT DOOR

2'-0"

BSMT. FLOOR

SECTION A - A

PLAN ABOVE ROOF

3'-4"

2'-0"

4" MIN.

8"X8" TERRA COTTER FLUE
12"X12"   "   "   "

PLAN AT FIRST FLOOR

6'-0"

2'-0"

AS DESIRED

BRICK MASONRY

FIRE
BRICK   ASH DP.

1'-6"

4"

4'-0"

H E A R T H

PLAN AT BASEMENT

6'-0'

2'-0"

ASH PIT

FOOTING

FOUNDATION

C.O. DOORS

Fig. 8-8. Chimney and fireplace details.

Treads	10″ wide, excluding 1″ nosing
Headroom	6′–8″ minimum
Stairs	3′–0″ wide
Scale	½″ = 1′–0″

First, draw the three floor lines at the height given from floor to floor, and assume a starting point on the first and second floors for the stair to begin its downward run. With a 7½-in. rise there will be thirteen risers between the basement floor and the first floor. Next, mark off thirteen equal spaces on a strip of paper, or use thirteen equal spaces on an architect's scale, for example, the ½″ = 1′–0″ scale. Place point 13 on the scale or the paper strip on the first-floor starting point and the 0 diagonally on the basement-floor line. Mark the thirteen spaces and draw the horizontal lines to be used for the treads. With thirteen risers there will be twelve treads, which at 10 in. each will give a total run of 10′–0″. Mark off the 10′–0″ on the first-floor line from the starting point, and draw a light line down to the basement-floor line. Now take a strip of paper, or the scale, and place it diagonally on the diagram from the starting point down to the end of the run on the first-tread line. Where the edge of the scale or paper strip intersects the tread lines, mark these intersections to locate the width of the treads. Complete the drawing with dimensions and all necessary notations as shown in Figs. 8-6 and 8-7.

Chimney and fireplace details

A house that is to be warmed with heat generated by some form of heating system which uses a coal-, oil-, or gas-fired furnace must be provided with a chimney to conduct the smoke and waste gas safely out to the atmosphere. The chimney, if properly designed, will provide a natural draft to aid the escape of smoke and waste gas. The most efficient chimney is round with a smooth interior surface and leads straight up to the outside air. However, rectangular or terra-cotta flue tiles are often used for chimneys as they provide a smooth surface, and regular brickwork can be built easily around them. A chimney in a residence should extend at least 2′–0″ above the roof or ridge line, but for industrial purposes chimneys are built much higher to comply with local building codes and to satisfy specific design requirements.

Figure 8-8 shows typical details of a chimney and fireplace for a residence. A fireclay lining of brick or terra-cotta tile should be built into the chimney and all joints should be tightly closed with fireclay cement to avoid deterioration due to the effect of hot gases on the regular brickwork of the chimney.

The chimney should be built from the ground up, and none of its weight should be supported by the building or framing. The flues from a range, stove, fireplace, or vent register should not be connected into the main chimney for the furnace, as any back draft from one to the other might be hazardous. Chimneys are often provided with two or more flues, in which case a 4-in.-thick division wall should be built between the flues.

Where the chimney extends through the roof, care should be taken to provide proper flashing and roofing material to make the joints between roof and chimney tight against the weather. However, the flashing must also allow for movement due to settling, which could damage the water seal. This can be accomplished by securing the cap or top flashing to the chimney brickwork and the base flashing to the roof. The cap flashing should be lapped over the base flashing.

The fireplace is a recess in a chimney in which a fire may be built and consists of the hearth or floor, sides, back, and an opening at the top into the chimney flue. But in addition to its utilitarian function the fireplace is often an outstanding or central feature in a house, and the architect should give special consideration to its treatment. The face of the chimney, around the fireplace opening, which is seen in the room can be treated in many ways, but as part of the fireplace it should be in keeping with the general architectural design of the house. A wood or stone mantel can be built into the brickwork over the fireplace opening, or the brickwork itself can be built out to form a shelf or mantel. The exterior parts of the fireplace have nothing to do with its successful operation but only serve as trimming.

Heat is thrown out from the fireplace by radiation and the movement of air. Therefore, the form, proportions, and materials must be such that the fuel for which the fireplace is designed will burn readily and while burning will not send smoke or gas out into the room. The sides should taper inward toward the back, and the back should be sloped to meet the throat. A damper should be provided in the throat for each flue, and the cross-sectional area of the throat when fully open should equal the flue area. The damper acts like a simple valve to vary the size of the throat opening and control the draft. The interior of the fireplace exposed to the heat should be lined with fireclay brick. Cleanout doors at the bottom of each flue and an ash drop in the hearth should be provided.

The dimensions of the fireplace depend on the size of the opening into the room. Figure 8-9 shows a table

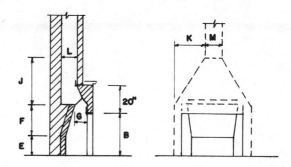

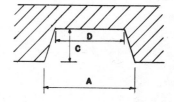

A	B	C	D	E	F	G	J	K	L M
2'-8"	2'-5"	1'-4"	1'-7"	1'-2"	1'-9"	8¾"	2'-0"	1'-1½"	8½"x12"
3'-0"	2'-5"	1'-4"	1'-11"	1'-2"	1'-9"	8¾"	2'-5"	1'-4½"	12"x12"
3'-4"	2'-5"	1'-4"	2'-4"	1'-2"	1'-9"	8¾"	2'-2"	1'-5½"	12"x12"
3'-6"	2'-8"	1'-4"	2'-5"	1'-2"	1'-11"	8¾"	2'-4"	1'-5½"	12"x12"
4'-0"	2'-8"	1'-6"	2'-9"	1'-2"	1'-11"	8¾"	2'-11"	1'-9½"	12"x12"

Fig. 8-9. Fireplace dimensions.

of dimensions which may be used as a guide for good proportions, but the exact dimensions may be varied somewhat to accommodate the materials used. A wood-burning fireplace should be approximately 18 in. deep. Another good guide is to have the area of the flue about one-tenth the area of the opening into the room.

Note in Fig. 8-8 that the hearth extends out into the room and that its parts are sometimes called the front hearth and the back hearth; also that the hearth is supported on a reinforced concrete pad to protect the building framing from the heat of the fire. The surface of the hearth may be made of a hard cement to which color has been added or of a special hard-burned floor tile.

Exercise

Select a set of fireplace dimensions from the table in Fig. 8-9 and make a drawing of a chimney and fireplace with details similar to those shown in Fig. 8-8. Use a scale of ½" = 1'-0".

9. symbols, conventions, and title box

In every field of endeavor there is a tendency to shorten or simplify the means or language used to explain the routine of the work. Words and expressions are abbreviated and symbols are introduced to speed up the task of preparing directions specifying the work and how it is to be done. This same simplification is carried out in the making of drawings, and we thus arrive at what are termed conventions and symbols, or standards, used to represent certain details.

These shortcuts are first developed by individuals and then are gradually adopted by other members of the trade or craft. Committees have been appointed by the various technical associations, including the American National Standards Institute and other related parts of the industry, to study and adopt certain suitable conventions and symbols as standards for everyone to use. Various departments connected with the federal government set up conventions and symbols; it is the task of the committees to try to reconcile all the various standards so that everyone will use and understand a particular symbol to mean just one thing.

Many drafting rooms furnish each draftsman with a set of standards used by that office. These standards cover the general procedure of that office in making drawings and include such items as sizes of drawings, border lines, title box, conventions and symbols for various items, revision procedure, and information which the draftsman may require on any other part of the work. From time to time the standards may be revised or new ones added.

When making shop or working drawings of mechani-

cal parts, that is, regular orthographic projection drawings, we show as many views as are necessary to depict the object. We draw all the lines necessary to show the visible and hidden edges or surfaces with complete dimensions so that every detail is made perfectly clear and definite to all concerned. But we also use symbols or conventions to indicate, for example, threads, sections, finished or machined surfaces, and dimensions which are not to scale. The alphabet of lines shown in Fig. 2-4 is really a representation of something it would take many words to express. When we cut through a wall or surface and draw what is known as a cross section of the area, we indicate the location as shown at F in Fig. 2-4.

Since we deal with many different kinds of materials, it has been found advisable to make up a set of standards, as in Fig. 9-1, which shows the kind of symbol to use in a section to indicate different materials. In addition to the symbols used for sections and plans we sometimes find it necessary to indicate the material in the elevations which are not sections. The symbols shown in Fig. 9-1, which are commonly used, have been adopted by the ANSI and are also shown in the "Military Standard for General Drawing Practice" of the U.S. Department of Defense.

It sometimes happens that one is required to show a material for which no symbol has been made up, in which case a new symbol may be devised, and a note added to the drawing stating the material depicted by the new symbol.

Quite often a whole drawing is used to list explana-

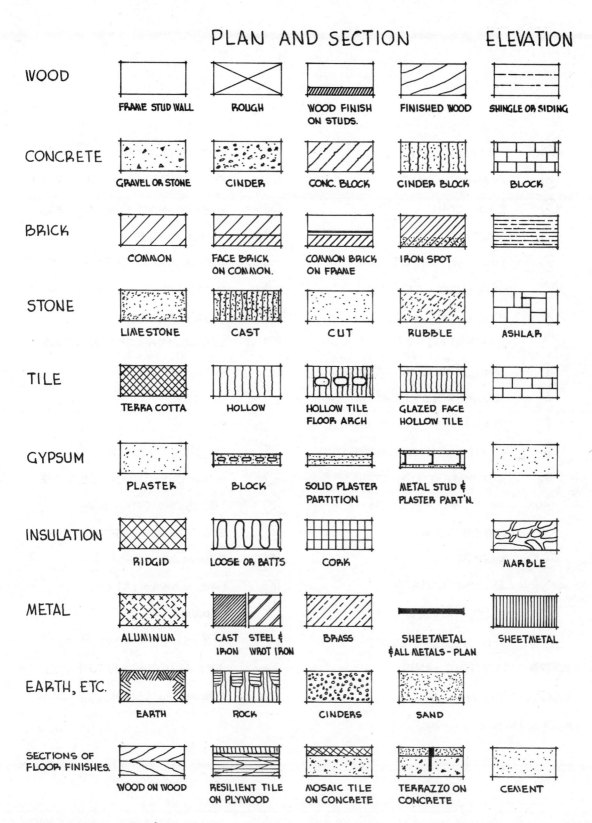

PLAN AND SECTION   ELEVATION

WOOD
FRAME STUD WALL | ROUGH | WOOD FINISH ON STUDS. | FINISHED WOOD | SHINGLE OR SIDING

CONCRETE
GRAVEL OR STONE | CINDER | CONC. BLOCK | CINDER BLOCK | BLOCK

BRICK
COMMON | FACE BRICK ON COMMON. | COMMON BRICK ON FRAME | IRON SPOT

STONE
LIMESTONE | CAST | CUT | RUBBLE | ASHLAR

TILE
TERRA COTTA | HOLLOW | HOLLOW TILE FLOOR ARCH | GLAZED FACE HOLLOW TILE

GYPSUM
PLASTER | BLOCK | SOLID PLASTER PARTITION | METAL STUD & PLASTER PART'N

INSULATION
RIDGID | LOOSE OR BATTS | CORK | MARBLE

METAL
ALUMINUM | CAST IRON STEEL & WROT IRON | BRASS | SHEETMETAL & ALL METALS - PLAN | SHEETMETAL

EARTH, ETC.
EARTH | ROCK | CINDERS | SAND

SECTIONS OF FLOOR FINISHES.
WOOD ON WOOD | RESILIENT TILE ON PLYWOOD | MOSAIC TILE ON CONCRETE | TERRAZZO ON CONCRETE | CEMENT

Fig. 9-1. Architectural symbols.

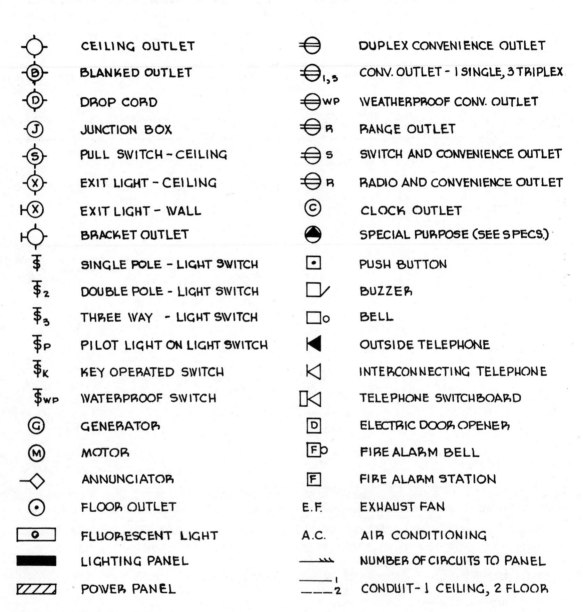

CEILING OUTLET		DUPLEX CONVENIENCE OUTLET	
BLANKED OUTLET		CONV. OUTLET - 1 SINGLE, 3 TRIPLEX	
DROP CORD		WEATHERPROOF CONV. OUTLET	
JUNCTION BOX		RANGE OUTLET	
PULL SWITCH - CEILING		SWITCH AND CONVENIENCE OUTLET	
EXIT LIGHT - CEILING		RADIO AND CONVENIENCE OUTLET	
EXIT LIGHT - WALL		CLOCK OUTLET	
BRACKET OUTLET		SPECIAL PURPOSE (SEE SPECS.)	
SINGLE POLE - LIGHT SWITCH		PUSH BUTTON	
DOUBLE POLE - LIGHT SWITCH		BUZZER	
THREE WAY - LIGHT SWITCH		BELL	
PILOT LIGHT ON LIGHT SWITCH		OUTSIDE TELEPHONE	
KEY OPERATED SWITCH		INTERCONNECTING TELEPHONE	
WATERPROOF SWITCH		TELEPHONE SWITCHBOARD	
GENERATOR		ELECTRIC DOOR OPENER	
MOTOR		FIRE ALARM BELL	
ANNUNCIATOR		FIRE ALARM STATION	
FLOOR OUTLET		EXHAUST FAN	
FLUORESCENT LIGHT		AIR CONDITIONING	
LIGHTING PANEL		NUMBER OF CIRCUITS TO PANEL	
POWER PANEL		CONDUIT-1 CEILING, 2 FLOOR	

Fig. 9-2. Electrical symbols.

PLUMBING SYMBOLS

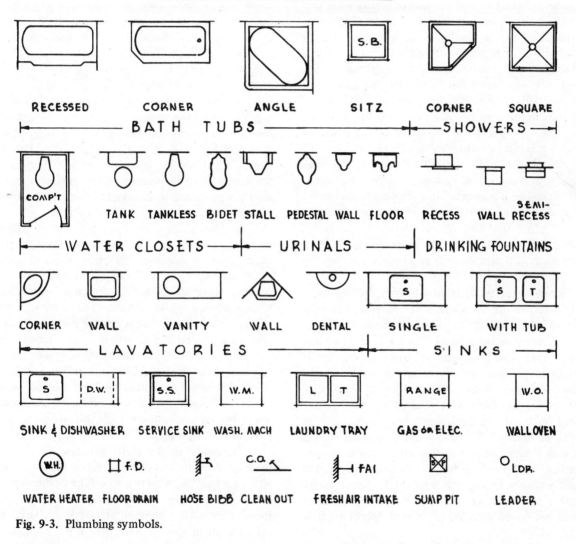

Fig. 9-3. Plumbing symbols.

tory notes, conventions, and symbols applying to a set of drawings made to cover a specific job or contract. Another method is to have each drawing carry a legend, or list, of standard symbols which apply to the work.

The architectural draftsman often has to indicate the electrical and plumbing facilities required for the project for which he is making the drawings. In fact, the desired arrangement of some of these features often affects many details of the plans. Therefore, symbols have been devised so that the desired arrangement and location of the electrical and plumbing facilities may be indicated in the simplest possible manner. Figure 9-2 shows a list of commonly used electrical symbols which have been taken from those approved by the ANSI, the American Institute of Electrical Engineers, and the "Military Standard for Electrical Symbols" of the U.S. Department of Defense. Dimensions are not given on the plans for the locations of the electrical items, as actual construction conditions will control the exact locations. For large installations an electrical engineer provides special drawings to cover the electrical work. The locations of the outlets are shown by symbols, and if necessary, special wiring diagrams designating wire sizes and the connections are made. Drawings for conduit may also be required. All these drawings incorporate symbols and conventions for the electrical trades.

The plumbing symbols shown in Fig. 9-3 represent only a few of the items which you may need to indicate on your drawings; additional symbols may be obtained from standard reference books. These plumbing symbols have also been approved by the ANSI. To facilitate proper planning of the arrangement of bathrooms and kitchens and determination of the size of the rooms, manufacturers' catalogs should be consulted for the overall dimensions of the facilities which are to be installed. The architectural drawings should show in a very simple way the general scheme of the electrical and plumbing features desired. The written specifications covering the work to be done should carry a definite description and list of the facilities which are to be installed. A typical specification is given in Chap. 16.

Figure 9-4 shows the different kinds of lines and combinations of lines and letters used to designate piping items. Figure 9-5 shows standard symbols and designations for heating and ventilating systems. This figure includes some piping designations which can be used on drawings for this service. Heating and ventilating installations require ductwork which is made of galvanized sheet metal or aluminum pipes of various shapes. The word *pipe* is usually associated with a round pipe or conductor, but ventilating ductwork may be round, square, or rectangular. The shape of the duct may vary in one run in order that a particular cross-sectional area may be maintained and that the duct may still pass through a restricted space.

Structural symbols are shown in Fig. 9-6. In Fig. 9-6a cross sections of the most commonly used steel shapes are shown. Conventional ways of drawing steel lintels over wall openings are shown in Fig. 9-6b. Lintels are necessary over wall openings, and they should extend beyond the opening on each side to support the load of the brick over the opening. A lally column, shown in Fig. 9-6c, is used to support floor beams or girders when bearing walls are not available for this purpose. Lally columns are made up of steel pipes with steel plates welded to each end of the pipe to provide adequate bearing surfaces, top and bottom.

The correct structural members for a building should be determined by the architect, the structural engineer, or the designer. The exact dimensions of any particular shape can be found in the "Manual of the American Institute of Steel Construction" or in a handbook published by one of the steel companies.

Very often separate drawings are made to show the plumbing, electrical, and structural-steel requirements of a project, and only the outline of the building is indicated on these special drawings. Structures with a reinforced-concrete or structural-steel framework require the preparation of special plans for the trades involved. Symbols and conventions applicable to these trades have also been adopted by the ANSI.

In nearly all the plates or drawings you have made previous to this, you have drawn various types of wall construction, windows, doors, and other items in detail. A knowledge of these details and how to draw them is essential, but when regular plans, elevations, and sections of structures are drawn, it is not practical to show complete details at all times, especially when the areas are drawn to a reduced scale. Therefore it has

SOIL OR WASTE	ABOVE GRADE	
	BELOW GRADE	
VENT		
COLD WATER		
HOT WATER		

ACID WASTE	ACID
SPRINKLER DRAIN	—— S —— S ——
VACUMN CLEANER	—— V —— V ——
GAS	—— G —— G ——

Fig. 9-4. Piping symbols.

RADIATORS OR CONVECTORS IN PLAN

RAD.	FREE STANDING
RAD.	RECESSED
RAD.	FLUSH
RAD.	RECESSED WITH ENCLOSURE
	UNIT VENTILATOR

PIPING SYMBOLS

FUEL OIL FLOW	———— FOF ————
FUEL OIL RETURN	———— FOR ————
FUEL OIL TANK VENT	———— FOV ————
HOT WATER SUPPLY	————————————
HOT WATER RETURN	— — — — — —
SUPPLY RISERS	O UP O DN
DRAIN	———— D ————
THERMOSTAT	(T)

DUCTWORK SYMBOLS

24 X 10	DUCT SIZE · 1ST FIG.-WIDTH, 2ND-DPTH.	REGISTER = R	GRILLE = G
→	DIRECTION OF FLOW	SUPPLY ‖→	EXHAUST ‖ ←∕—
R D	RISE OR DROP IN DUCT	LOUVER OPENING ⌐L→	

Fig. 9-5. Heating and ventilating symbols.

become the custom to shorten the drafting time and simplify the drawing by adopting certain conventional pictures to indicate certain types of construction.

Some of the more commonly used conventions are shown in Fig. 9-7. These conventions should be studied and kept in mind for use when making architectural drawings. Note that for concrete and brick walls it is customary to dimension to the outside face of the wall, while for frame construction, dimensions are given to the face of the studs. Doors and windows are located by a dimension to the center of the opening because the frames are made up off the job and later set into rough openings in the structure as it is built. A great deal of information is required for items, such as windows and doors, which cannot be placed directly on the working drawings. This information can be conveniently listed in schedules, where the information can be arranged logically and located in one place. For win-

dows and doors all the information can be placed in a table as shown in Figs. 9-8 and 9-9. Another method used is drawing simple small-scale pictures of the different types of doors and windows, adding the required information to the drawing by dimensions and notes. For large structures with many rooms, corridors, and other areas, a schedule is made up of the finishes for the walls, floors, and ceilings for each area.

When you have made the necessary drawings to show the structure which is to be built or the alterations to be made in an existing structure, you have not entirely finished the drawings. These are plans which others will use to carry out the work involved, and they must have an identity easy to recognize. No drawing is completely finished until it has a title box or similar arrangement containing all the information necessary for the correct future handling of the drawing.

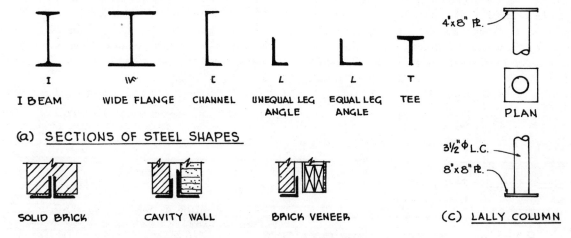

I	W	C	L	L	T	
I BEAM	WIDE FLANGE	CHANNEL	UNEQUAL LEG ANGLE	EQUAL LEG ANGLE	TEE	PLAN

4'x8" PL.

(a) SECTIONS OF STEEL SHAPES

SOLID BRICK	CAVITY WALL	BRICK VENEER	

3½"ɸ L.C.
8'x8" PL.

(c) LALLY COLUMN

(b) STEEL LINTELS OVER WINDOW & DOOR OPENINGS

Fig. 9-6. Structural symbols.

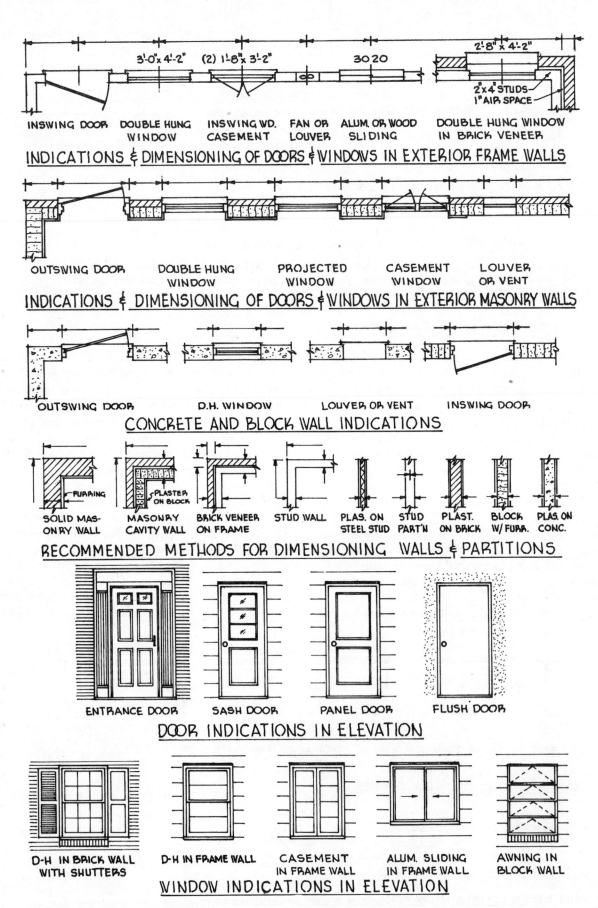

3'-0"x 4'-2"   (2) 1'-8"x 3'-2"   3020   2'-8" x 4'-2"

2"x4" STUDS
1" AIR SPACE

INSWING DOOR   DOUBLE HUNG   INSWING WD.   FAN OR   ALUM. OR WOOD   DOUBLE HUNG WINDOW
WINDOW   CASEMENT   LOUVER   SLIDING   IN BRICK VENEER

INDICATIONS & DIMENSIONING OF DOORS & WINDOWS IN EXTERIOR FRAME WALLS

OUTSWING DOOR   DOUBLE HUNG   PROJECTED   CASEMENT   LOUVER
WINDOW   WINDOW   WINDOW   OR VENT

INDICATIONS & DIMENSIONING OF DOORS & WINDOWS IN EXTERIOR MASONRY WALLS

OUTSWING DOOR   D.H. WINDOW   LOUVER OR VENT   INSWING DOOR

CONCRETE AND BLOCK WALL INDICATIONS

FURRING   PLASTER
ON BLOCK

SOLID MAS-   MASONRY   BRICK VENEER   STUD WALL   PLAS. ON   STUD   PLAST.   BLOCK   PLAS. ON
ONRY WALL   CAVITY WALL   ON FRAME   STEEL STUD   PART'N   ON BRICK   W/FURR.   CONC.

RECOMMENDED METHODS FOR DIMENSIONING WALLS & PARTITIONS

ENTRANCE DOOR   SASH DOOR   PANEL DOOR   FLUSH DOOR

DOOR INDICATIONS IN ELEVATION

D-H IN BRICK WALL   D-H IN FRAME WALL   CASEMENT   ALUM. SLIDING   AWNING IN
WITH SHUTTERS   IN FRAME WALL   IN FRAME WALL   BLOCK WALL

WINDOW INDICATIONS IN ELEVATION

Fig. 9-7. Architectural conventions.

WINDOW SCHEDULE

MARK	SIZE	TYPE	DESCRIPTION	GLAZING	MAT'L.	REMARKS
A	3'-6" x 4'-0"	DBL. HNG.	UALCO	S.S.'B".	ALUM.	SOUTH. SASH S&S CO. OR EQUAL
B	3'-0" x 3'-4"	SLIDING	UALCO	OBSCURE	ALUM.	"
C	2'-2" x 3'-1"	AWNING	UALCO	S.S.'B".	ALUM.	"

Fig. 9-8. Window schedule.

DOOR SCHEDULE

MARK	SIZE	TYPE	DESCRIPTION	HEAD	JAMB	SILL	FINISH	REMARKS
D/1	3'-0" x 7'-0" x 1¾"	WOOD PANEL COLONIAL	FIR	¹/₁	¹/₁	⁴/₁	PAINT	MORGAN OR EQUAL
D/2	2'-6" x 7'-0" x 1⅜"	FLUSH WOOD HOLLOW CORE	BIRCH VENEER	²/₁	²/₁	—	STAIN	U.S. PLYWD OR EQUAL
D/3	2'-0" x 6'-8" x 1⅜"	FLUSH WOOD HOLLOW CORE	BIRCH VENEER	³/₁	³/₁	⁵/₁	PAINT	U.S. PLYWD OR EQUAL

Fig. 9-9. Door schedule.

NAME OF SCHOOL		
CITY		STATE
TITLE		
DRAWN BY	DATE	
TRACED BY	SCALE	
CHECKED BY	DWG. NO.	

Fig. 9-10. Title box, school.

DRAWN BY	SCALE	SHEET TITLE	
CHECKED BY	DATE		
		JOB TITLE	
JOHN J. DOE REGISTERED ARCHITECT NEW YORK CITY NEW YORK			SHEET NO. OF

Fig. 9-11. Title box, professional.

The form and contents of the title box will vary with different offices. The one shown in Fig. 9-10 is a simple one which might be used for schoolwork. The title box in Fig. 9-11 would be more suitable for professional use and illustrates the features commonly incorporated in one of this type. The title box should include the name of the architect or firm responsible for the work just as a letterhead contains the name of a company or person and indicates the origin of the letter. So that everyone using the drawing will be able to identify it, there should be a space for a job or drawing title. In organized offices, drawings are produced under a regular procedure and a space is provided for the draftsman's and checker's name or initials. If all the drawing is made to one scale, the scale is marked in a space provided in the title box. When several different scales are used on one drawing, the scales are noted under the section of the drawing to which they apply, and the scale in the title box is given thus, "as noted." A numbering system for the drawings produced should be adopted and the drawings numbered accordingly. Sometimes an initial letter, such as L for large, H for half size, and Q for quarter size is used, but a consecutive system of numbers will provide the simplest method of identification for filing purposes and for reference in all correspondence. To facilitate handling and filing, the number should be located in the lower right-hand corner. The number is often inverted and also placed in the upper left-hand corner of the sheet. This is done to facilitate the handling of prints when many copies of drawings must be sorted for distribution.

There is another method of numbering drawings that uses the contract or job number in conjunction with a series of numbers applying only to one particular contract. For example:

Contract No. 1221
Sheet No. 1 of 10

While the dates of any revisions are not a part of the title box, it is well to provide a definite form for recording the date when a change or an addition is made after the original completion date of the drawing. All such changes in a drawing should be carefully checked and dated. Extra care should be exercised to see that everyone concerned with the work is notified of a change and that superseding copies of the drawings are sent to everyone who received a copy of the original drawing. Proper handling of revisions is most important and will avoid many costly errors.

It is a good practice to adopt standard-size sheets for drawings, such as multiples of size 8½ by 11 in., which is letter size. This facilitates filing and the folding of prints for mailing. The finished drawing should have a border line ½ in. inside the edge of the paper; quite often the left-hand border is made 1 or 1½ in. wide to allow for the binding of prints in sets. Many firms have their tracing paper or tracing cloth printed with border lines and title box. This might seem an extra expense, but it saves considerable drafting time.

When making drawings for government contracts, it is well to ascertain beforehand what standards have been established for drawing sizes and what arrangements have been made about title box and style of lettering. In some cases the requirements are very definite and may not agree with the usual practice of the office.

Check each drawing carefully to see that all words have been spelled correctly. A word spelled incorrectly always stands out as a glaring error. Words that are often used on drawings and frequently mispelled are *symmetrical* and *supersede*; *gauge* is the preferred spelling for architectural drawings.

10. reproduction of drawings

If you stop to think about the drawings which you have made and the building plans which you will make, you will realize that in each case you have an original pencil drawing which is good for use in the drafting room. But additional copies will be required for many purposes if you are to have your plans carried forward to completed structures. After the drawings are completed, it will be necessary to file copies with the local building authorities and other interested departments to obtain the required permits to allow the actual building construction to proceed. The contractors will require a set of plans in order to prepare a bid to cover the work and to build the structure after the contract is awarded. The field men representing the owner and the architect will also need drawings to check the work as it progresses. Various subcontractors and suppliers will have to have copies of different drawings which pertain to certain parts of the work in which they are directly interested.

Hence, it can be readily seen we must be prepared to have numerous copies made of the pencil drawings. This should bring us to the subject of tracing, but before we take up the chapter on tracing, it will be well to take a little time to discuss various ways and means available, and frequently used in drafting rooms, to obtain the necessary additional copies of the drawings which will be required.

If the pencil drawings have been made on tracing paper, or vellum, we can have blueprints made directly from the vellum drawings. A blueprint is made in a manner similar to a photographic print in that the tracing is placed in contact with a prepared paper, exposed to the light, then developed, washed, and dried.

However, this prepared paper is not as sensitive as photographic paper and may be handled in an ordinary lighted room. Most prints are made with white lines on a blue background, hence the common name "blueprint." Variations can be made, such as blue lines on a white background or black lines on a white background. Then there are vandyke prints, which have white lines on a brown background; if the vandyke paper is thin, it can be used as a negative to obtain a print with brown lines on a white background.

Keep in mind that all of the aforementioned paper prints are made by developing and washing process which requires drying, and therefore the paper may shrink or stretch. The equipment for processing the work also requires a water supply for the developing solution and washing.

Another process has almost replaced the original blueprint process, in which ammonia fumes are used to develop the prints. Specially prepared paper is used to produce blue or black lines on white or tinted backgrounds. Also used are sepia and black line duplicate originals on vellum, cloth, or film, and colored acetates for overlays for projection. The ammonia-fume method does not require washing or drying, and the equipment for making the prints may be set up in any available space in the office. The special paper is sensitized with a diazo compound and color coupler which, after exposure, is developed with ammonia fumes. Diazo compounds are obtained by the action of nitrous acid on a salt of certain amino compounds. One of the diazo-type printing processes is called the Ozalid process. In commercial printing establishments where quite large machines are used, some means of ventilating the space

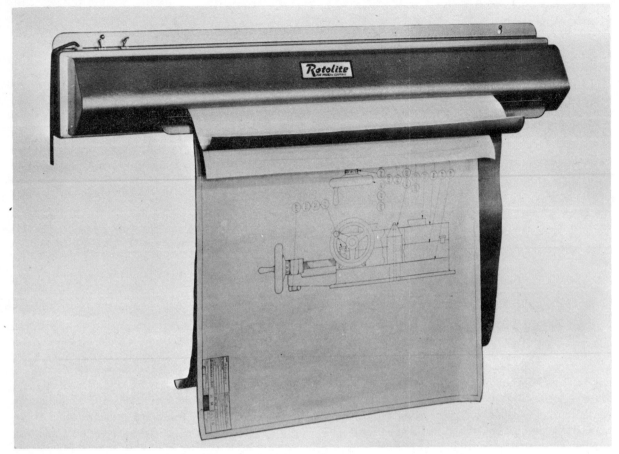

Fig. 10-1. Early model whiteprinter. *(Rotolite Sales Corporation, Sterling, N.J.)*

should be provided to clear away the ammonia fumes.

The machines originally used in commercial establishments were too large and costly to be used in the average office or drafting room. In 1953 R. M. Ellis, President of Rotolite Sales Corporation, developed a small machine which could be used in moderate-sized architect's offices and drafting rooms. Today nearly every architect's or engineering office has its own do-it-yourself white printing equipment.

Figure 10-1 shows a model of the early do-it-yourself printer invented in 1953. Figure 10-2 shows how easily the original drawing and the diazo paper may be inserted into the bottom of the latest-model combined printer and developer, and in Fig. 10-3 the print only is run through the top of the machine for developing. Copies up to 42 in. wide and of any length may be made on this machine. The equipment for handling the ammonia is so arranged that there is practically no annoyance from the ammonia liquid or fumes. The do-it-yourself printer can be obtained in wall-mounted or table-mounted models for office use.

As mentioned above, prints or copies can be made from vellum pencil drawings, but it will be readily seen that the vellum drawing would not last very long if we made numerous prints or if it were filed and refiled

many times. The vellum tends to become brittle and tear or split around the edges. Not too many years ago transparent vellum papers were not available, and pencil drawings were usually made on a heavy buff-colored mat-surfaced paper. Since prints could not be obtained from this heavy paper, it was customary to make tracings of the drawings on cloth that had been coated to give it a smooth surface which would readily take the drawing ink. The best grades of tracing cloth are made of very-fine-staple cotton known as batiste. Sometimes tracing cloth is mistakenly called linen. Linen, which is made from fibers of the flax plant, may have been used originally but not for many, many years past. You might ask, Why not use a regular photographic process for making duplicate prints? The cost of any photographic process would rule it out without considering other disadvantages, such as size limitations and excessive time required for processing.

A copying process which produces copies known as photostats has its place in the field. These copies are more expensive than so-called blueprints but may be made directly from any picture or printed matter. The original material may be enlarged or contracted within the limits of the copying machine. The cost is not excessive if only one or two copies are to be made. Some-

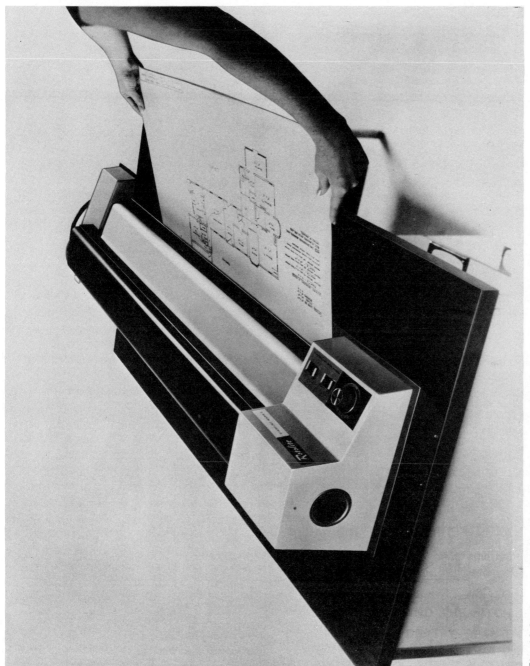

Fig. 10-2. Combined whiteprinter, loading. *(Rotolite Sales Corporation, Sterling, N.J.)*

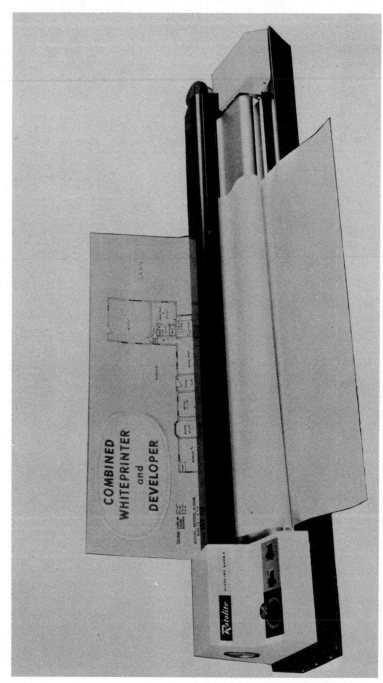

Fig. 10-3. Combined whiteprinter, developer. (*Rotolite Sales Corporation, Sterling, N.J.*)

times this process is useful if it is required that various-size drawings be reduced or blown up to one uniform size for a report.

There are still other methods of reproducing drawings which while not always used by every draftsman, are frequently very useful in helping to expedite the work of producing the necessary drawings which may be required. Of course, these various methods of reproducing drawings are not part of learning how to draw. However, as a draftsman acquires experience and becomes familiar with all phases of the work of actually producing the plans which can be used to build the structures he has designed, he will find that a knowledge of all these reproducing processes may be used to advantage at some time or other. There is, for instance, a process by which ink tracings on tracing cloth can be made from pencil drawings on vellum. These reproductions are called lithoprints. If the pencil vellum drawings have sharp black lines, very good reproductions, or lithoprints, on cloth can be obtained. If the lines in the original drawings are not sharp and black, then the reproductions will require more or less touching up with drawing ink. This process, however, will save money over the cost of actually tracing and rechecking the tracing against the original drawing. There is in addition a time-saving element to be considered if these short cuts are used. There is also a photographic process of reproducing ink tracings on cloth which is more expensive than the ordinary method of making reproductions on cloth but which can be used when the vellum drawings are poorly made and do not have sharp black lines.

There are times when long bills of material or a long series of notes are required as part of a set of plans. The lettering of the material on tracing cloth by hand, or even by a mechanical lettering set, requires a great deal of laborious work and expensive time on the part of a draftsman. One way this may be avoided is to have the material typed on a Varitype machine on a strong bond paper that is fairly transparent. The typed copy can then be reproduced in black ink on tracing cloth. A regular typewriter may be used, but a Varitype machine will be found to be more flexible for this work especially if there is a continuous use for it. This type of work is more likely to be encountered in the preparation of bills of material for piping and electrical drawings than in architectural drawings. Blueprints also may be obtained from specifications typed on bond paper and backed up with carbon paper.

There is still another process used to make reproductions known as C-B's. In this process a tracing cloth with a specially prepared surface is used together with a special C-B ink to obtain the reproduction. The C-B ink may be removed from the cloth to make changes in the drawing by the careful use of a very small amount of water applied with a felt pad. Special C-B ink must be used to add to or change the reproduction.

11. tracing

When we speak of tracings in the drafting room we usually refer to ink tracings on regular tracing cloth. In other words, tracings in ink of drawings which were originally drawn in pencil. The pencil drawings are copied, that is, actually traced on cloth in order to produce better prints and as many copies as may be required. The cloth will stand wear and tear longer than tracing paper, called vellum, and may be kept indefinitely as a record and for future use. Drawings on tracing cloth may be revised or changed to record corrections or to incorporate design changes if any are made. We mentioned in Chap. 10 that tracing cloth is not made of linen but is a fine cotton cloth specially coated to take drawing ink. The ink is really applied on top of the coating, with care being taken not to cut or break the coating and allow the ink to penetrate into the fibers of the cloth. A good grade of tracing cloth should be used so that it will stand up under filing and refiling many times, the making of many prints or copies, and the erasures due to revisions and changes which may have to be incorporated in the drawing from time to time.

Drawing ink is composed of very finely ground carbon suspended in water with a gum added for waterproofing. It may be purchased in pint- or quart-size bottles, but the draftsman should be provided with a standard ¾-oz. bottle that has a plastic squeeze stopper with a dropper attached. The dropper is used to transfer ink from the bottle to the ruling pen, pen compass, or straight pen. Ink-bottle holders may be purchased, or the bottle can be fastened to a piece of cardboard with drafting tape so that it will not be upset accidentally. Do not dip the pen or instruments into the ink bottle as this may leave ink on the sides of the pen which can soil the fingers and smear the tracing. Sufficient ink can be transferred from the bottle to the pen with the dropper, and in this way messy blots may be avoided.

The large compass usually comes with one removable leg so that it may be changed from pencil to pen, or vice versa. It may also have an extension bar which may be inserted to make very large circles. The small bow pen is an instrument entirely separate from the bow pencil or bow dividers. The ruling pen and pen compass usually have correctly sharpened points as the instruments come from the factory. The points should not be too sharp or they will cut the cloth. Slight burrs may be removed by the careful use of a smooth honing stone, but it is recommended that pens be sent to a reliable supply house for any real resharpening work. However, a good pen can be used for many years without resharpening.

Now that we have the tracing cloth, ink, and ruling pen and pen compass ready for use, the next step is to place the drawing to be traced on the board, line it up, and fasten it with drafting tape. Place the tracing cloth over the drawing with the dull side upward, and secure the cloth to the board with tape, being careful to avoid making any creases or wrinkles in the cloth.

Shake some pounce over the cloth, rub in gently with a cloth and dust off any excess powder. Pounce is a combination of finely ground pumice and chalk. It is rubbed into the cloth to provide a good surface to take the ink smoothly and hold it as the pen is drawn over the surface. In past years the draftsman scraped pumice or chalk alone from a cake or stick onto the drawing and rubbed the scrapings in. But now a prepared ground mixture of the two may be purchased in shaker cans for convenient use.

Next put a small quantity of ink in the pen with the squeeze stopper. Do not put too much ink in a pen, or the weight of the ink will cause it to run out too quickly and make a blot. Try to finish a line with one complete stroke of the pen. It is a good plan to start at the top of the drawing and work downward and from left to right because it is necessary to work carefully and allow the ink to dry before going back over the work to put in additional lines.

As in pencil work the outlines should be heavy or wide with the hidden, or dash, lines slightly thinner for contrast. Then the center lines, dimension lines, and crosshatching lines should be the really thin lines. The American National Standards Institute has recommended these three thicknesses of lines. Center lines should be put in first, then the circles and arcs of circles. Straight lines can be drawn to match up with arcs quite readily, but it will be found difficult to put arcs in correctly when the straight lines are drawn first. The straight lines and arcs should match exactly at the tangent points and should be of the same thickness. If the correct centers for the arcs cannot be easily seen, it will be advisable to stop and relocate the centers in pencil before proceeding.

Hold the ruling pen nearly vertical and draw upward or from left to right in the manner previously recommended for pencil use and shown in Figs. 1-1 and 1-2. Always use the ruling pen with the T square and triangles. Do not press in against the T square or triangle, but use them as a guide. Ruling pens have a natural curved shape, and if used correctly, the points are held away from the triangle and T square so that the ink will not run under the edges and blot or smear. Before starting the work, try out the pens for thickness of the lines on a small piece of tracing cloth, and retain this as a guide or template to reset the pen if it is necessary to change the setting from time to time. Because ink will have a tendency to dry in the pen if not kept in use, the pen should be wiped out between fillings. A pen should be kept clean at all times. If the ink should dry on the pen, it can be softened in warm water or in a purchased pen-cleaner solution.

Work slowly and carefully, allowing the ink to dry on the cloth before trying to put in additional lines in a section of the drawing previously inked. After the solid lines and dash lines for the outlines of the object have been inked, then ink the dimension lines. In general the ruling pen should only be used for straight lines. If there are any curved lines which were drawn with an irregular curve from plotted points, be very careful in trying to trace them with a ruling pen. If the curve is rather flat, it is possible to draw the ruling pen around the outer edge of the irregular curve, using short sections of the curve at a time and then moving to an adjacent section. The sectioning, or crosshatching, lines should be inked in last after the lettering has been completed, especially if any section lines are to be omitted to clear dimensions or lettering.

Lettering, dimensions, and arrowheads should be inked with a straight lettering pen. There are many kinds of lettering pens, two of those in common use being the 303 Gillotte and the crow quill. Ball-point pens are used for large headings and titles. It will take practice to use the pen properly and let the ink flow onto the tracing cloth. Remember that the dimensions and letters must be drawn carefully and not written. Use fresh guidelines and do not try to copy the penciled letters exactly, but try to improve the lettering when inking. It is also a good time to relocate or rearrange dimensions to make them more readable and to improve the appearance of the drawing.

There are lettering guides, many special pens, and mechanical lettering sets, such as the Unitech, Leroy, and Wrico lettering sets, which may be used to advantage. However, the beginner should first try to perfect his freehand lettering with a straight pen and his linework with a standard ruling pen which is adjustable for various line widths. Do not try to hurry the inking. It is better to do careful, accurate, neat work and to allow speed to develop with experience. The illustration in Fig. 11-1 shows a Unitech lettering set with lettering templates, scriber, lettering pens, and an ink cartridge. Each template should be used with the recommended pen size. Technical or tube-type pens may be used to draw lines or to letter, instead of the standard ruling pen or straight lettering pen point. These tube-type pens have replaceable points similar to those in the lettering sets, each pen point making a definite line width. Figure 11-2 illustrates a tube-type pen set consisting of a handle, a pen adapter, seven pen sections, and a bottle of ink. The pen points in the pen sections are removable and can be replaced by other points. Figure 11-3 shows the line widths which can be made with the eight different pen points available.

Naturally one tries not to make errors, draw the wrong lines, or make blots, but these things do occur. Again, it is often necessary to make changes in or additions to a completed ink tracing. In any event erasing is a necessary part of a draftsman's work, and you should learn to erase carefully to avoid marring the surface of the tracing cloth. It is best to use a good pencil eraser and rub evenly, using an erasing shield to cover lines which are to be retained. When erasing, place the tracing on a smooth hard surface. After erasing on cloth, rub in some pounce to restore the surface for the

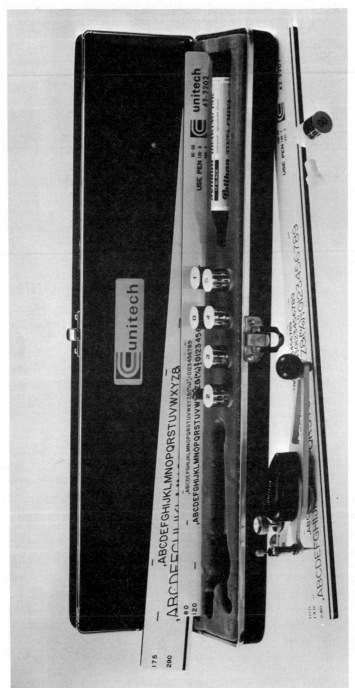

Fig. 11-1. Lettering set. *(Charvoz-Carsen Corporation, Fairfield, N.J.)*

Fig. 11-2. Tube-type set. *(Charvoz-Carsen Corporation, Fairfield, N.J.)*

000   00   0   1   2   2½   3   4

Fig. 11-3. Line widths. *(Charvoz-Carsen Corporation, Fairfield, N.J.)*

new inking. So-called ink erasers contain too much abrasive material, have a tendency to scratch the surface of the cloth, and make it difficult to ink over the erasure. Ink eradicators are also unsatisfactory. There are electrically operated erasing machines on the market, which if handled properly, may be used to advantage when there is considerable erasing to be done. Metal scrapers or razor blades are definitely not recommended.

It might be well to note at this time that a special tracing cloth can be obtained which is suitable for pencil drawings. It is whiter in color than tracing cloth for ink, which usually has a slightly bluish tint. The pencil cloth is stronger than vellum but in general not quite as transparent. Drawings are made on pencil tracing cloth when it is not intended or necessary to make ink tracings of the drawings. Necessary prints or copies may be made directly from the pencil tracing.

The following is a list of some of the things that should not be done when inking or tracing drawings.

Do not use a blotter on tracing cloth. Allow the ink to dry thoroughly before starting to erase.
Do not close the points of a ruling pen beyond the point of contact.

Do not hold the pen over a drawing while filling with ink.
Do not leave the stopper out of the ink bottle.
Do not contaminate the drawing ink by adding regular writing inks, and do not stick a ball-point pen in the ink bottle.
Do not put instruments or pens away without cleaning them. This applies especially to pens of all kinds.

Exercises

Regular tracings are made on tracing cloth, but as the cloth is expensive it is recommended that you first practice inking on tracing paper. An application of pounce will not be required on tracing paper. Start to practice lettering by drawing letters and numerals with a straight lettering pen (such as a Gillotte 303) on tracing paper. Lettering with a pen and ink requires a different touch, or technique, from that required for lettering with a pencil. Hold the pen so that the points do not dig into the paper, and allow the ink to flow smoothly onto the paper. After sufficient practice on paper, continue the practice, using tracing cloth.

On tracing paper, practice tracing several of the drawings previously made for exercises in Chaps. 7 and 8. Fasten the original drawing to the drawing board with drafting tape, at the same time smoothing out all wrinkles. Then lay the tracing paper over the drawing and fasten it to the board with drafting tape. Review the instructions given in this chapter on tracing with ink, and when you have become proficient, trace several drawings on tracing cloth.

12. frame garage

Before the advent of automobiles it was customary for the owner of a horse and carriage to build a carriage house, or stable, on his property. A stable would house horses and rigs, and it might also include living quarters on a second floor for a full-time groom or coachman. In some countries the house and stable used to be grouped around a wall-enclosed courtyard. This was done for convenience and also for protection against intruders. In other instances, the stable was located at some distance from the house for sanitary reasons. When automobiles, or as we now call them cars, came into general use people began to turn their stables into houses for their cars. Or lacking a stable, the owner built a new structure for the car, usually at some distance from the house. At the same time we began using a word derived from the French, "garage," meaning a place for housing automobiles and originally even an airship or a flying machine.

Hence, we can define a garage as primarily a place to house automobiles, but it should also include some additional room for storage space. Garages for commercial use must be built to accommodate other functions that contribute to the maintenance of automobiles, in addition to providing housing for them. This chapter will deal with private garages for houses and leave the larger types for other texts.

A separate garage may not add to or enhance the architecture of a house, but it should not clash with the design of the house. Rather, the garage should look as if it fitted in with and belonged to the house.

There are reasons for having a garage separate from the house, such as:

It might not be feasible to add an attached garage to an existing house.

The owner of a large house having several cars might wish to have the garage at some distance from the house.

The size or shape of the plot might make it undesirable to attach the garage to the house.

There are also many good reasons which can be cited in favor of the attached garage, some being:

An attached garage usually makes a small house appear larger than it really is.

It will avoid a walk between the house and garage, which is especially undesirable in inclement weather.

In most cases it will decrease the lengh of driveway required to be installed.

An attached garage can be readily heated from the house heating system.

From the foregoing it would seem that the question of a separate or an attached garage is a matter of individual choice, but unless one has a very definite preference for a separate garage, it would be better to plan on making the garage a part of the house. In that case it should harmonize and fit in with the general scheme and design of the house. A garage large enough to house two cars will require approximately 20 by 22 ft of floor space, which may seem to be a large area when compared with the rest of the house. One arrangement is to place the garage at one corner of the house and increase the apparent length of the house. The garage could also be separated from the house by a covered walk, or breezeway If the breezeway, or space between the house and the garage, were enclosed by screened sash, it could be utilized as extra living space.

While the garage should be designed and built primarily to house cars, it should be remembered that the house and grounds must be maintained and kept in good condition and repair. This means that there will be an accumulation of tools and equipment, such as a lawn mower, wheelbarrow, and ladder, for which it will be necessary to have a storage space. Therefore, be farsighted: provide some room for shelves and closet space in the garage to stow miscellaneous equipment, and thus encourage good housekeeping habits.

In some sections of the country, where the weather is not too severe during the winter season, an enclosed garage has been superseded by a carport. This consists of a roofed-over area adjacent to the house under which the car can be stored when not in use. A carport is less expensive than a complete garage.

In connection with planning and laying out any type of structure, a great deal of detailed information will be required. Much of the needed information can be obtained by consulting such reference books as:

"Architects and Builders Handbook," F. E. Kidder and H. Parker, John Wiley & Sons, Inc., New York.
"Architectural Graphic Standards," G. G. Ramsey and H. R. Sleeper, John Wiley & Sons, Inc., New York.
"Blueprint Reading for the Construction Trades," Herbert F. Bellis and Walter A. Schmidt, McGraw-Hill Book Company, New York.
"Building Codes," National Board of Fire Underwriters, New York.
"Building Construction Handbook," Frederick S. Merritt, Editor, McGraw-Hill Book Company, New York.
"Reinforced Concrete and Masonry Structures," G. A. Hool and W. S. Kinne, McGraw-Hill Book Company, New York.
Sweet's Catalog Service–Architectural, F. W. Dodge Corporation, New York.
Local building codes.
Manufacturers' catalogs and bulletins for details and directions covering the use of special materials.

Figures 12-1 and 12-2 show the plan, section elevations, and details for a frame garage. Assume that the owner has requested the architect to prepare plans for a one-car garage situated some distance from the house but with roofing and siding similar to that used for the house. The architect decides that the overall dimensions of the garage should be 14'–0" wide by 22'–0"

long. He has either made a freehand sketch or verbally instructs you, the draftsman, to proceed with the preparation of the plans. It will be your problem to draw the plans for the garage as shown in Figs. 12-1 and 12-2 to the scale specified.

Keep in mind that you should make notes of the instructions you receive, and as you proceed with the work make notes and freehand sketches of what you propose to draw before you start the actual drawing. Approximate the overall size of the views which you intend to draw in order that you will be able to arrange the views neatly and logically on the drawing. Make a rough sketch showing the arrangement of the views on the sheet. A good arrangement of the various views will enhance the appearance of the finished drawing. Retain all your notes and sketches for future reference. With experience you will find that a mental picture of your drawing will come to mind at the beginning of the work and that many lines can be drawn in their final form immediately. Until such a time, however, draw in the lines lightly, using a 4H pencil, until you are sure of their location and extent. Then darken the lines for the final drawing, using an H pencil.

First prepare two sheets of drafting paper or vellum, size 11 by 17 in. with a ½-in.-wide border at the top, bottom, and right side, and a 1-in.-wide border at the left-hand side. Rule off a ¾-in.-wide space at the bottom of the sheet for the title and number.

Start with the plan shown in Fig. 12-1, and lay out the 14'–0" rectangle to show the outside of the garage walls using the scale of ¼" = 1'–0" as noted. Because it is a frame garage, you decide to use 2- by 4-in. studs spaced 16 in. center to center and covered on the outside with ¾-in.-thick tongue-and-groove sheathing. The final covering will be asbestos shingles over a layer of building paper. The studs will be exposed on the inside of the garage since it is not necessary to apply a finishing material on the inside face of the studs. With this information you can now draw the inner rectangle on the plan with a wall thickness of 5 in. Next indicate a stock-size double-hung window located at the midpoint of each side of the garage. In the front wall locate an overhead entrance door 8'–0" wide by 7'–0" high, and in the rear wall a small door for use when it is not necessary to open the large door. Check manufacturers' bulletins for the stock sizes of the doors and windows.

At this point start to draw section A-A and refer to Figs. 7-2 to 7-4 for typical details. First draw the outside wall lines 14'–0" apart, and draw a line to represent the established grade. The garage walls should rest on a foundation wall extending under all four upper walls. The foundation wall should project a minimum

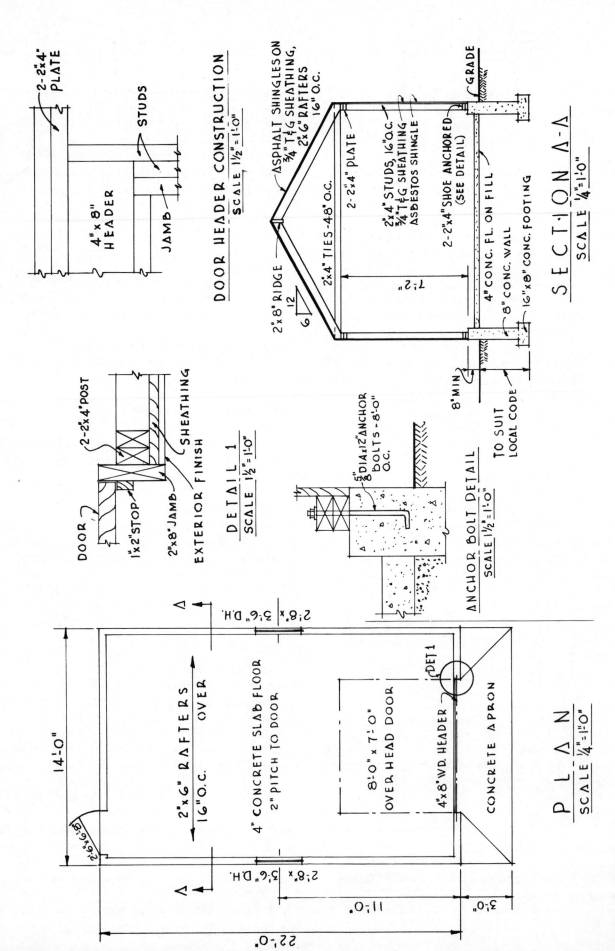

2-2"x4" PLATE

STUDS

4"x8" HEADER

JAMB

DOOR HEADER CONSTRUCTION
SCALE 1½"=1'-0"

ASPHALT SHINGLES ON ¾" T&G SHEATHING, 2"x6" RAFTERS 16" O.C.

2-2"x4" PLATE

2"x4" STUDS, 16" O.C. ¾" T&G SHEATHING ASBESTOS SHINGLE

2-2"x4" SHOE ANCHORED (SEE DETAIL)

GRADE

4" CONC. FL. ON FILL

8" CONC. WALL

16"x8" CONC. FOOTING

7'-2"

2"x4" TIES-48" O.C.

2"x8" RIDGE

12
6

8" MIN.

TO SUIT LOCAL CODE

SECTION A-A
SCALE ¼"=1'-0"

2-2"x4" POST

SHEATHING

1"x2" STOP

2"x8" JAMB

DOOR

EXTERIOR FINISH

DETAIL 1
SCALE 1½"=1'-0"

⅝" DIA.x12" ANCHOR BOLTS - 8'-0" O.C.

ANCHOR BOLT DETAIL
SCALE 1½"=1'-0"

2"x6" RAFTERS 16" O.C. OVER

4" CONCRETE SLAB FLOOR 2" PITCH TO DOOR

8'-0" x 7'-0" OVER HEAD DOOR

4"x8" WD. HEADER

CONCRETE APRON

DET 1

2'-8" x 3'-6" D.H.

2'-8" x 3'-6" D.H.

14'-0"

2"x6" RFTR.

22'-0"

11'-0"

3'-0"

PLAN
SCALE ¼"=1'-0"

Fig. 12-1. Frame garage.

106

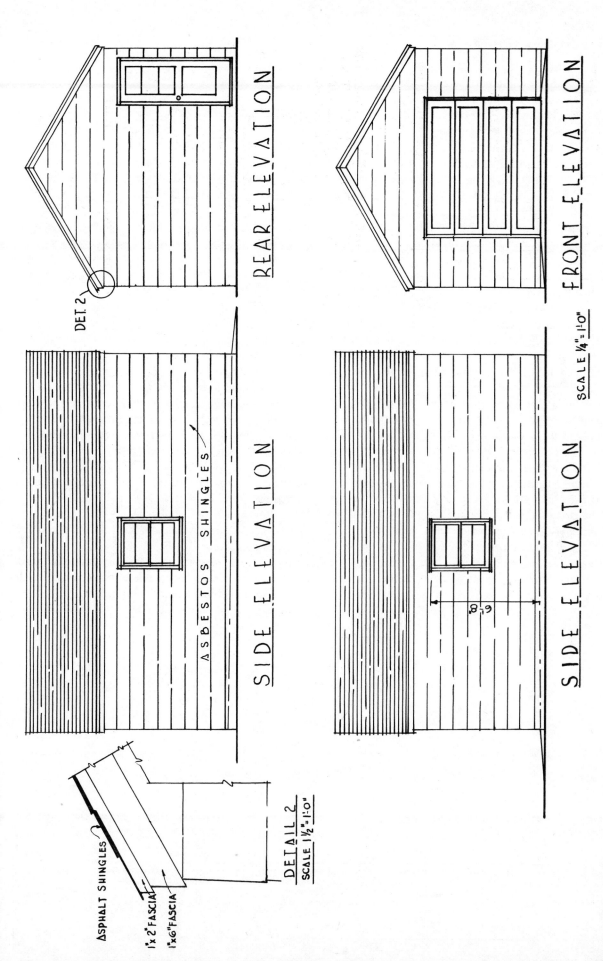

REAR ELEVATION

FRONT ELEVATION

SCALE ¼" = 1'-0"

DET. 2

ASBESTOS SHINGLES

SIDE ELEVATION

SIDE ELEVATION

9'-8"

ASPHALT SHINGLES

1" x 2" FASCIA

1" x 6" FASCIA

DETAIL 2
SCALE 1½" = 1'-0"

Fig. 12-2. Frame garage.

of 8 in. above the ground line and extend down into the ground the distance required by the local building code. For a one-story structure of this type an 8-in. poured-concrete wall or concrete blocks will be acceptable, but the foundation wall proper should be built upon a poured-concrete footing 16 in. wide by 8 in. deep. The 4-in.-thick concrete floor can be poured directly over the firmly tamped fill inside the foundation walls. If desired, a light wire mesh may be laid in the concrete for reinforcement. The front wall will be notched out 8 in. deep for the width of the door opening, and the concrete floor will be continued outside the garage to form the sloping apron for the car approach.

Now that you have the foundation wall drawn, proceed to draw in the garage walls and the roof, outlining the studs, rafters, ridge, and ties. Since the shoe upon which the studs rest must be fastened securely to the foundation, you make a sketch of the anchor-bolt detail to be added to the drawing later. The slope of 6 in 12 for the roof was selected because it is a ratio commonly used, that is, a roof pitch of one fourth, as explained in Fig. 7-8. This pitch may be varied so that it will blend architecturally with the roof slopes of the main house. The sizes selected for the rafters, ridge, and ties are ample for a structure of this size and can be checked in reference books on frame construction.

Up to this point you have drawn only the outlines of the structure, but all the dimensions and notes have been preserved on freehand sketches. Add the anchor-bolt detail to the drawing. The carpenter will provide standard framing construction for the windows and the single door, and this should be noted in the specifications. You feel, however, that additional information

should be added to the drawing for the wide overhead door. Therefore, draw detail 1 showing a section through the jamb and the detail showing the door header construction. Indicate the 4- by 8-in. header over the door opening in the plan and the location of detail 1 by a small circle at the side of the door opening. Next, from your notes and freehand sketches add all the necessary dimensions and other information shown on the drawing. Mark the location of section A-A on the plan, and show the symbolic sectioning for the concrete and lumber where indicated. Add the subtitles and note the scale used for each view. Then complete the drawing by adding the main title and drawing number.

Having completed Fig. 12-1, proceed to draw the two side elevations and the front and rear elevations of the garage to the scale of $\frac{1}{4}'' = 1'-0''$ as shown in Fig. 12-2. Indicate the asbestos shingles covering all four sides of the garage and the asphalt shingles used on the roof. Also give a dimension locating the height of the top of the windows above the floor line. Note the sloping apron in front of the garage from the top of the concrete floor to the ground line. Next, draw detail 2 showing the size of the fascia boards and the asphalt shingles which will be laid over a layer of building paper covering the $\frac{3}{4}$-in.-thick tongue-and-groove sheathing noted in section A-A in Fig. 12-1. Add the subtitle for each view and note the scale used. Complete the drawing by adding the main title and the drawing number.

Now check the two drawings very carefully to see that the views drawn are complete and correct, with all necessary dimensions and other information.

13. frame residence

When drawing the plans for a house, there will be different conditions to be considered for locations in various sections of this country. That is, there are regional variations in construction practices in the United States, and the same idea would apply to other countries. Simplified, this means that an architect must adjust the design and details to conform to local conditions.

The U.S. Federal Housing Administration, called FHA, has set up seven different regions or areas in this country. These regions have basic construction details in common, but some variations must be made due to different conditions, such as the prevailing weather of the region, soil conditions, available building materials, and other possible items peculiar to the local area. Variations caused by these conditions are also reflected in the local building codes. Following are some of the main points which should be considered.

Foundations and footings

Any of the various foundation and footing designs may be employed in the different regions, but certain designs predominate in each region because of local building practices and local codes. In areas subject to freezing weather the frost line determines the depth of the footing. As frost has a tendency to lift the footing, the building codes set a mandatory depth for footings, which should be below the established frost line for the area. Foundation walls built of poured concrete, concrete blocks, cinder blocks, or brick require larger footings than frame walls because of the greater weight to be supported. Concrete-block and cinder-block walls

are used extensively in tropical regions because of the prevalence of termites or other destructive insects. Swampy lands, spongy soil, filled-in lands, and beaches usually require that foundations extend down to stable soil. This often means that piling must be used under a footing as explained in Chap. 7. In freezing climates, footings are usually formed and poured separately from the foundation walls. Concrete blocks are used in basement walls for their insulating properties. While they require the use of more waterproofing than poured concrete, they may cut down the cost of construction. Poured concrete can be made impervious or watertight by the addition of waterproofing compounds to the mixture. Waterproofing can also be accomplished by the application of hot asphalt mopped or troweled over the outside of the walls. In regions of heavy snowfall, waterproofing of the exterior foundation surfaces below the snow level or grade is necessary to prevent seepage through the walls due to melting snow. Where the soil is spongy or swampy, special precautions should be taken to spread the chimney footing so that the footing will not settle and the chimney pull away from the house.

Wall framing and covering details

Wall framing and the finish covering vary for many reasons. The majority of houses, especially in the East, are sheathed with ¾-in. tongue-and-groove wood or ½-in. gypsum board. The sheathing is then covered with building paper and wood siding, shingles, stucco, or a brick veneer. Braced framing is especially good for regions of prevailing high winds, but it is more difficult to erect and usually more costly. The western, or platform, framing is a variation of the braced framing. It provides a rigid structure and with solid or panel sheathing is effectively braced. Because of the simplicity of its erection, this design of framing has gained in popularity throughout this country. Modular wall framing with prefabricated panels is also used, especially in wet, cold, or snowy regions. Erection time and cost for modular constructions may be considerably reduced, but the fabricator's recommended directions and specifications should be followed with the utmost care.

Roof framing

Roof framing is basically the same throughout the country, and all variations of pitch are used. There is, however, a tendency to specify a steeper roof pitch in sections where there may be frequent and heavy snow loads. The steeper pitched roof tends to clear itself of snow quicker than flat types. When cement tile or other heavy materials are used, the supporting rafters must be sized to suit the load of the unsupported roof span.

Window frames and sash

In mild climates window frames without built-in weatherstripping may be used to cut down costs. Window frames in brick walls are made tight against the weather by sealing the joints with oakum or jute and a caulking compound. Metal sash and frames are being used more and more for residences and have some advantages over wood sash.

The remarks in Chap. 12 regarding reference books, building codes, and manufacturers' catalogs apply equally well to the preparation of plans for a residence. Figures 13-1 to 13-7 comprise a set of plans to cover the drawings for a frame residence of the Cape Cod type. The house covered by these plans is a plain and simple structure of a basic design which has been popular with builders because of the ease with which it can be built. It illustrates basic construction, and when you have mastered these details it will be easy to vary the layout in many ways to add more style and modernization to the design. However, many people feel that in the proper setting the very simplicity of a Cape Cod cottage is in itself charming.

In an architect's office, plans are usually started as the result of a request from a client who desires to build a house and commissions the architect to prepare the necessary plans. Before approaching an architect, the client has usually selected or purchased a parcel of land and has had the property surveyed. The surveyor will have made a map or drawing showing the dimensions of the plot and noted the contours and any special features, such as large trees, a creek, or large rocks which are exposed. The architect will be given a copy of the property map for the purpose of locating (orienting) the proposed residence on the property. He will know from previous experience the required setback for the front, side, and rear yards. These requirements vary with each city, township, and village and must be checked carefully with the local building department. An initial check will avoid a possible revision of the plans and relocation of the residence on the property before the necessary building permit is issued.

Many items are taken into consideration in the discussion between the architect and his client. The client should state his needs regarding the space required for living, sleeping, eating, and recreation facilities. This will establish the general size of the house and will enable the architect to make freehand sketches on graph paper to show the client the general floor-plan arrangement that will provide for the facilities he has in mind. The architect, with his background and experience, will be able to fit rooms together to make a smooth, workable plan which will avoid waste space and utilize each area to the best advantage. Construction limitations, lumber sizes, and building restrictions have to be taken into consideration during this early discussion period to avoid the necessity of drastic changes when the floor plan is drawn to scale by the draftsman. Materials, such as the type of foundation, wall and roof construction, exterior and interior wall finishes, type of windows and doors, kitchen equipment, bathroom fixtures, and electrical and heating systems, are discussed, and notes are made regarding these items for future reference as the work on the plans progresses.

At this stage sufficient information has been assembled to start drawing the preliminary plans for the house. The architect gives his sketches and material requirements to one of his experienced draftsmen, who draws the plans in pencil on tracing paper, or vellum, usually to a scale of $\frac{1}{4}'' = 1'-0''$. These preliminary plans consist of the floor plan, a partial construction section, and a front elevation. When completed, blueprints or Ozalid prints (blue lines on white background) are made from the pencil tracings for the purpose of further discussion. A meeting is arranged with the client to discuss the plans, and if the preliminary plans are approved as drawn, the architect is authorized to proceed with the project and complete the finished plans. In the event the client requests changes in the preliminary plans, this may necessitate another meeting for further approval of the preliminary plans after the changes have been made. After approval of the preliminary plans, the drawings are given back to the drafts-man who made the drawings with the necessary in-structions to complete the entire set.

In large offices employing many draftsmen, the job may be turned over to a junior draftsman who will complete the work under the supervision of a senior draftsman or a job captain. In small offices a senior draftsman may complete the whole project by himself or with the help of a junior draftsman who may draw parts of the project, such as the elevations, lettering, and titles. The beginning draftsman will start on some of the simpler drawings. His progress will depend on his ability and ambition, both of which are necessary to further his progress toward the goal of becoming a first-class senior draftsman.

A student has usually taken little or no notice of windows, stairs, and other construction details on existing buildings before he makes drawings of these details, which are covered in Chaps. 7 and 8. Therefore when a beginning draftsman starts out to draw his first set of plans, he often finds them quite confusing. It is easy to understand that many questions enter his mind that cannot be answered at once. But now, as you begin to draw a set of house plans, the detail drawings you made previously will begin to fit together and have more meaning. If you take pains to complete the fol-lowing figures carefully and accurately, transcribing the plans, sections, elevations, and details, you will lay a good foundation for much of your future work.

Redraw or transcribe the plans, sections, elevations, etc., shown in Figs. 13-1 to 13-7 to a scale of ¼″ = 1′–0″, following the procedure given for each figure. Before starting each drawing, study the text carefully, and refer to it frequently to avoid mistakes and to accustom yourself to follow directions so that you can do the job correctly. Use vellum size 11 by 17 in. with the same borders that were specified in Chap. 12 for the two plans of the frame garage. You will note as you continue to read that the proper grade of pencil to use for various parts of the drawing has been speci-fied. There is no hard-and-fast rule on the grade of pencil which must be used for different lines, but the suggestions made are the result of the authors' experi-ence when working on vellum.

Floor plan

Figure 13-1. Fasten a clean sheet of vellum to your drawing board with drafting tape and, with a 4H pen-cil, lightly draw the border lines specified in Chap. 12. Draw a light line between the right and left border lines 1¼ in. below the upper border line. Mark the center of the space between the right and left border lines and from that point locate the rear left-hand corner of the

building. Draw the outside perimeter of the floor plan lightly with a 4H pencil. This should be a con-tinuous line disregarding the door openings. Draw the exterior-wall thickness, which is shown as 5 in., and on the front wall add the additional 4 in. for the brick veneer. Locate and draw the interior partitions 4 in. thick, but note that part of the bathroom wall is 8 in. thick. Continue to use the 4H pencil, and again disre-gard the openings for the doors and arches.

Using an H pencil, locate the door and window cen-ter lines on the exterior walls, and then establish the width of each one according to the sizes specified on the plan. Always use a pencil with a sharp point, keep rolling the pencil as previously instructed in Chap. 2, and avoid making double lines. Locate the chimney and the front- and rear-entrance stoops from the di-mensions given on the foundation plan. Next locate and draw the lines to show the interior doors and arches. The short stub at the side of the door is usually 3 in. for interior doors and 4 in. for exterior doors to allow for the jamb and the double stud.

Draw in the kitchen equipment and the bathroom fixtures using dimensions which you can obtain from the reference books and catalogs available. Locate the electric outlets and wall switches as shown in Fig. 13-1. Information for the electrical requirements will be found under Electrical Wiring later in this chapter.

Now darken all object outlines with a sharp H pen-cil, and dimension all windows and doors and the out-side of the building. Use a 2H pencil for extension and dimension lines and an F pencil for lettering, numerals, and arrowheads. Keep your pencil point sharp for all lines, but round the point slightly for lettering. Re-member that dimension lines should be thin black lines to contrast with the object outlines. It is preferable to start the first line of dimension ¾ in. from the building outline and to allow ½ in. space to the next line of dimensions. However, this rule applies as space permits, and there will be instances where it will be necessary to reduce these allowances proportionately to suit the space available. Dimension the interior of the building as shown. Draw the doors as indicated, using a 30° triangle for the doors and a compass for the arc. To make the proper swing, set the point of the compass at the point where the door hinge would be. Doors may also be shown with a 45 or 90° swing if the space permits. Indicate the stairs down to the basement and up to the attic, using a tread width of 9 in. The dimen-sions for the size and location of the chimney, which is 2′–0″ square, are shown in Fig. 13-2. Fill in the section lines for the chimney, the brick veneer, and the bricks for the front stoop.

Letter the room names, and add all other dimen-sions and notes as shown and noted in Fig. 13-1. Check

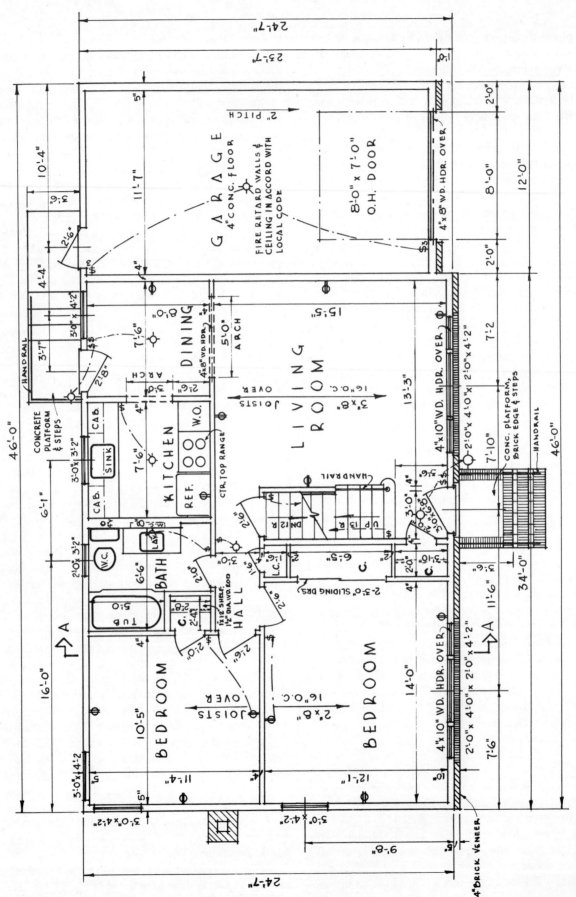

Fig. 13-1. Frame residence. Floor plan. (Scale: $1/4'' = 1'-0''$.)

112

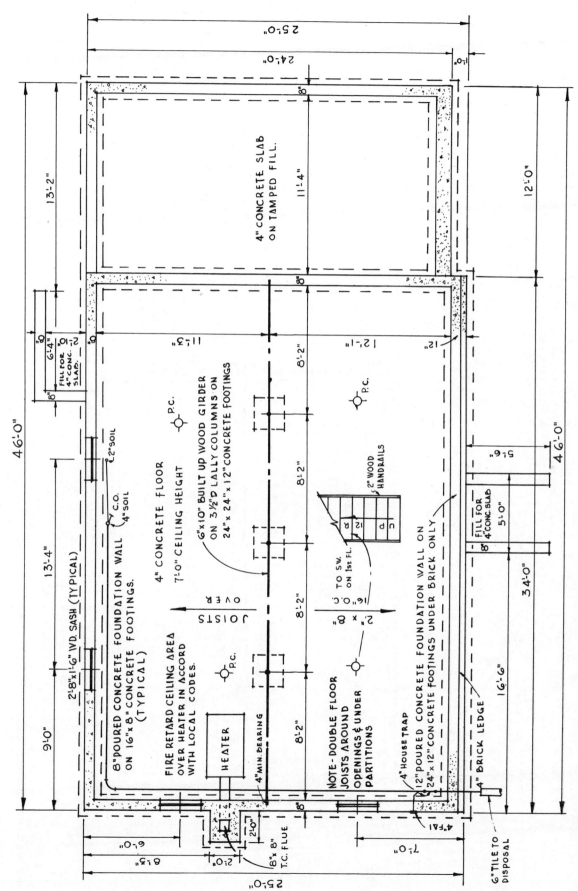

Fig. 13-2. Frame residence. Foundation plan. (Scale: 1/4" = 1'-0".)

113

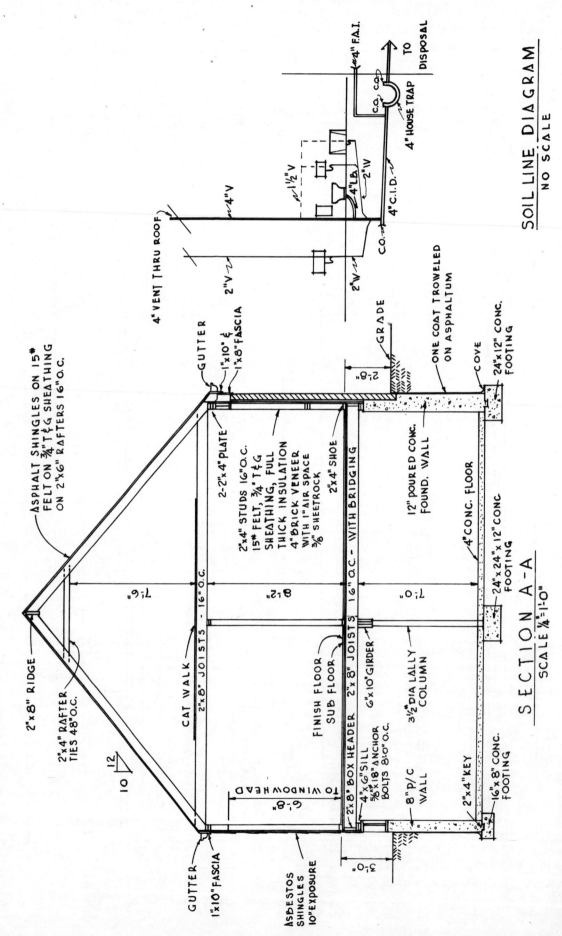

Fig. 13-3. Frame residence.

114

over the drawing carefully to be sure that you have indicated every line and item. Darken the border lines which you made when you started the drawing.

Do not remove the drawing from your drawing board.

Foundation plan

Figure 13-2. Place a clean piece of vellum over the drawing of the floor plan and fasten to the board with drafting tape. Then trace the perimeter or outer line of the floor plan. Measure in 8 in., using the scale of $\frac{1}{4}'' = 1'-0''$, for the side and rear walls and 12 in. for the front wall. On the front wall draw a line 4 in. from the outer edge to indicate the ledge for the brick veneer above.

You will note that the stairs leading to the basement has twelve risers. From Fig. 8-7, stair details, you learned that there is always one less tread than riser. Hence, there are eleven treads, and using a width of 9 in. for each tread you will have a run of 99 in. from the top riser to the bottom riser. From the floor plan, measure 99 in. from the first riser. This will locate the bottom riser in the basement. Draw only a few treads with a break line indicating that the stairs disappear above the eye level. Add the arrow indicating up, the handrails, and the note, and you have completed the stair indication.

Note that the girder has been located under the center of the wall between the two bedrooms. Draw a heavy center line, with long and short dashes, to indicate the girder, and locate the lally columns and the footings to the dimensions shown. Trace the outer edges of the front and rear stoops and the return with an 8-in. thickness to form the cheeks, or side foundation walls, for the stoops. The outer line of the building foundation wall continues past the stoop cheeks since they are usually lower than the top of the foundation wall. However, the cheeks are poured at the same time as the foundation wall and are tied into the wall with bent steel bars to prevent settling. This same condition is shown where the foundation for the garage is connected to the main building's foundation wall. Draw the dash lines around the perimeter of the house and the garage on both sides of the foundation wall to indicate the footing. Draw the footing 4 in. wide on each side of all 8-in.-thick walls and 6 in. wide on each side of the 12-in. front wall.

Locate and draw the chimney foundation, the footing and flue, the heater, the windows, the electric outlets, and the 4-in. soil line. Add all other dimensions and notes shown in Fig. 13-2, and draw the border lines as you did for the floor plan. As a timesaver, the border lines for each sheet may be traced from a previous drawing of the same size or from master forms prepared in advance for the standard sizes of sheets which are to be used. Check your foundation plan thoroughly to see that all the information given in Fig. 13-2 has been included in your drawing.

Section and soil line

Figure. 13-3. Fasten a third sheet of 11- by 17-in. vellum to your drawing board and draw the views shown in Fig. 13-3. The border lines may be traced from one of the previous drawings. Start section A-A $1\frac{1}{4}$ in. above the title space in the lower left-hand corner of the sheet. Draw section A-A, often called the construction section, from the bottom up, as if you were actually building the house.

Start with the poured-concrete footing and the foundation walls, using the dimension of $25'-0''$, outside to outside of the walls as shown on the foundation plan. Add the 4-in. concrete floor, the lally column, and the built-up wood girder. Draw the bottom line of the floor joists $7'-0''$ above the concrete floor line with the ends of the joists supported on the 4- by 6-in. sills at the top of the foundation walls. The basement windows may be placed directly beneath the sills as indicated by the window shown in the rear wall. Continue by completing the floor joists, the headers, the 2- by 4-in. shoes, the studs, the siding and shingles on the rear wall, and the brick-veneer construction on the front wall. Show the top and bottom of the window in the front wall with the header at the top. Draw the ceiling joists with the lower edge $8'-2''$ above the top of the floor joists, with the ends supported on the double 2- by 4-in. plates. Note that the lower edge of the rafters starts at the top inner corner of the figure. Draw the rafters, to the slope shown in Fig. 13-3, and the ridge; add the rafter ties, the catwalk, or rough flooring, for the attic, the gutters, the fascia boards, and the shingle line. Indicate the asphaltum waterproofing for the foundation walls by solid lines and add the grade lines.

Complete section A-A by adding all the dimensions and notes, including the roof-pitch symbol and the section designation with the scale below it, as shown in Fig. 13-3. The construction section A-A is a very important drawing and should be drawn as accurately as possible since it will be used in drawing the elevations of the house. The accuracy with which you draw this section will be reflected in the drawings of the elevations.

The soil-line diagram in Fig. 13-3 showing the waste system should be transcribed as shown to the right of section A-A. You will note that it is not drawn to scale, and no attempt has been made to show the exact run or location of the pipes, which is the reason it is called

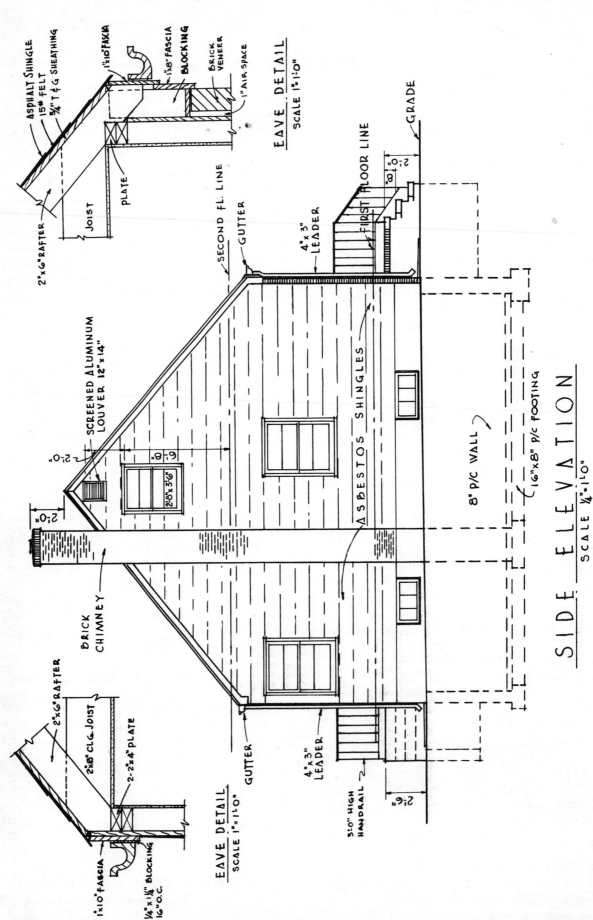

EAVE DETAIL
SCALE 1"=1'0"

EAVE DETAIL
SCALE 1"=1'0"

SIDE ELEVATION
SCALE ¼"=1'0"

Fig. 13-4. Frame residence.

116

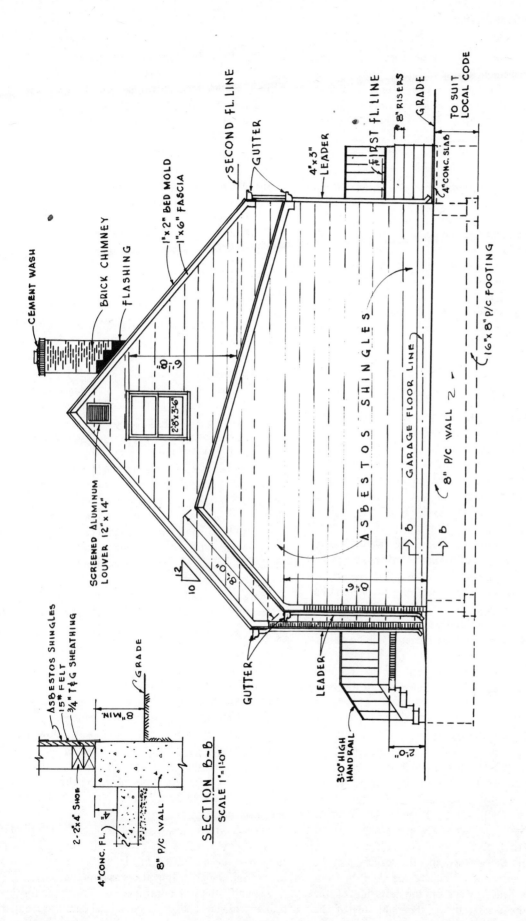

CEMENT WASH

BRICK CHIMNEY

FLASHING

SCREENED ALUMINUM
LOUVER 12" x 14"

2'-8"x3'-6"

6'-8"

12
10

8'-0"

ASBESTOS SHINGLES

1" x 2" BED MOLD
1"x 6" FASCIA

SECOND FL. LINE

GUTTER

4"x 3"
LEADER

FIRST FL. LINE

8" RISERS

GRADE

TO SUIT
LOCAL CODE

4" CONC. SLAB

GARAGE FLOOR LINE

8" P/C WALL

0'-6"

16"x 8" P/C FOOTING

GUTTER

LEADER

3'-0" HIGH
HANDRAIL

2'-0"

SIDE ELEVATION
SCALE ¼"=1'-0"

ASBESTOS SHINGLES
15# FELT
¾" T&G SHEATHING

GRADE

8" MIN.

2-2"x4" SHOE

4" CONC. FL.

4"

8" P/C WALL

SECTION b–b
SCALE 1"=1'-0"

Fig. 13-5. Frame residence.

117

a diagram. It is drawn in this manner because the method of arrangement of the different connections is more important than the scale. The fixtures are shown in their general relationship rather than in relation to the dimensions on the floor plan. The local building departments require such a diagram to show them that proper back venting will be incorporated in the plumbing work.

The complete understanding of plumbing piping, including waste lines, hot- and cold-water lines, cesspools, and septic tanks, requires further study, which you should pursue to become an advanced draftsman. There are many good reference books and handbooks available, as well as local building codes, which cover plumbing requirements. Figures 13-8 and 13-9 show plumbing requirements in more detail for a residence of this size. Add to your drawing all dimensions, notes, symbols, lettering, title, scales, and border lines shown in Fig. 13-3.

Side elevations

Figures 13-4 and 13-5. The elevations of a residence or any building are exterior views or pictures of the completed structure. These drawings should be accurate in size and shape and should reflect the locations of the doors, windows, stoops, chimney, and roof lines as shown on the floor plan and the section. Draw the elevation of the left side shown in Fig. 13-4 on a clean sheet of vellum 11 by 17 in., using the same dimensions for the outline of the house that were used to draw section A-A on the previous drawing. Start by drawing the grade lines 2¼ in. above the title space. Add the windows from the locations shown on the floor and foundation plans, the stoops, and the chimney. The window and door indications for all elevations should be carefully drawn after checking manufacturers' catalogs for the stile, rail, muntin, glass, sill, and trim sizes for the windows, and for the stile, rail panel, and glass sizes for the doors. Draw the eave details for each side of the house to a scale of $1'' = 1'-0''$, and add the gutters and leaders to the side elevation. Complete the elevation by adding all the dimensions, the lines denoting shingles, lettering, title, scales, notes, and border lines shown in Fig. 13-4.

Figure 13-5 shows the elevation of the right side of the house looking at the garage, and should be drawn on a clean sheet of vellum 11 by 17 in. Draw the grade line 2¾ in. above the title space as for the previous drawing. The roof of the main house, the chimney above the roof, the gutters, and the leaders may be taken from the elevation of the left side. Add the front stoop and the brick veneer on the left side of the drawing and the rear stoop on the right side of the

drawing. Draw the roof line for the garage, and note that the front of the garage is set back $1'-0''$ from the front of the house as shown in Figs. 13-1 and 13-2. The foundation wall for the garage only is shown on the right side elevation, and it should not be carried down any deeper than the frost line specified in the local building code. Complete this elevation by adding the attic window and screened louver in the same location as on the left side elevation, and by adding the lines denoting shingles, chimney flashing, lettering, section B-B, title, scale, notes, and border lines as shown in Fig. 13-5. Do not remove this drawing from your drawing board.

Rear elevation

Figure 13-6. Place another sheet of vellum 11 by 17 in. over the completed drawing of the side elevation and proceed to draw the rear elevation as shown in Fig. 13-6. Use the side elevation to trace off the grade line, floor line, and roof heights. Locate the windows and doors from the floor and foundation plans. Not only is this procedure time-saving, but, more important, it reduces errors as you trace from your carefully drawn side elevation. The brick, siding, and roofing indications are purposely shown in the dash lines and not drawn continuously from corner to corner and edge to edge. This avoids the look of a mechanical drawing. With practice you will gain the ability to add softness and realism to the elevation drawings and make them more pleasing to the eye. Remember that the client must like what he sees and must be sold by your drawings. Include the outlines of the foundations, the stoop, gutters, leaders, chimney, dimensions, lettering, notes, titles, scale and border lines, all as shown in Fig. 13-6.

Front elevation

Figure 13-7. Remove the side elevation drawing from your board, but retain the rear elevation as you may use it to locate the grade line, roof, door, window, stoop, and chimney heights. Place a clean sheet of vellum over the drawing of the rear elevation and draw the doors and windows in the location shown on the floor plan. Add the gutters, leaders, stoop, chimney, foundations, and dash lines for the brick veneer. Complete by including all dimensions, lettering, title, scale, and border lines as shown in Fig. 13-7. Note that nearly all dimensions have been omitted in Fig. 13-7 as these may be taken from the preceding plates as required.

Assemble the seven drawings you have made for this frame residence, and give them a final check to see that

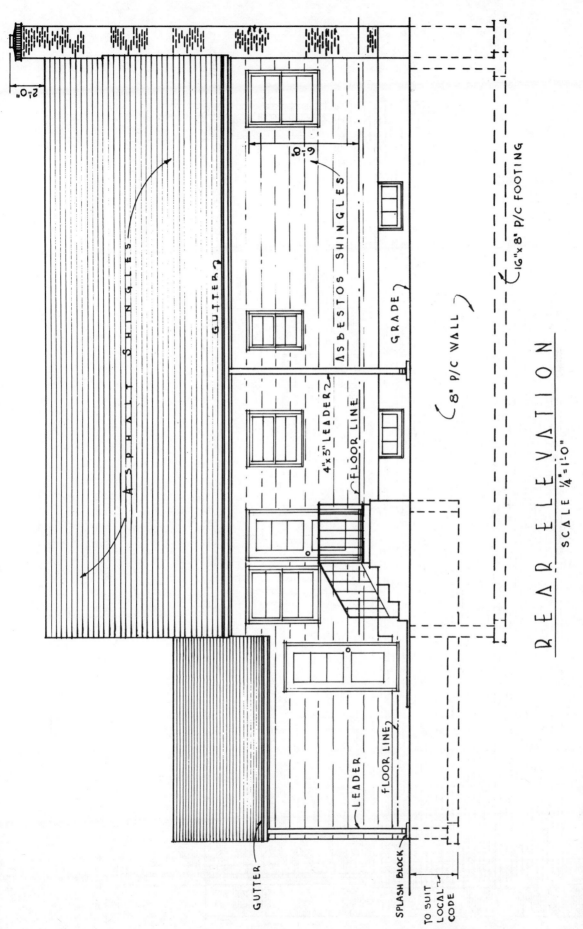

Fig. 13-6. Frame residence.

119

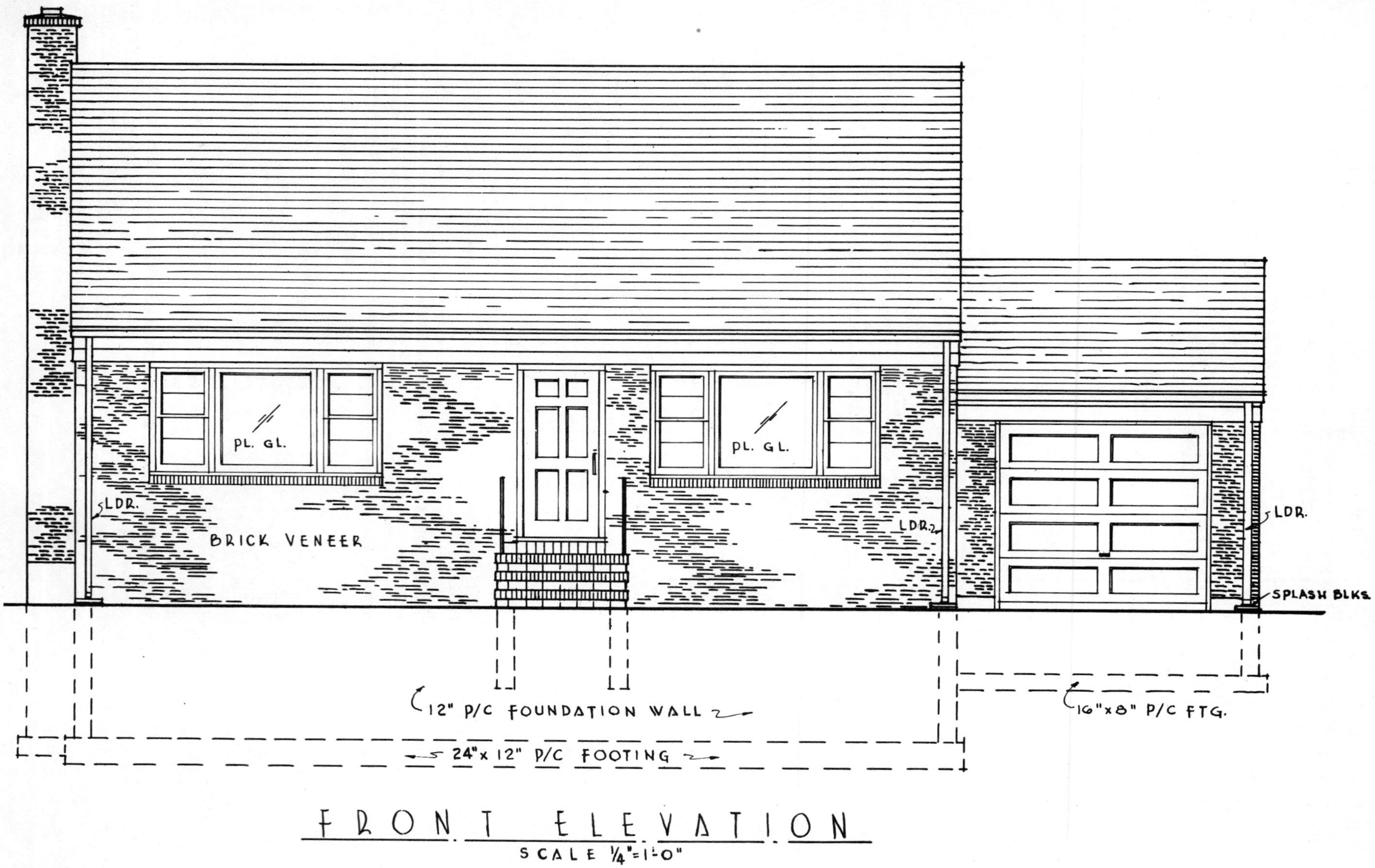

PL. GL.
PL. GL.
LDR.
BRICK VENEER
LDR.2
LDR.
SPLASH BLKS.
12" P/C FOUNDATION WALL
16"x8" P/C FTG.
24"x 12" P/C FOOTING
FRONT ELEVATION
SCALE 1/4"=1'-0"

Fig. 13-7. Frame residence.

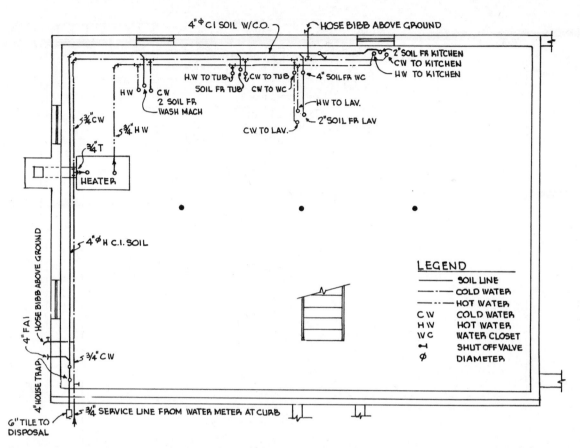

Fig. 13-8. Frame residence. Plumbing and waste piping. Foundation plan.

everything shown in Figs. 13-1 to 13-7 has been included in your drawings.

Plumbing

In addition to the soil-line diagram shown in Fig. 13-3 and the soil line shown in Fig. 13-2 the following drawings have been made to show plumbing information with a minimum of building details.

Figure 13-8 shows the plumbing and water piping in the foundation plan. The water supply for the residence is piped in from the street through a meter installed in a pit at the curb, or the meter may be placed inside the basement. A main shutoff valve should be located inside the foundation wall to permit the entire supply service to be cut off in the event of an emergency. The water from the main is cold; therefore a diverting tee is installed to provide water to be heated by the heating system for the hot-water supply line. The two supply lines, one for cold water and the other for hot water, run horizontally, suspended from the basement ceiling or the wall near the ceiling. They turn out or up to the fixture they supply, as shown in Fig. 13-8. Shutoff valves are located at various places in both the hot- and cold-water lines at basement level

and usually at each fixture to permit replacement of washers and faucets. The piping shown in Fig. 13-8 takes care of the disposal of waste water from each plumbing fixture. A cleanout plug is placed at one end of the waste line for emergency cleaning. Before the waste line leaves the basement there is a trap with a water seal for preventing the return of odors. The fresh air inlet (FAI) maintains fresh air in the waste (soil) piping and also serves as a warning system for trouble in the disposal piping. The hose bibbs are faucets above ground line on the exterior of residences for watering lawns, etc. The legend on the drawing will identify the different symbols and abbreviations used in Figs. 13-8 and 13-9.

Figure 13-9 shows the bathroom and kitchen fixtures on the first floor with the required plumbing connections. It is sufficient to indicate which fixtures require hot- and cold-water connections, drain lines, and the locations of the vent lines. The outside hose bibbs are repeated on this plan. Every set of construction plans must include a set of detailed specifications which should in turn include a special plumbing section. The specifications describe the plumbing in detail, giving sizes and material for all piping, valves, and fittings. A list of fixtures and special fittings should be included in the specifications. The method of running

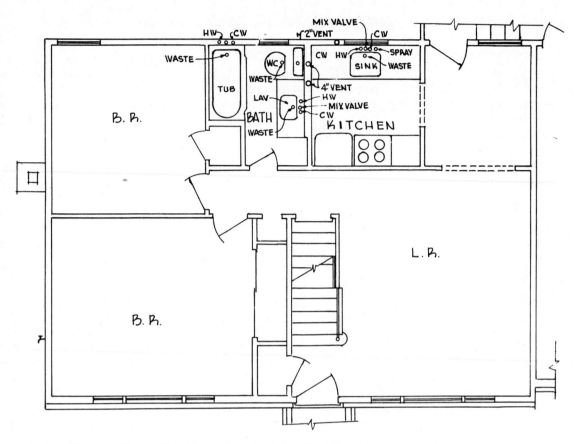

Fig. 13-9. Frame residence. Plumbing and waste piping. First-floor plan.

the lines for proper drainage, the supports, traps, clean-outs, insulation, and any trenching for outdoor lines are also described. The specifications also cover obtaining building permits and guarantees of materials and workmanship.

When a steam or hot-water heating system is installed in a building, additional supply and return lines are required, and these should be shown on the drawing. The installation of this piping is also included in the work for the plumbing contractor. Most air conditioning systems require some piping connections, which should also appear on the plans.

Exercise

Plumbing

Use your drawings of the first-floor plan, Fig. 13-1, and the foundation plan, Fig. 13-2. Place a sheet of vellum over each of these drawings and trace off the outlines of the building and the fixtures as shown in Figs. 13-8 and 13-9. Then add all the piping lines, designations, notes, and title to make complete drawings of the plumbing and waste piping.

Electrical wiring

The electrical connections indicated on the floor and foundation plans do not represent the electrical fixtures, but only the locations of the outlets and switches required. The installation of electrical wiring and electrical outlets should conform to the rules of the National Electrical Codes and the National Board of Fire Underwriters, which, as a rule, set minimum requirements. The installation must also be able to pass inspection by the local building or fire inspection bureau. For most small structures it is not necessary to make a separate electrical layout drawing, but the number and locations of the outlets, the arrangement of switches, and the locations of incoming lines, distribution panel, and fuses can be shown on the floor plans. The sizes of wire and other pertinent information may be given in the accompanying specifications or listed on the drawings. All electrical devices and materials used should have the approval of the Underwriters Laboratories, Inc. This information is sufficient for the installing licensed electrician.

The National Electrical Code specifies definite rules for computing loads, and the size of the main service is determined by the utility company. In addition, local ordinances usually require that electrical installations be made by licensed electricians. These precautions have been set up for reasons of safety and fire prevention, and if carefully observed will make fire insurance more readily obtainable and less costly.

The following specifications may be used as a guide for providing electrical circuits and outlets in a house. The specifications given here follow the code for a particular area, and, therefore, in applying this example, you must check local requirements. There are three classifications of circuits required in wiring a small house:

1. General-purpose circuits
2. Appliance circuits
3. Individual circuits

1. General-purpose circuits

These circuits are used primarily for lighting but will also service portable appliances of small demand, such as clocks, radios, television sets, and vacuum cleaners. The number of circuits required is computed as follows:

Determine the area to be lighted by multiplying the outside dimensions of the house by the number of floors. Do not include the garage, basement, storage space, or attic. However, that part of the basement which will be used as a recreation room and any part of the storage space or attic which may later be used for living space should be included in the calculation of the total area.

The code requires 3 watts per square foot of area; therefore, the total watts needed equals 3 times the total area. If 15 amps per circuit at 115 volts is allowed, by multiplying we find that 1,725 watts is needed per circuit. Divide the total watts required by 1,725 and round off the answer to the nearest whole number to find the minimum number of circuits required.

Use No. 14 wire for these 15-amp circuits, although the trend is toward using No. 12 wire. Note that the code recommends, but does not require, one circuit for every 500 sq ft of area.

These general-purpose outlets consist of (1) ceiling outlets; (2) duplex convenience outlets for lamps, clocks, radios, and television sets (antennas and grounds may be combined with these outlets); (3) wall outlets for lighting mantels, vanity tables, mirrors, etc.

Mounting requirements

One ceiling outlet is required for each room except where the length of the room equals or exceeds twice the width, when two or more outlets are required. Note that wall-cove or valance outlets may be substituted for ceiling outlets. Some living rooms have no ceiling outlets but depend on light from floor and table lamps. In a room having a single doorway, or two doorways not more than 10 ft apart, install a two-way switch at each doorway. When the doorways are farther apart and it is desired to control the outlet from either of two locations, install three-way switches. If an outlet is to be controlled from any of three locations, four-way switches will be required. Wall switches should be located about 4 ft above the floor line.

One or more convenience outlets in each room may be two- or three-way-switch-controlled at the doorway. A switch with a small pilot light allows the switch to be easily located in the dark or it may be used to alert the user that a light has been left on in the basement or a closet. Locate convenience outlets so that no point, measured at the floor line in any usable wall space (unbroken by a door) is more than 5 or 6 ft from an outlet. Duplex convenience outlets allow two appliances to be connected to the same outlet.

In the basement provide one ceiling light for each 150 sq ft of floor area, spaced as equally as is practical, but there should be at least one light in each area partitioned off.

Provide one or more lights in the laundry at work centers and one light each located at the furnace, cooling unit, home freezer, and workbench. If part of the basement is made into a recreation room, it should be treated in the same way as the living room.

In the kitchen it is unlikely that one ceiling outlet will provide adequate lighting; therefore, additional outlets should be spotted over the sink and under wall cabinets for surface lighting.

Each closet which is 6 sq ft or more in area or 30 in. or more deep requires one light with a pull chain or a door switch.

A group of two or more single-pole switches placed together under a single cover plate to protect the switches is commonly called a *gang switch*. The metal box set in the wall to enclose a switch, convenience outlet, or ceiling outlet is called a gem box.

The front entrance should have exterior lighting outlets as the doorway architecture demands. An exterior outlet should be provided at the garage entrance, for exterior decoration or other special purposes. All exterior outlets should be weatherproof.

2. Appliance circuits

The increased use of air-conditioning units, electric heaters, electric blankets, and cooking units, washing machines, clothes dryers, and other appliances has tended to overload the usual 110-volt circuit. It is therefore advisable to provide 220-volt circuits for all appliances to avoid overloading of circuits. In the case of all-electric houses this provision is especially desirable.

3. Individual circuits

An individual circuit should be provided if electric panel heating is to be installed. A workshop in the basement with motor-driven tools should also have an individual circuit. The electrical code requires use of an individual circuit for an oil-burner installation. This is advisable so that continuous service can be maintained if a fuse blows out in other circuits.

There are a number of other items which should be considered in specifying the electrical requirements. In frame houses flexible nonmetallic covered cable of the Rome type is generally used. Flexible cable is easily installed by boring holes in studs and joists. The nonmetallic covered cable has largely superseded the use of flexible metal armored BX cable. The insulated wires of BX cable have a metal spiral-wrapped covering, which allows the cable to be bent easily. The metal covering also protects the wiring if nails are driven in the walls at a later date and accidentally strike a BX cable. A nail would slide off the metal and not be liable to pierce it. In masonry buildings wires are usually run in rigid metal conduit, a thin wall pipe that can be bent readily. The radius of the bend should be not less than 6 times the diameter of the conduit. After the conduit is in place, the insulated wires are pulled through it to junction boxes or to the terminal blocks. A conduit may also be buried in a concrete floor and the wires pulled through after the concrete has been poured.

The National Electric Code requires that in systems supplying wiring circuits, one wire of the circuit shall be grounded. This means that a connection must be made between the wire and a conductor that extends into the earth or ground. A continuous metallic underground water line should be used where available.

All electrical equipment installed outdoors must be protected by weatherproof cases or covers. These will protect all insulation and exposed parts from deterioration which might be caused by rain, snow, sleet, or any condensation of moisture in the air. If electrical equipment is not properly protected, severe damage may be caused by short circuiting of the line.

During lightning storms high voltage may be electrostatically induced in the outdoor electric lines. These voltages produce surges of high voltage which travel along lines and into electrical equipment whether it is outside or inside. The high-voltage surges can puncture the insulation of equipment, cause fires, and be dangerous to life. Lightning arresters are used to limit these voltages to a safe value and to provide a path to the ground for dissipation of the electrical energy of the surge.

If wiring to lights on the lawn or to other facilities outside the house is placed underground, it must be installed with lead-coated cable at least 12 in. below the finished grade. In the case of outdoor systems there may be local ordinances forbidding overhead wires for safety reasons and for avoiding unsightly poles and exposed wires. There are several methods of installing wires in underground systems including:

1. Burying properly protected cable in the ground
2. Wiring ducts which have been installed underground
3. Locating conduit in underground tunnels

Installing underground systems is more expensive than installing overhead lines on poles or towers. However, underground systems are not subject to damage by wind and other storms, and the maintenance cost may be lower. When overhead lines are run through wooded areas, there is a recurring cost for tree trimming to provide a clear area around the lines. Lines placed underground allow the ground area to be free of obstructions and available for other uses.

Exercise

Check the electrical requirements of the frame residence, discussed above, using the information given under Electrical Wiring.

14. orientation

It is not the function or purpose of this book to delve into the question of whether a person should first decide on the house he wants to build and then look around for a suitable plot or whether the plot should be selected first and the house made to fit the lot. This question has many aspects and differs with each situation. It is a question that the prospective owner or builder should study and decide before the project reaches the drafting stage.

It is the function of the draftsman to make a drawing of the plot using the map of the property which the surveyor has prepared from measurements taken in the field. The surveyor's map should show the property lines and measurements, including the direction of the lines or angles with respect to the points of the compass. If there are any depressions or elevations, they should be noted by means of contour lines with the elevations related to the elevation of an established base point. Contour lines are lines connecting points which have the same elevation or level. All large trees, shrubbery, or protruding rocks too large to be removed should also be noted on the surveyor's map.

You will note that surveyor's measurements are taken in feet and decimals of a foot, and the plot plan should be laid out with a civil engineer's scale using the same decimal system.

Whether to build in a certain location is of course the owner's choice, but the architect can advise on the suitability of a particular kind of house for the size, character, and location of the plot. The architect should check on the zoning restrictions for the neighborhood and examine the deed for any use or building restrictions. The architect should also advise on the way the house should be located on the plot in order to make use of all its best natural features.

In northern climates windows facing south receive more desirable winter sunlight and less undesirable hot summer sunlight. Hence it might be considered better to put the living room on the south side or the bedrooms on the south side of the house. But there are other factors to be considered in addition to the question of which rooms should face the sun. The direction of the prevailing summer breezes and winter winds should be considered; also, whether greater protection is needed from extreme heat or extreme cold. The proximity of the neighboring houses might also influence the location of the house on the plot.

If there are trees on the plot, they are valuable assets and it would be wise to retain some of them. The possible location of a flower garden or other type of garden should be given consideration. The type and nature of the outdoor recreation for the family and the location of a play area, such as a tennis court or swimming pool, should not be left to be added as an afterthought. The shape and contour of the plot may have considerable influence on the location of the front- and rear-yard areas, the service entrance, and the location of the garage and driveway.

Assume that the owner has purchased the plot which he desired and has settled generally on the size and type of house which would be suitable for the plot. The next step is to prepare a map or plan of the plot to scale, with the contour lines and the location of any trees or other distinguishing features. There might even be a small brook on the property. Next prepare a cardboard template of the proposed floor plan of the house, drawn to the same scale used for the plot plan. Place the template on the plot plan with the intention of moving it around to various locations and of considering in each location the items noted in the previous paragraph.

In a cold climate, try to place the living quarters so that they face south, receiving the winter sun, and are protected from the prevailing winter winds. Therefore, existing trees on the north side of the house could well be retained to act as a screen against the winds. In a warm climate, this procedure would be reversed to have the living room receive the benefit of summer breezes, retaining the trees to provide shade.

Formerly the tendency was to build a more compact and easier-to-heat house in cold climates, and the rambling-type house was usually found in warm climates. However, with modern insulating materials and methods the rambling- or ranch-type house is found in all sections. The same house on opposite sides of the street should usually be turned 180° in order to be placed equally well with respect to the sun.

It is not a fixed rule that the front of the house or the front entrance should face the street. In many cases the entrance is from the side, or the rear of the house may face the street if this arrangement affords a better orientation on the plot.

The contours of the plot sometimes influence the type of house or its location on the plot. The moving of earth from one location to another is expensive, but a certain amount of excavation is usually necessary and the excavated soil may be used to fill in low spots. Always remember to note that the contractor must save the top soil before excavating. Natural grades should be taken into account and related to the final or finished grade. Short driveways save money and use up less valuable ground than picturesque long driveways. However, short steep driveways are hard to maneuver on, especially during severe winters, and may provide a natural place for snowdrifts to accumulate.

Many local building codes establish a definite distance that the house must set back from the curb line, but the tendency has been to allot less room for spacious front lawns and allow for larger play and work areas in back of the house. The requirements and the ideas of a family change as the years go by. Accordingly, it is good practice to keep the work and play areas of the plot as large as possible so that rearrangements can be made by the owner as the need arises.

Exercise

Plot Plan

Figure 14-1. Place a clean sheet of vellum size 11 by 17 in. on your drafting board, fasten with drafting tape,

and draw the border lines as for previous sheets of the same size. Transcribe all of the information shown in Fig. 14-1. First lay out the plot lines using a 4H pencil, making the lines black but very thin. The plot is made up of four regular lots each 20 ft wide by 100 ft deep. Note, however, that the boundary lines on the street are wider black lines. The plot dimensions are given in feet and hundredths of a foot, and you must use a civil engineer's scale to mark off the dimensions. The plot is 172.50' east of the Fulton Street corner, as indicated by the break in the wide black line.

Next draw the outline of the house to the dimensions shown, the dimensions being those of the frame residence described in Chap. 13. Note that the left front corner of the house is located 25.00' back of the southerly lot line and 8.12' inside of the westerly lot line. The right front corner of the house is located 25.03' back of the southerly lot line which will place the house at a slight angle to the street line. This alignment will place the left rear corner of the house 8.09' inside the westerly lot line. Mark the lot numbers for the plot and the adjacent lot numbers at the rear. Spring Lane is 40 ft wide, and the elevation of the center of the street is given at each side of the plot. Add all the elevations and angles as indicated, and note that a permanent stake or marker shall be placed at the northwest corner of the plot. Draw the north-south arrow, and complete by including all dimensions, notes, street names, title information, and scale, all as shown in Fig. 14-1.

The Perspective

Figure 14-2. The perspective is the architect's conception, or mind's-eye view, of the building. It may serve several useful purposes. The architect may use a perspective drawing to show his client a picture of the proposed residence. It is especially useful when a client is unable to visualize the completed building from the flat or orthographic drawings. Sometimes perspectives are colored or tinted and framed for a client. You will see many perspectives or renderings in newspapers and magazines to advertise new houses. The perspective has other commercial values, especially for industrial plants and commercial buildings. It may be enlarged and painted on a sign placed on the property to announce the erection of a building and to give credits to the architect and builders.

When you apply for your first position as a beginning draftsman, the knowledge and ability to turn out a pleasing perspective will not usually be one of the requirements specified. Nevertheless, as with many other things in life, the more background and knowledge you have, the more easily you will progress. It

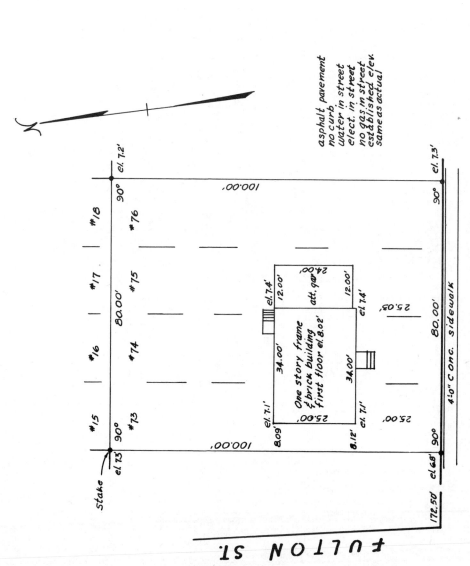

Fig. 14-1. Plot plan. (Scale: 1" = 20'-0".)

Fig. 14-2. Perspective.

takes time and practice to accomplish a pleasing, realistic perspective, and the ability to add shading or coloring, shrubs, trees, people, and vehicles to the drawing will do much to enhance the finished work.

Exercise

At this time review Chap. 6, referring to Fig. 6-3, which illustrates the two-point method of drawing a perspective of a house. Using this same method and the information in Figs. 13-1 to 13-7 for the Cape Cod cottage, draw the perspective as shown in Fig. 14-2. This perspective drawing was made using the floor plan drawn to a scale of ¼″ = 1′–0″ at an angle of 30° to the picture plane and with the southwest corner of the house on the picture plane line. The horizon line was drawn 5′–6″ above the ground line. This information is given only as a guide, and you may vary the angle at which you set the house on the picture plane depending on the view you wish to obtain. The distance of the station point from the picture plane in the plan view is usually determined by the size of the drawing board you have available. The farther away from the picture plane you locate the station point, the smaller the resulting picture will be. You may place the station point to the right or left of the southwest corner of the building and in so doing change the depth of the side or front of the house. The heights of the different parts of the building may be taken from the elevations after the lines have been correctly carried down through the picture plane as described in Chap. 6.

It may be necessary to make several preliminary perspectives in order to select the one which will present the most pleasing appearance. Complete the drawing as shown in Fig. 14-2 by adding the same border lines and title space used on previous drawings for a sheet 11 by 17 in.

15. masonry building

Figures 15-1 to 15-4 show the plans for a commercial building of masonry construction. Assume that an architect has a client who wishes to construct a building on property which he owns. A number of meetings will take place during which sketches and notes will be prepared, in a manner similar to the procedure outlined in Chap. 13 for the frame residence. The building materials will differ from those used for the residence because this building will be used for a different purpose. All materials must be checked for size in reference books and manufacturers' catalogs. The types and dimensions of the windows and doors should be studied before you attempt to lay them out on the drawings. In commercial buildings concrete blocks or sometimes cinder blocks are often used for the exterior walls above grade. The sizes for steel girders, lally columns, steel lintels over doors and windows, roof beams and their spacing should be calculated by the architect or his designer. This information should be noted on the sketches prepared for your use as the draftsman. All steel must have a minimum bearing of at least 4 in. Your problem will be to transcribe the plan, section, elevations, etc., shown in Figs. 15-1 to 15-4 to the scale of $\frac{1}{4}'' = 1'-0''$ in accordance with the following instructions.

Prepare four sheets of vellum, size 17 x 22 in. with a ½-in.-wide border at the top, bottom, and right side and a 1-in.-wide border at the left side. Instructions for the grade of pencil to be used for various lines will not be repeated as this should be fairly well established by this time from the practice gained on the previous drawings. However, some instructions will be repeated several times because a draftsman should acquire cer-

tain definite work habits which will help him proceed in a methodical manner, covering all necessary points, checking as the drawings progress, and thus avoiding errors and omissions.

Floor plan

Figure 15-1. Fasten a sheet of the prepared vellum to your drawing board with drafting tape. Draw a light line between the right and left border lines 1 in. below the top border line. Mark the center of the light line and from that point locate the rear left-hand corner of the building. From this point lay out and draw the outside perimeter of the floor plan lightly, disregarding the door openings. Note that two 16- by 12-in. brick pilasters are used on each long wall and a pilaster of the same size in the middle of each end wall. The brick pilasters are bonded into the exterior walls to strengthen them. Between the pilasters show the wall built of 8- by 8- by 16-in. cinder blocks. The front wall is built of 4- by 8- by 16-in. cinder blocks with a 4-in. brick-veneer facing. The brick veneer bonded to the cinder block will give the building a finished appearance. Duro-wall, a chicken-wire-type reinforcement, should be specified in the cinder-block courses to help retard wall cracking.

Locate and draw the partitions in the lower left-hand corner of the building for the office, lavatory, and locker room. These partitions will be made up of 2- by 4-in. studs with $\frac{3}{8}$-in.-thick sheet rock on the interior and exterior faces. If the purpose and use of the building require interior partitions to be of fire-

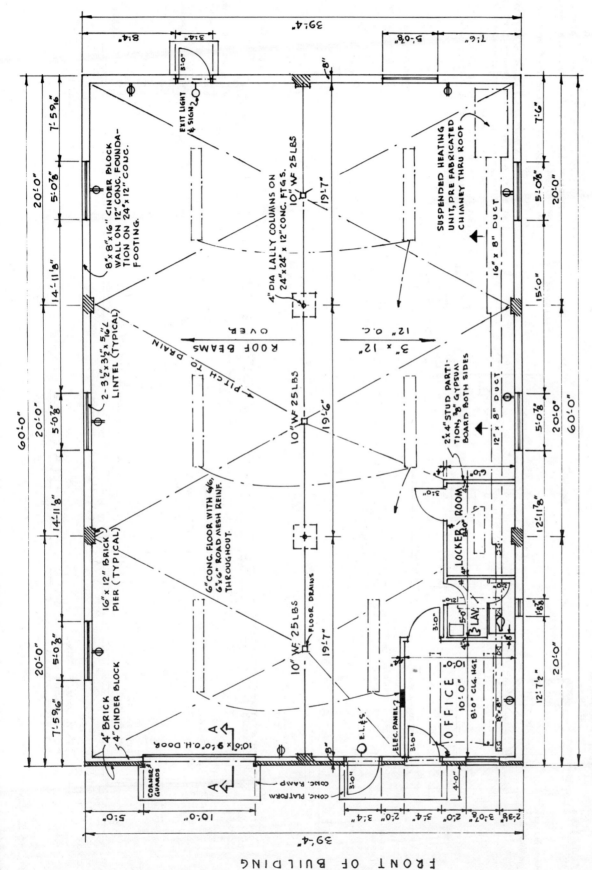

Fig. 15-1. Masonry building. Floor plan. (Scale: $\frac{3}{16}'' = 1'-0''$.)

131

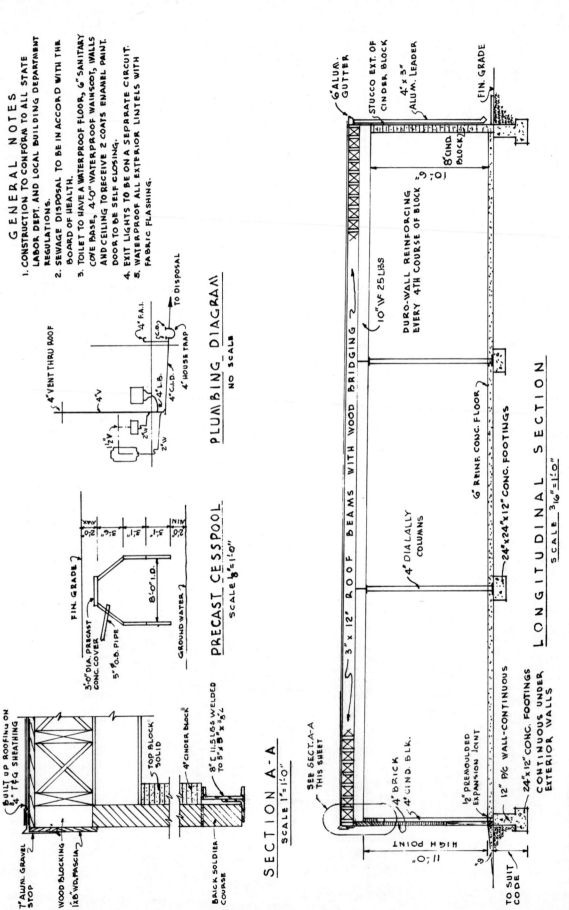

Fig. 15-2. Masonry building.

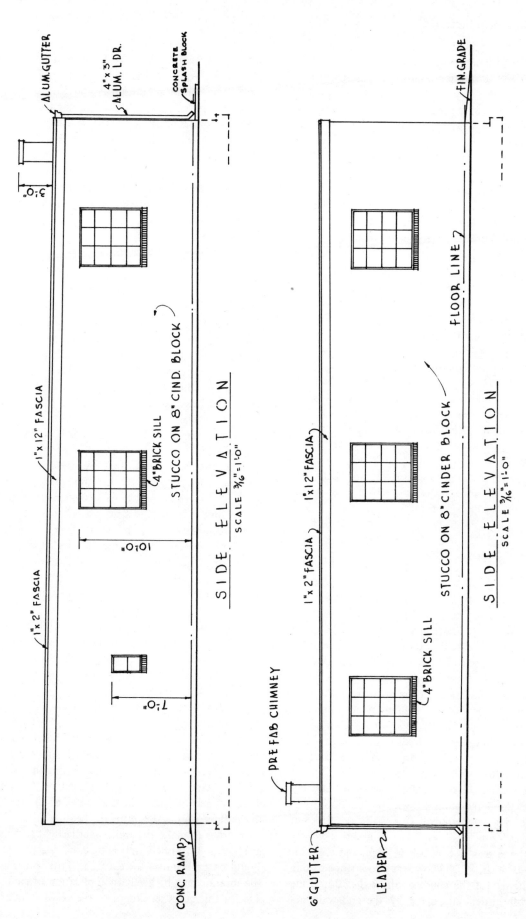

Fig. 15-3. Masonry building.

133

retarding construction, they can be built of 4-in.-thick cinder block. The interior lavatory partition will be a metal enclosure. Through the center of the building show the 10-in. wide-flange 25-lb roof girders supported on the end pilasters, and the 4-in.-diameter lally columns set on 24- by 24- by 12-in. concrete footings. Note the 3- by 12-in. roof beams on 12-in. centers.

Locate and draw all windows and doors in the outside walls using the center-line dimensions shown. Draw the doors in the interior partitions and the lavatory fixtures. Show the direction of opening for each door. Indicate the large overhead door and the channel lintel over the door opening. Section *B-B* in Fig. 15-2 shows a detail of the lintel. Darken all wall and equipment outlines and add the lighting sockets, wall convenience outlets, and the designation for the electric panel located in the office partition.

The heating system necessary to take care of the requirements of the building and its occupancy should be selected by the architect. A suspended heating unit has been indicated in the lower right-hand corner of the building with a hot-air duct extending the length of the building. Side outlets have been indicated for the main building and the office, while bottom vents have been shown for the lavatory and locker room.

Complete the drawing by adding all dimensions, sectioning for brick, notes, titles, and scale shown in Fig. 15-1. Remove the drawing from the board.

Section, plumbing, and notes

Figure 15-2. Fasten a second sheet of the prepared vellum to your drawing board, lining up the lower border line with your T square. Draw a light line about 2 in. above the border line, and start the outer wall footing on this line. Locate the center of the line and mark off $60'-0''$, the face-to-face distance of the outer walls, and extend these lines down to the 24-in.-wide by 12-in.-deep concrete footing. The depth of these footings will vary in the local code requirements, but $4'-6''$ is the usual depth for the Middle Atlantic states.

Draw the 12-in.-thick poured-concrete walls up to the finished grade level and the 6-in.-thick concrete floor from wall to wall. Locate the 24-in. by 24-in. by 12-in.-thick concrete footings for the 4-in. lally columns, to the dimensions shown on the floor plan. Draw the 8-in. cinder-block rear wall and the 4-in. cinder-block front wall with the 4-in. brick veneer. Note that the rear wall is $10'-6''$ high, and the front wall $11'-0''$ high which allows for a roof slope of 6 in. toward the rear of the building. Show the 10-in. wide-flange 25-lb girders supported by the end walls and

lally columns, and the 3- by 12-in. roof beams 12 in. on centers. Indicate the ¾-in. roof sheathing by a double line, and draw the gutter and downspout at the rear of the building. Add the sectioning for brick, concrete, and cinder block.

Draw the plumbing diagram and the cesspool as shown in Fig. 15-2. Add all dimensions, section *A-A*, lettering, and notes shown in Fig. 15-2, including the general notes listed in the upper right-hand corner, the titles, and scales. Remove the drawing from the drawing board.

Elevations

Figure 15-3. Fasten another of the prepared sheets of vellum to your drawing board, taking care to line up the lower border line with your T square. Start by drawing the finished grade line of the lower side elevation 2 in. above the border line, and the grade line for the top side elevation 6½ in. above the border line. Locate the center of the line and mark off the length and height of the building from the dimensions on the floor plan and section, and complete the outline of each elevation. Show the fascia boards, gutter and leader.

Draw the floor line 6 in. above the finished grade, and locate the windows to the dimensions shown on the floor plan and at the heights noted in Fig. 15-3. Each window is to have a brick sill formed by a rowlock course, that is, the bricks are laid on the narrow side. The window frames and sash are usually of the projected or pivoted type made of steel or aluminum for this kind of building. The window designations noted on the floor plan are standard and denote the type of window to be furnished. A casement window has been specified for the office. The building specifications should contain a window-and-door schedule listing the exact type, including finish and hardware. A security-type window can be used, which will prevent entrance at these points.

The exact location of the chimney will depend on the heating unit installed. The builder will leave an opening in the roof for the chimney, which should be installed before the roofing contractor finishes his work in order that the necessary flashing may be provided to make the opening weathertight. Locate the chimney approximately in the center of the rectangle on the floor plan representing the heating unit.

In order to make the walls weathertight and also to give them a finished appearance, a coat of stucco should be applied over the exterior of the cinder block. The interior may be given an application of paint suitable for this purpose. Complete the drawing by adding

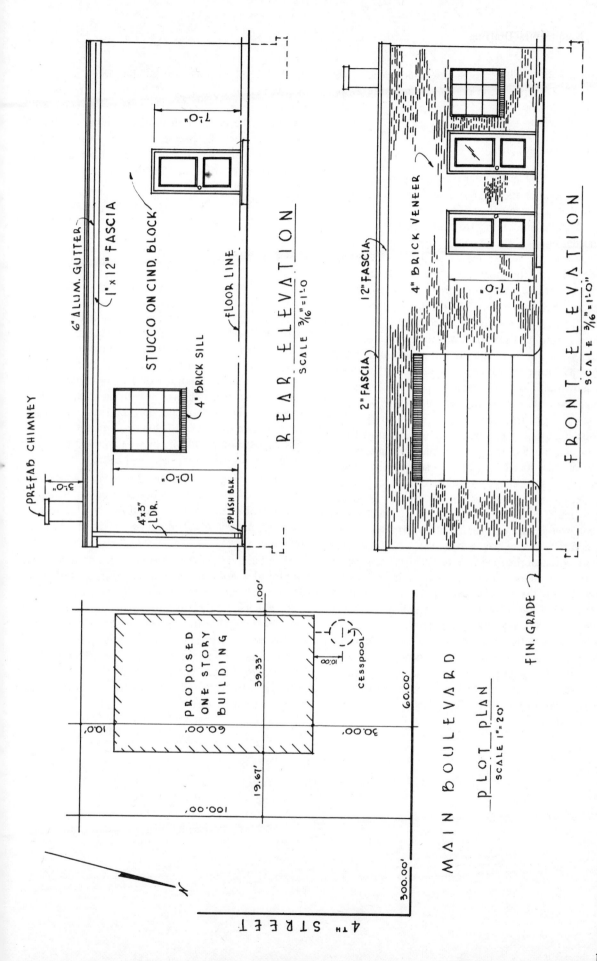

Fig. 15-4. Masonry building.

all dimensions, lettering, notes, titles, and scales shown in Fig. 15-3. Remove the drawing from the drawing board.

Elevations and plot plan

Figure 15-4. Fasten the fourth of the prepared sheets of vellum to your drawing board, and line up the lower border line with your T square. Start by drawing the finished grade line of the front elevation 2 in. above the border line, and the grade line for the rear elevation 6½ in. above the border line. Draw these two views on the right half of the sheet. Draw the side of the building 1 in. from the right border line. Then mark off the width and height of the building from the dimensions on the floor plan and section, and complete the outline of each elevation. Draw the fascia boards, gutter, and leader. Draw the floor line 6 in. above the finished grade, and locate the windows and doors to the dimension shown on the floor plan and at the heights noted in Fig. 15-4. Show the brick sills under the windows the same as on the side elevations. The exterior and interior door bucks or frames should be steel for a commercial building rather than the wood jambs and entrances used for residences. The large OH door will be made of steel and constructed to fold or roll up easily to a horizontal position overhead. All other doors should be kalamein type, that is, sheet metal covered over a wood core, or a hollow-metal type, both designed to be fire retarding. Note that a soldier course of brick laid with the long edge vertical has been shown over the large door. Draw the chimney in each elevation and show the brick veneer for the front elevation as indicated in Fig. 15-4. On the left half of the sheet draw the plot plan as shown in Fig. 15-4.

You will note that small dots have been used at the ends of dimension lines in place of arrowheads. This is not a standard practice, but it is used here because many offices use this method in place of arrowheads, especially on plot plans. This type of plot plan is drawn to show the location of the building and is not as informative as a surveyor's map. It is used only by the building contractor. The architect uses the surveyor's map to study the orientation of the building on the plot before starting the preparation of the finished drawings. Complete the drawing by adding all dimensions, lettering, notes, titles, and scales shown in Fig. 15-4. Remove the drawing from the drawing board.

Now that you have completed the four drawings for the masonry building, check over each drawing thoroughly to see that the picture has been drawn in correctly and is complete. Also check all dimensions, notes, and other lettering.

It is assumed that the architect has consulted with the owner and a lighting specialist regarding the locations and types of lighting fixtures required. This information should be covered in the building specifications for the guidance of the electrical contractor. The electrical panel located in the office should control all the lighting circuits, and the exit lights should be on a separate circuit which may be left on at all times. The wiring to the wall outlets may be run through rigid conduits laid in the floor before the concrete is poured. The exposed overhead wire may be armored cable (BX) or insulated wire run through rigid conduit.

The building specification should also contain full information for the plumbing contractor, listing the type of toilet fixtures to be installed, together with the size and material of all supply, wastes, and vent piping required.

The building in the problem covered by this chapter employed a roof construction consisting of steel girders and wood beams, but there are other types of construction which could have been used. New materials or combinations of materials are on the market, such as laminated wood beams, light-steel-bar joists, built-up plywood beams and girders, all designed to support any required roof load. These materials should be investigated, and the ease and speed of erection may warrant their use in many cases.

16. specifications

Now that you have completed plans for two different types of structures, you will readily understand that there is a considerable amount of additional information needed to obtain bids, award a contract, and finally accomplish the building of the project. Certain parts of the structure require a written description or reference to a manufacturer's catalog number. Other parts require written instructions covering the manner in which the work is to be performed. All these instructions and descriptions can be put down in writing and will form the specifications covering the project. Some items, such as electric or plumbing fixtures, can be listed in the specifications. This supplementary information in the form of a specification should accompany the drawings and be considered as part of them. The specifications may be typewritten or in some cases printed so that the necessary copies for all concerned may be obtained readily.

The work to be performed must be described under separate headings for the various trades, and general conditions which apply to all trades must be stated. The more detailed information you can incorporate into the drawings and the specifications, the less chance there will be for errors and misunderstandings. In other words, the contractor or builder should be able to obtain a clear understanding of what his work includes. Any items added or changes made in the drawings or specifications after the contract has been awarded are liable to prove costly.

The specification writer must know the materials available and how to use them properly in the building under consideration in order that the project may be completed as intended by the designer and as shown on the drawings. When writing the specifications, keep in mind the following points:

The specifications should help to avoid dispute between the contractors and the architect or his representatives.

The specifications enable the inspectors or architect's representatives to check the materials and workmanship as the construction proceeds.

The specifications are also used by the estimator to "take off" materials and quantities to figure costs.

The specifications help to avoid conflicting opinions regarding the way the work shall be done and the extent of the work.

As stated before, the specifications supplement and accompany the drawings and are sent out to contractors with a letter requesting bids. The covering letter should include all the terms and conditions under which the bids must be submitted. After the desired bidder is selected, a contract should be drawn up stating the price, manner of payments, insurance, and all other pertinent items. The contract is a legal document, and contract items should not be included in the specifications. If the standard contract of the American Institute of Architects is used, it can be referred to as such in the specifications.

Following is a sample specification for a residence. Note the general outline and various subdivisions which the specification covers.

**SPECIFICATION
FOR A ONE-STORY RESIDENCE
TO BE BUILT FOR
MR. AND MRS. J. B. NOE
322 MAIN ST., PLACE, N.Y.
AT 3 ELM ST., ELDER, N.Y.**

Specifications

General conditions

The general conditions of the contract of the American Institute of Architects, latest edition, shall be deemed a part of these specifications together with the general conditions of the contract for this project and shall apply to each subdivision of the specifications.

Reference to the contractor in the specifications shall mean the general contractor who shall be responsible for the performance of the work of all of the subcontractors employed by him. All interests of the owner shall be referred to the architect or the architect's representative who shall act in the owner's behalf.

All building insurance and compensation insurance shall be provided as specified in the contract. It shall be the duty of the contractor to see that any part of the work subcontracted is covered by the insurance required in the contract, and he shall be responsible for the same.

All materials shall be first class as herein specified, and all labor shall be performed in a thorough, workmanlike manner by skilled workmen in accordance with FHA standards. (Note: Reference to Federal Housing Authority standards may be omitted if the house is not required to have FHA approval.)

All work and material shall be in accordance with local building laws and regulations notwithstanding anything hereinafter specified to the contrary.

Anything which is not shown on the drawings but is mentioned in the specifications, or vice versa, shall be furnished and performed as though specifically mentioned in both. The drawings referred to shall be those drawings which were sent to the contractor for the purpose of bidding upon the work to be done. Any work which develops defects, except from ordinary wear and tear, within one year from date of certification of approval, shall be replaced without additional charge.

In the event of any differences between the data shown on the drawings and those noted in the specifications, all such questions shall be referred to the architect or his representative for the correct interpretation.

Scope

The contractor shall furnish all materials, labor, transportation, scaffolding, and equipment of every description required for the full performance of the work covered by the specifications.

The contractor shall lay out the work, as indicated on the plot plan, from the surveyor's stakes and be responsible for the correctness of the layout. All necessary permits to carry out his work shall be obtained by the contractor, and all fees for the permits shall be paid for by the contractor unless stated otherwise in the contract. The contractor shall afford the architect or his representative every facility for inspection while the work is in progress. The contractor shall be responsible for any and all violations of the law and any damage to adjoining property, sidewalks, curbs, etc., caused by him or his employees. The contractor shall protect his work from the weather during its progress by the use of rough enclosing doors, tarpaulins, or other adequate means.

The contractor shall clear the building site of all buildings and other obstructions, including trees, as agreed upon with the owner. All trees which it is agreed shall be left standing shall be protected from damage by the contractor or his workmen at all stages of the work.

The contractor shall clean out any of his rubbish or other debris when requested to do so by the architect or his representative and shall leave his work in perfect condition and broom clean at completion.

At the completion of the work the contractor shall rough-grade the ground to the established grade line with soil furnished by the owner. Before rough-grading, the contractor shall remove all lumber, brickbats, wire, pieces of plywood, and other building debris and rubbish from the plot and cart it away.

The general conditions of the specifications shall form an integral part of each and every subdivision hereinafter described whether the work shall be performed by the general contractor or by a subcontractor.

Excavation

The contractor shall excavate the ground to the depth required by the foundations and footings as shown on the drawings. All top soil shall be removed first and stored at a suitable location on the site so that it will be available for use when the plot is graded by the contractor at the completion of the work.

Foundations and footings

All footings for the walls, lally columns, and chimney shall be of poured concrete to dimensions shown in the drawings. Concrete mix shall be one part portland cement, two parts sand, and four parts clean gravel.

All foundation walls shall be 12-in. poured concrete. Concrete mix shall be one part portland cement, two parts sand, and four parts clean gravel.

Carpentry work

All general framing lumber shall be Douglas fir or yellow pine. Main sills shall be western red cedar or California redwood. The sizes of all lumber shall be taken from the drawings and checked with the sizes noted in the specifications.

The floor beams shall be 2 by 10 in., 16 in. on centers, of clear long-leaf yellow pine. The girders shall be 6 by 10 in., built up of three pieces of 2- by 10-in. lumber supported on lally columns as shown and noted on the drawings. The sill shall be of the box type, 4 by 6 in. The rafters shall be 2 by 6 in. and 16 in. on centers.

All enclosure studs shall be 2 by 4 in. and 16 in. on centers. The studs shall be spiked to plates and sills and set double at the sides of all door and window openings. All plates shall be 4 by 4 in.

All headers and trimmers shall be doubled and properly framed and spiked together, leaving all openings of sufficient size for the stairs, chimney, etc.

All partitions shall be made up of 2- by 4-in. studs, 16 in. on centers. All door studs shall be set double and properly blocked to receive the trim. All openings over 4 ft wide shall be provided with wood headers as noted on the plans.

All exterior woodwork shall be first-quality white pine, free from oil shakes and large, black, or unsound knots. All joints shall be square.

All exterior walls and roofs shall be covered with sound shiplap or tongue-and-groove North Carolina pine sheathing, not to exceed 8 in. wide and nailed to each and every bearing.

The carpenter shall do all necessary cutting of beams, joists, studs, etc., that may be required by other trades. He shall also install all necessary grounds required by the plasterer or other trades.

The roof shall be framed and constructed in accordance with the drawings and in the most thorough, workmanlike manner. All cornices, eaves, and overhangings shall be made of $7/8$-in.-thick white-pine boards.

One layer of 24-lb Johns-Manville, or equal, felt waterproof building paper shall be laid under all cornices, door and window casings, shingles, etc. The paper shall have an overlapping of at least 2 in. and shall be well tacked down.

The sides, roofs, dormers, and all other areas noted on the drawings shall be covered with Johns-Manville,

or equal, asphalt shingles applied in accordance with the manufacturer's directions. The color shall be as selected and approved by the architect or owner.

All door frames shall be made of clean white pine except the interior parts which shall match the interior trim of the house. The jambs shall be solid blocked to receive the hinges. Door frames shall be made as shown on the drawings and in stock designs with molded casings. Exterior door frames shall be caulked with oakum and mastic and made weathertight and watertight.

The contractor shall furnish and install all aluminum casement windows and frames as shown and specified on the drawings. The picture windows shall be installed complete with glazing.

The rough flooring for all rooms on the first floor shall be 1- by 6-in. tongue-and-groove lumber. All rooms on the first floor except the kitchen shall have 1-in. oak-finish flooring laid over a layer of 15-lb felt paper, Johns-Manville, or equal.

The rough flooring in the kitchen shall be covered with vinyl tile cemented in place over a layer of 15-lb felt paper in accordance with the manufacturer's recommendations. Pattern and color shall be as selected by the architect or owner.

All interior walls, except the tile work in the bathroom, shall be finished with ½-in.-thick gypsum wallboard as indicated on the drawings. The wallboard shall be fastened to the studs in accordance with the manufacturer's specifications. All joints shall be neatly taped and sanded for painting or papering by others.

All exterior doors shall be of the size and design shown on the drawings and shall be made of No. 1 white pine or ponderosa pine 1¾ in. thick. Panels shall be solid if required.

All interior doors shall be flush panel, birch veneer, $1\frac{3}{8}$ in. thick, paint grade.

Molded oak saddles shall be provided for all exterior doors.

All interior trim shall be No. 1 kiln-dried white pine of stock design. Molding type ¾ by 3½ in. shall be as approved by the architect. All rooms shall receive a $5/8$- by 3-in. base. All door trim shall be carried down to the floor without blocks and receive molded stops for the doors.

All closets shall have plain ¾- by 2½-in. casings and $5/8$- by 3-in. base. Install one shelf in each clothes closet with hat-and-coat strips with hooks for same and a clothes pole under the shelf. The linen closet shall have five shelves.

Furnish and install all kitchen cabinets as shown and indicated on the drawings.

All exposed soil and waste pipes in the rooms shall

have the partitions furred out to enclose the pipes. Under no conditions shall pipes stand out in any room.

All locks, butts, knobs, escutcheons for doors, sash fasteners, drawer pulls and catches, window hardware, etc., shall be selected by the architect and fitted and installed by the contractor. The contractor shall furnish all necessary nails, building paper, and rough hardware to complete the project.

Insulation[1]

All exterior walls and the ceilings exposed to unheated areas shall be insulated with 4-in.-thick rock-wool bats installed between the studs and joists in an approved manner, including the floors over unheated spaces such as a garage, crawl space, or basement. A vapor barrier shall be installed under all living-area concrete slabs, and all insulated surfaces shall include a vapor barrier protection on the inner side of the insulation. Paper sill sealers shall be provided between the foundation walls and the floor slabs.

When the structure is equipped for electric heating, the uppermost ceiling insulation shall be increased from 4-in. to 6-in. thickness.

Masonry

All brickwork for the steps and chimney shall be selected common red brick. The front entrance, fireplace, and chimney above the roof shall be veneered with Westchester stone. All joints shall be of cement mortar composed of one part cement, one part hydrated lime, and six parts clean sharp sand. All joints shall be well buttered and made tight against the weather and shall be tooled. Upon completion, the brickwork and stonework shall be cleaned with mild acid and left in perfect condition.

The walls of the bathroom shall be prepared to a height of $4'-0''$ for tile by covering with wire lath and one rough coat of portland cement plaster. The walls around the bath tub shall be tiled to a height of $6'-0''$.

The floor of the bathroom shall be prepared for the tile by chamfering the tops of the joists and then laying a concrete slab (1:2:4 mix) on sheathing between the joists. The sheathing shall be well supported and covered with waterproof paper. The tile shall be laid level with the adjoining finished wood floors.

The color of the wall tile shall be selected by the architect. A complete list of the built-in wall fixtures and medicine cabinet shall be submitted to the architect for approval and installed by the contractor.

[1]Year-round Comfort System specifications and insulation recommendations by Long Island Lighting Company.

Plumbing

This specification shall include all the necessary labor and material required to complete the plumbing for the entire building. All work shall be done in a thorough, workmanlike manner as shown and indicated on the drawings. All materials required shall be of first-class quality.

The plumbing contractor shall give the proper authorities due notice relating to the work in his charge, and obtain the necessary permits for temporary obstructions and pay all fees for the permits. He shall carry out his work as rapidly as possible at all times in order not to hold up the work of other trades.

The plumbing contractor shall do all necessary digging of trenches for the laying of the sewer pipes and the water main and shall backfill the earth after the work has been completed, including the necessary inspection.

The plumbing contractor, when installing all piping, must take care not to undermine and weaken walls, piers, or supports of any kind. The cutting of all beams or any framing shall be done by the carpenters where required.

The plumbing contractor shall provide and install all necessary hangers and supports for the piping best suited to meet the job conditions.

The soil piping shall be 4-in. extra-heavy cast iron and shall be installed as indicated on the drawings with the vent piping extending up through the roof. The vent piping shall be provided with necessary aluminum flashing at the roof to make a watertight seal. The aluminum flashing shall carry at least 8 in. under the roof shingles. The 4-in. extra-heavy drain pipe shall start 4 ft outside the foundation wall and run through the wall to the soil pipe. A 4-in. cleanout trap shall be provided in the cellar floor with a screwed brass cleanout cap, and the 4-in. cast-iron fresh-air vent pipe shall be connected to the drain on the house side of the cleanout trap. The fresh-air vent pipe shall extend outside of the cellar wall and be capped with a metal strainer one foot above the grade line. All pipe branches shall be Y branches. All cast-iron pipe joints shall be bell-and-spigot type and shall be caulked with oakum and molten lead. All soil and drain piping shall be well supported.

The plumbing contractor shall connect all outside leaders on the building to the tile drain piping and shall install the tile drain piping as indicated on the drawings.

The plumbing contractor shall furnish and install the water-supply piping from the street main to the house including the inverted curb cock, curb box, and rods, and all hot- and cold-water piping inside the house, all as shown and noted on the drawings. All hot- and cold-water-supply piping inside the house shall be ¾-in. copper, K type with ½-in. branches to all fixtures. All exposed pipe shall be supported by pipe hangers. A hose bibb connection for cold water shall be provided outside the house. A gate valve shall be installed inside the house in the main water-supply line and a shutoff valve in all water pipes leading to each separate group of fixtures. All lines shall be graded for draining at a low point. Any branches of the hot- and cold-water piping which must be located in exterior walls shall be insulated against freezing. Exposed cold-water piping in the basement shall be properly wrapped with felt insulating material to prevent dripping from condensation of moisture on the outside of the piping. No exposed piping shall run in the finished part of the house.

The plumbing contractor shall provide and install the necessary gas service from the gas company's meter and shall properly connect same to the gas range, gas-fired boiler, and domestic hot-water heater.

The plumbing contractor shall furnish and install a 5-gallon-per-minute tankless heater to be operated by the hot-water heating boiler with winter and summer controls.

The plumbing contractor shall furnish and install the following plumbing fixtures complete with necessary valves and fittings. All fixtures shall be Crane Company, or equal, and shall be installed in the locations shown on the drawings. All exposed pipes, fittings and valves, faucets, etc., shall be chromium plated.

Kitchen sink. 42- by 21-in. flat-rim sink with center outlet, chromium-plated cup-and-deck-type combination faucet. The sink shall be set in a formica top as indicated on the drawings.

Laundry tray. One cast-iron white-enameled laundry tray with hot- and cold-water connection with chromium-plated faucets.

Bathroom. One wash-down closet bowl and tank with shutoff valve and pearlite seat. One 20- by 18-in. lavatory basin. One bathtub complete with shower head. The lavatory fixtures and shower head shall be chromium plated.

The plumbing contractor shall submit a complete list of the above fixtures and fittings for the kitchen and bathroom to the architect for approval before installation.

Electrical equipment

This specification shall cover furnishing and installing the complete electrical equipment by the electrical contrator, as shown and indicated on the drawings for the following electrical work.

Electric lighting. Provide and install all necessary outlets complete with wiring for all lighting and convenience outlets. The wiring system shall be General Electric, or equal, low-voltage remote-control relay-operated wiring system. Only 120-volt wiring shall be BX cable. Two- or three-conductor 24-volt wire with thermoplastic insulation shall be used for all remote-control wiring.

Wall switches of the silent toggle type shall be mounted 4'–0" above the floor. Convenience outlets shall be of the duplex or other multiple type. Final location of the wired outlets shall be as approved by the architect.

Bell system. Provide and install the following electric chimes together with necessary wiring and transformer and connect to the 120-volt electric system.

For front door. Push button to ring 5-in. chimes in the hall.

For kitchen door. Push button to ring 3-in. chimes in the kitchen.

All wiring for the bell system shall be damp-proof type, run through and between the beams and studs. All joints and splices shall be covered with rubber tape.

Utility system. Provide and install necessary 220-volt wiring together with outlets for the furnace, washer, and dryer in the utility room; wall ovens and exhaust fan in the kitchen; and ventilating fan in the attic.

All cover plates for push buttons, toggle switches, and convenience outlets shall be solid brass except those in the kitchen and bathrooms which shall be chromium plated.

All wiring shall be installed in accordance with the latest rules and regulations of the National Board of Fire Underwriters and local codes and ordinances. No electric device or material shall be used that has not been approved by the Underwriters Laboratories, Inc.

All electric lighting fixtures shall be selected and furnished by the owner, and they shall be properly installed or hung by the electrical contractor.

The contractor shall obtain a satisfactory certificate of inspection from the local building department and the local Board of Fire Underwriters and shall pay all necessary fees.

Painting

This specification shall cover the furnishing by the painting contractor of all necessary materials and labor required to accomplish the painting as described herein.

All paints and painting materials required for the completion of this work shall be of the best quality as recommended by the manufacturer for the service required.

The painting contractor shall not mix any paints on the floors of the building. At the completion of his work he shall clean down all woodwork, floors, sash, etc., of any paint and do all necessary retouching of painting work in the building, leaving his work in perfect condition.

All exterior painting shall be done in dry weather. No paint shall be applied to lumber that is not dry and no painting shall be done until the inside plastering, if there is any, shall be dried out. At least twenty-four hours shall elapse for drying between each coat of paint. The outside trim shall be painted first so that the main body color may be laid neatly against the trim.

Before applying any priming coat of paint the painting contractor shall go over all woodwork and apply one coat of white shellac over all knots.

All exterior woodwork including the front and side doors shall be given one priming coat of paint and two finishing coats of approved paint of the color selected by the architect.

All interior trim, woodwork, and doors of the building shall be properly cleaned and made ready for finishing. All interior trim and woodwork shall receive one priming coat and two finishing coats of approved paint of the color approved by the architect. All woodwork shall be properly sandpapered and cleaned between coats of paint.

After all priming coats for exterior and interior work have been applied and before the first finishing coat is applied, the painting contractor shall go over all the woodwork and putty up all nail holes or other defects.

The interior walls shall be given one priming coat and two finishing coats of approved paint of the colors selected by the architect.

All finishing coats for exterior and interior woodwork, walls, and ceilings shall be flat paint, except for the bathroom and kitchen which shall have a gloss finish.

All finished wood floors shall be sanded, thoroughly cleaned, and finished with two coats of Minwax, or equal finishing material, approved by the architect.

Year-round comfort system

This specification shall cover the furnishing by the heating and cooling contractor of all material and labor required to install a complete forced-air system consisting of a natural-gas fired furnace and cooling equipment, with a multiple-speed fan, supply and return ducts, filter, registers, power humidifier, thermostat, and all additional fittings, piping, wiring, and controls.

The ducts and registers shall be sized according to the respective requirements of each room and shall not be of less carrying capacity than the furnace fan rating. The ducts shall be concealed in the walls and insulated when located in an outside wall, attic, or other unheated space. Supply registers shall be located so as to supply a blanket of air across the major heat-loss areas without interference by such articles as furniture or drapes.

All equipment and materials furnished shall be installed in accordance with the manufacturer's recommendations.

All heat-loss and heat-gain calculations shall be made according to the recommended standard methods of the American Society of Heating, Refrigerating and Air-Conditioning Engineers.

Heating. The air heating system shall be complete in every detail and shall be of sufficient capacity to heat the house interior to $70°$ Fahrenheit when the outdoor temperature is at $0°F$ and there is a wind of 15 mph.

Cooling. The cooling system shall be centrally included and complete in every detail and shall be of sufficient capacity to cool the house interior to $80°F$ and a relative humidity of $50°F$ when the outdoor temperatures are $95°F$ dry bulb and $75°F$ wet bulb.

The evaporator coil shall be included in the discharge plenum of the furnace. It shall incorporate a suitable condensate collection system and shall be connected to the outdoor located condenser-compressor with correctly charged and designed tubing.

The condenser-compressor assembly shall be located on a concrete slab outdoors on the north side of the house. The unit shall be correctly wired and grounded in accordance with the electric code and manufacturer's recommendations.

A manual throw-over switch and the house thermostat shall be designed for controlling both the heating and the air conditioning systems.

Driveway and grading

The contractor shall construct the driveway and all retaining walls as shown and noted on the plans.

Before completion of the work, the contractor shall rough-grade the plot by removing all brickbats, chunks of cement and plaster, pieces of lumber, and other debris accumulated during the building and shall then bring the plot to the finished grade shown on the plans by using the topsoil on the property or necessary additional fill or topsoil provided by the owner. The contractor shall carefully protect all trees from damage during the grading.

17. curtain walls and steel construction

In previous chapters we have discussed wood-frame structures, brick and concrete or concrete-block structures, and structures made of combinations of these building materials. A few steel members have been used as girders, lally columns, doors, and windows. The use of a structural-steel skeleton or framework for many buildings has been common practice for a long time. However, a more recent development has been the idea of designs for steel component systems, capable of wide adaptability together with the use of new shapes for steel members which can be made with modern high-speed production methods. Wall panels can be made using light-gauge roll-formed steel sections for sash, mullion, jamb, and head of the windows. Steel roof-ceiling systems and a combination of reinforced-concrete and steel-panel floor slabs can be designed making use of these lighter, stronger, and more economical steel shapes and sections. The necessary ducts for the heating and ventilating systems can be incorporated in the floor slabs.

These systems can be readily used for warehouses, light manufacturing plants, and similar structures, with office spaces included within the building for the use of the supervisory and design staff. The systems are also adaptable for residential construction, both for single units and for group housing such as garden-type apartments. The aim of the manufacturers is not to provide an all-steel structure but to use steel harmoniously with other materials to reduce the cost of construction, maintenance, and replacement. The goal with each type of building is to make the maximum intelligent use of steel and at the same time to make a real effort to improve the mechanical efficiency, livability, and appearance of the completed structure.

Wall panels

The example illustrated in Fig. 17-1 is a manufacturing plant with offices for the engineering and supervisory staff. For the front and entrance passageway, stonework and sculptured Steelox[1] wall panels have been used to give a pleasing appearance. The side walls and back wall are built entirely of sculptured Steelox wall panels. All panels have a factory-applied color and for this building a light blue baked-on plastic-base enamel was used. Other colors are available.

Figure 17-2, the floor plan, shows the general layout of the interior space. The offices are finished inside with plywood and decorative hardboard applied to furring strips, as shown in the enlarged section *A-A*, Fig. 17-3. The wood furring strips can be attached to the Steelox side panels with special Helyx[1] nails which will penetrate the wood and the Steelox ribs.

A plan view of the arrangement at the masonry wall is shown in the enlarged section *B-B*, Fig. 17-4. The unique interlocking ribs of the Steelox wall system make this type of wall finish easy to achieve. These ribs form a framework inside the exterior wall on a 16-inch module, permitting the use of regular insulating and finishing materials.

The manufacturer's Liner panels are used throughout the production area. These efficient steel finishing panels are insulated at the factory and quickly put in place on the rib framework formed by the exterior wall panels. This is shown in the enlarged section *C-C*, Fig. 17-5. The Liner panels provide a plant interior finish for both comfort and practicability.

[1] Steelox and Helyx are trade names for items manufactured by Armco Steel Corporation.

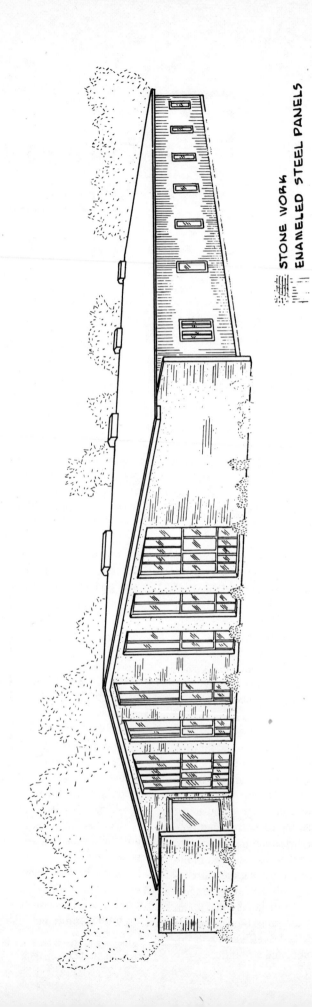

STONE WORK

ENAMELED STEEL PANELS

Fig. 17-1. Factory building. perspective.

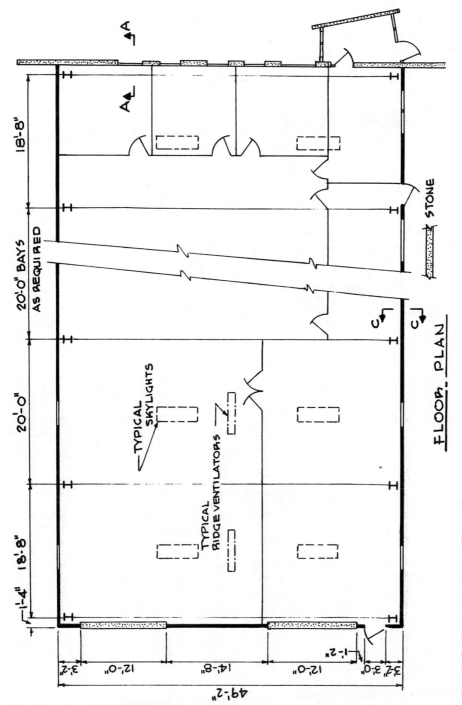

Fig. 17-2. Factory building. Floor plan.

145

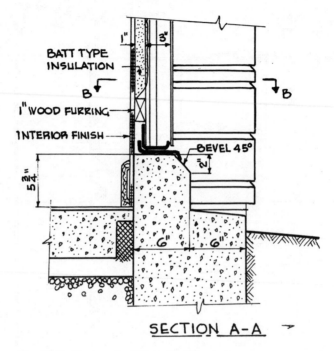

BATT TYPE
INSULATION

1" WOOD FURRING

INTERIOR FINISH

BEVEL 45°

SECTION A-A

Fig. 17-3. Factory building. Section *A-A*.

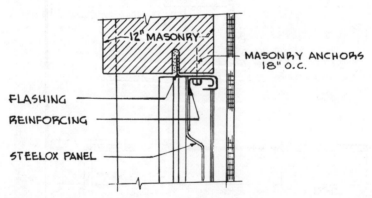

12" MASONRY

MASONRY ANCHORS
18" O.C.

FLASHING

REINFORCING

STEELOX PANEL

Fig. 17-4. Factory building. Section *B-B*.

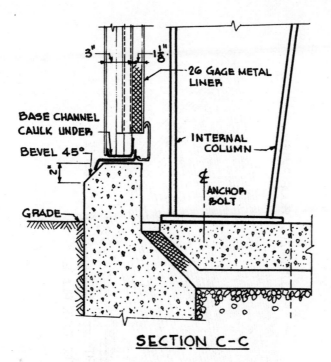

Fig. 17-5. Factory building. Section *C-C*.

This building may be readily expanded for future needs as the business volume grows. Steelox panel construction will permit the addition of more bays at the end, or an additional span alongside the initial building. Entire walls can be moved and rearranged, with a minimum of inconvenience, to accommodate new requirements.

Roof ceiling system

Figure 17-6 illustrates a roof ceiling system that is unique from the top down. It is a simplified, easily constructed truss network, covered by special Aluminized steel panels. This aluminum-coated steel defies weather and corrosion, reflects the heat, and provides top strength for the roof. The panels also serve as structural components, a double service that adds strength without adding weight or complicating the construction. A ceiling of gypsum board may be fastened to the steel "hat-section" furring strips which are attached to the underside of the trusses parallel to the length of the structure. Ventilation is carefully engineered to permit airflow either from the eaves to the ridge or in the reverse direction. Reversible airflow eliminates condensation which presents a problem with most construction methods.

Floor ceiling system

Figure 17-7 illustrates a floor ceiling system made up of Steelox interlocking modular-construction panels. It will be noted that the panels interlock and therefore can be quickly assembled. These panels are weathertight and no bolts are required. The Steelox panels form the ceiling of the lower floor and the floor structure for the upper floor. In this construction the panels are flat and rest with the smooth side down on the beam and column supports. The panels also interlock tightly to create a 16-in.-wide full-length section of the floor-ceiling system. This section provides a space for conduit or other piping and may serve as airflow channels. Because of the steel panels there is no chance for the ceiling to crack, chip, or buckle. The upper floor may be finished in a simple two-step process. First, the plywood subflooring is attached to the interlocked flanges of the Steelox panels. Then the finished flooring of either tile or carpet can be applied over the subflooring. The subflooring can be nailed directly to the ribs of the Steelox panel flooring with the Helyx nails which penetrate the wood and the Steelox ribs.

Windows and walls

The windows and walls, like the roof and the ceiling system, are modular units, and the Steelox for wall panels is sculptured, giving it a pleasing shadow appearance. The 16-in.-wide panels interlock to form a full-length section of the wall that stretches from eave to foundation. The window frames are roll-formed steel segments, accurately fabricated to bolt into the wall system without additional framework. Once in place the window frames, which have been developed specifi-

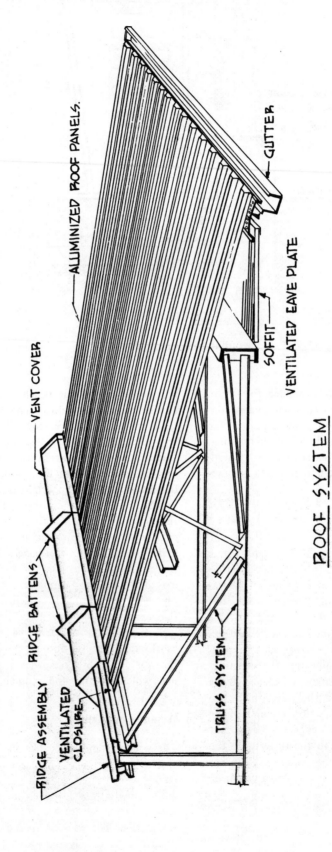

RIDGE ASSEMBLY
VENTILATED CLOSURE
RIDGE BATTENS
VENT COVER
ALUMINIZED ROOF PANELS.
GUTTER
VENTILATED EAVE PLATE
SOFFIT
TRUSS SYSTEM

ROOF SYSTEM

Fig. 17-6. Factory building. Roof ceiling system.

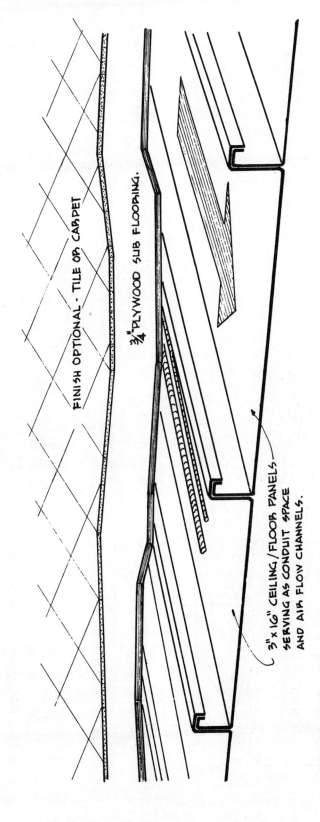

FINISH OPTIONAL - TILE OR CARPET

¾" PLYWOOD SUB FLOORING.

3" x 16" CEILING/FLOOR PANELS
SERVING AS CONDUIT SPACE
AND AIR FLOW CHANNELS.

Fig. 17-7. Factory building. Floor ceiling system.

149

Auto Sales Building, Fayetteville, North Carolina

Ink Factory Building, Toronto, Ontario

Office Building, Kinston, North Carolina

Beer Distribution Center, Denver, Colorado

School Bus Garage, Pike Township, Indiana

Electric Cooperative, Friendship, Wisconsin

Fig. 17-8. Modern steel structures. *(Armco Steel Corporation, Middletown, Ohio)*

Restaurant, Parson, Kansas

Showroom and Supply Depot, Tulsa, Oklahoma

Tractor Building, Valdosta, Georgia

Packaging Factory, Madison, Wisconsin

Aircraft Hanger, Dayton, Ohio

Aircraft Factory, Charleston, North Carolina

Fig. 17-9. Modern steel structures. *(Armco Steel Corporation, Middletown, Ohio)*

cally for the modular component system, readily accept glass or color panels. Door frames also are prefabricated fully protected steel and fit the wall system without on-site modification.

Improved residential construction

The traditional materials for residential construction such as wood, stone, and brick have been used because they were readily available or simply because they were there first. Design, construction methods, and building schedules have been established by the use of these traditional materials. Residential houses built of these materials present a good initial appearance, but the big problem of maintenance starts almost immediately. The maintenance problem is a long-term headache.

With the modular steel components previously described, residential houses may be designed using a material that combines permanence, textural warmth, and architectural flexibility. Steel can be used in its many forms to provide handsome appearance and brute resistance to weather. Steel coated with zinc, steel coated with aluminum, and steel coated with baked-on enamel are also available. Steel is also available in fluted form or embossed, flat and smooth on the one hand, textured for warmth on the other hand.

The modular steel components can be erected in minimum time by the builder, stay in place for the home owner, and provide design versatility and the warmth required for residential construction. The entire system is designed for simplicity, accuracy, and permanence. Figures 17-8 and 17-9 include illustrations of a variety of structures using Armco steel and panel construction.

Exercise

Design a small residence using modular steel components. First select the style of house, whether ranch-type or two-story, and the desired arrangement and size of the rooms, that is, the floor plan. Make freehand sketches of the floor plans and general appearance of the house. Check these sketches with your instructor before proceeding with the drawings. After the sketches have been approved, make the necessary floor plans, foundation plan, sections, and exterior elevations. All additional information required in order to complete the plans should be obtained from manufacturer's bulletins.

glossary

Every profession develops a language of its own but at the same time makes use of many words and terms employed elsewhere. It may seem that the borrowed terms have been given a different meaning, but careful study will reveal a similarity or kinship in their use.

Aggregate	The gravel or broken stone used in concrete.
Altitude	The perpendicular distance from the base of a figure to its summit.
Anchor bolt	A round rod, threaded on one end and having a nut, used to secure the sill plate to the foundation.
Angle	Geometry—the enclosure formed by two lines extending from the same point.
	Structural shape—a piece of steel shaped to form a 90° angle.
Apron	The concrete ramp in front of a garage.
	Also the trim below the window stool.
Arch	An arrangement of a structure which carries the weight over an opening.
Area	A level surface, or piece of ground.
Area wall	The masonry surrounding or partially surrounding an area.
Areaway	An enclosure built to admit light to a basement.
Asbestos	An incombustible fibrous mineral substance used for siding materials and fireproofing.
Attic	The space directly beneath the roof of a house.
Awning window	An out-swinging window hinged at the top.

Backfill	The earth used to fill in around foundation walls after they are completed.
Back hearth	The portion of the hearth inside the fireplace.
Backing	Usually used in referring to a portion of a wall which reinforces the front of the wall.
Balloon frame	A type of building framework in which the studs extend from the foundation to the eaves without interruption by horizontal members.
Balustrade	A row of balusters supporting a top rail.
Base	The bottom or supporting part of a structure.
Baseboard	The finishing board that covers the wall where it joins the floor.
Basement	The lowest story of a building. It may be above the ground, partially above the ground, or entirely below ground level.
Base molding	A molding used to trim the bottom edge of a baseboard.
Base shoe	A molding strip used next to the floor for interior baseboards.
Bat	A piece of broken brick.
Batten	A narrow strip of wood used as a cleat across parallel boards or to cover joints between boards.
Batten boards	Boards set up at the corners of a new construction from which are stretched the lines marking off the wall.
Beam	A horizontal building member which supports a load.

Bearing partition	A partition supporting a vertical load.
Bearing plate	A flat piece of wood or metal used between a building member and the supporting structure below it.
Bench mark	A point of reference used by surveyors when establishing lines and grades.
Beveled siding	Siding cut at a slant along each edge.
Bond	The arrangement of bricks in a wall. The joint between the courses.
Bridging	The cross bracing between joists or studs to align and stiffen them.
Btu	British thermal unit, a unit used to measure heat.
Buck	The frame for a door, usually metal.
Building line	The line on a plot, established by law, beyond which the building must not extend.
Building paper	A heavy water-repellent paper used over sheathing before siding is applied and between final floors.
Butt	A hinge.
Calcimine	A white powder made up of a whiting and glue size, mixed in water, used as a binder.
Caulking compound	A nonhardening paste used to fill cracks and crevices.
Cantilever	An overhanging part of a structure supported at one end only.
Carriage	The horizontal part of the stringers of a stairs that supports treads.
Casement	The glass frame of a window which turns on hinges fastened to one edge of the frame.
Casing	The frame around a door or window which is set into the wall.
Catch basin	A cement, wood, or cast-iron receptacle which receives the water draining from a roof, floor, etc. Usually connected to a sewer or drainage line.
Catwalk	A partial rough floor in an attic.
Cellar	A story of a building entirely below ground.
Center of vision	The vanishing point used in one-point perspective.
Center to center	Refers to measurements taken from the center of one member to the center of another member, noted oc.
Ceramic tile	Tile made of clay.
Channel	A structural-steel shape formed like a rectangular box with only two sides and no top cover.
Chase	A furred space in a wall to allow for passage of pipe or electric conduit.

Chord	The bottom horizontal member of a truss. A straight line joining any two points on an arc of a circle.
Circuit	The path over which an electric current may pass.
Circuit breaker	A device for opening and closing an electric circuit.
Clerestory	A windowed space which rises above lower stories to admit air and light.
Client	A person who employs an architect.
Collar beam	A beam tying together two opposite rafters of a roof.
Column	A vertical supporting member.
Concrete	Sand, cement, gravel or broken stone, and water. When the mixture hardens, it is concrete.
Conductor	Architecture—a drainpipe leading from the roof. Electricity—any material which will transmit an electric current.
Conduit	Tubing used to protect electric wires; usually metal.
Contractor	Someone offering to perform specified work for an agreed sum of money.
Convector	A surface designed to transfer heat to surrounding air largely or entirely by means of air currents.
Corbel	Often used to denote brickwork when each course projects a little beyond the course below to form a supporting bracket.
Corner bead	A metal strip fastened to exterior corners before plaster is applied, serving to protect the corners from chipping.
Cornice	That part of the roof which extends horizontally beyond the wall.
Counter flashing	Sheet metal placed over flashing and returning into the masonry to stop moisture from entering the structure.
Coursed ashlar	Regular-shaped stones for veneer masonry.
Cove molding	A concave molding used on inside corners.
Crawl space	The space between the floor joists and the ground when a cellar or basement is omitted.
Crosshatching	Lines usually drawn at 45° and close together to indicate a sectional view.
Curtain wall	An enclosing wall which provides no structural support to the house.
Dado	A plain, flat surface at the base of a wall. Sometimes decorated.
Damper	A movable plate placed in a chimney or vent pipe to regulate the draft.
Detail	A fully dimensioned view of a particular portion of a project.

Dimension line A line drawn between two points to show the beginning and end of the dimension.

Dividers One of the drafting instruments used for transferring or marking off dimensions.

Door buck The door frame (usually metal).

Double-hung window A window made up of an upper and a lower sash which slide past each other vertically.

Drain A pipe or other contrivance which carries away waste water.

Dressed and matched Lumber, squared and finished smooth to size.

Drip cap A wood or aluminum member installed over windows and doors and designed to deflect water from the face of a building.

Dry wall A wall finished with wallboard instead of plaster.

Dry well A pocket dug in the earth to help drain off water which is being returned to the earth.

Ducks Lead weights used to hold a spline in position. See spline.

Ducts Sheet-metal tubes to distribute cool or warm air.

Eave The projecting lower portion of a roof beyond the wall line.

Elbow A section of pipe or a fitting in the shape of an L.

Elevation Measurement—the height of a point above sea level or some other datum point.
Drafting—a drawing or orthographic view of any of the vertical sides of a structure.

Ellipse A closed plane curve differing from a circle in that it has a major and a minor axis.

Enamel Paint with a considerable amount of varnish in it that produces a hard, glossy surface on wood or other materials.

Escutcheon plate The plate at a keyhole which covers the rough opening.

Excavation A hole in the ground made by removing the earth.

Eye level The level of the horizon line.

Face brick Brick used for the outside face of the wall exposed to view.

Fascia (or facia) A vertical board used at the ends of rafters.

Fenestration The arrangement and proportion of windows in solid-wall areas.

Firebrick A special brick made of fireclay and hard-burned to resist heat.

Fireclay A grade of clay that can withstand a great deal of heat. Used in fireplaces and boiler linings.

Fire cut The angular cut at the end of joists.

Fire door A metal-clad door designed to resist fire.

Fire stop Cross members between joists intended to retard the spread of fire.

Fixture An electric or plumbing item which is attached in a definite location.

Flange The horizontal parts of an I beam or a channel section.

Flashing Sheets of metal which are installed to seal building joints tight against the weather.

Floor plan A drawing or orthographic view of a horizontal floor of a structure showing partitions, doors, windows, etc.

Flue An interior opening in a chimney.

Flush door A door in which both surfaces are flat planes.

Folding door A door made of fabric, wood sections, or plastic in such a manner that it will fold to one side of the opening.

Footing The lower part of the foundation which rests on the ground.

Foundation The supporting wall or part of the structure.

Framing The bare wooden or metal skeleton of a structure.

Frieze That part of the wallboard directly under the cornice.

Furring Wood strips fastened to a wall for the purpose of attaching covering material.

Fuse A strip of soft metal inserted in an electric circuit and designed to melt and open the circuit if the current exceeds a predetermined value.

Gable The triangular portion of an end wall formed by a sloping roof.

Gable roof A roof that slopes up from only two walls of a building.

Girder A wood or steel horizontal member designed to carry a load between two supports.

Girt A horizontal member in a wall.

Grade The level of the ground around a building.

Ground line A horizontal line representing the supporting plane.

Grounds Strips of wood fastened to the frame to act as nailing strips for the baseboard.

Grout A thin mortar used to fill up spaces that cannot be sealed by heavier mortar.

Guidelines	Light lines drawn to serve as a guide for lettering.
Gusset	A flat surface of plywood or metal used to reinforce the joints of a truss.
Gutter	A trough designed to carry off water.
Hangers	Metal straps used to support pipes, gutters, etc.
Header	Horizontal cross member used to frame over openings.
Header course	A row of bricks placed endwise to the face of the wall.
Headroom	The vertical clearance for a door or on a stairway.
Hearth	The masonry part of a floor in front of a fireplace.
Hexagon	A plane-geometric figure with six equal sides.
Hip rafter	The rafter at the junction of two sloping roofs that form an exterior angle.
Hip roof	A roof that slopes up from four walls of a building.
Hollow-core door	A flush door made of two outer plywood surfaces over a core of glued strips which form a honeycomb.
Hood	A ventilated canopy.
Hopper window	An in-swinging window with hinges on its lower side.
Horizon line	Perspective drawing—a line parallel to the ground line representing the level of the vanishing points.
Horizontal	Parallel to or measured in a plane of the horizon, that is, where the earth appears to meet the sky.
Humidifier	A mechanical device which adds water vapor to various materials or to the atmosphere.
House drain	The piping inside a building that carries off the discharge from all waste and soil piping.
I beam	A steel beam shaped in the form of an I.
Insulation	A special material placed in walls, floors, or ceilings to reduce transfer of heat between two surfaces. Also used to cover pipes and ducts.
Isometric	A three-dimensional drawing with parallel isometric lines and no perspective.
Jack rafter	A short rafter placed between the hip rafter or valley rafter and the roof ridge.
Jamb	The vertical sides of a door or window frame.
Jerry-built	Built poorly, of cheap materials.
Joggle	A point made between two surfaces of wood, stone, etc., by cutting a notch in one and making a projection in the other to fit into it.
Joggle post	A post with shoulders to receive the feet of studs.
Joiner	A carpenter who finishes interior woodwork.
Joist	The wood framing members which support the floor.
Journeyman	A worker who has finished learning his trade.
Kalamein door	A metal-covered door.
Kerf	A cut or notch made by an axe or a saw.
Key	Something that completes or holds together the part or parts of another thing, as the keystone of an arch.
Keyed	Fastened or reinforced with a key.
Keystone	The center top stone of a masonry arch.
King post	A vertical supporting post between the apex of a triangular truss and the base.
Knee brace	A brace between two members joined in the form of a knee.
Knock down	To take apart for convenience in shipping.
Lally column	A vertical supporting member made from steel pipe and usually filled with concrete.
Laminated	Consisting of several layers of material glued or cemented together.
Landing	A platform at the top of a flight of stairs.
Lath	Wood strips or sheets of metal with holes nailed to studs and joists to hold plaster.
Lavatory	A place for washing one's face and hands.
Leader	A vertical conductor of water from a gutter. A downspout.
Lean-to	A shed or small building adjoining the side of a larger building.
Lineal	A term applied to measurements along a single line.
Lining	A covering over the interior surface of an object.
Lintel	A horizontal member placed above a masonry opening to support the load above.
Lite	A pane of glass.
Load bearing	A term applied to an exterior wall supporting the roof and upper floors. Also interior walls with joists tied directly to them.
Longitudinal	A term applied to the length of an object.
Lookout	A short wooden extension which

supports the overhanging portion of a roof on the gable end.

Lot lines The boundary lines of a parcel of land.

Louver A screened slotted opening usually at the gable ends of a house for the purpose of ventilation. An opening covered by ventilating slats to keep out rain.

Lowercase Describing the small letters of the alphabet as distinguished from the capital letters.

Lumber Wood that has been cut into usable sizes for the builder; usually less than 8 in. wide, and 4 to 5 in. thick.

Manhole An opening in a pipe, sewer, or other structure to allow access for a man.

Mantel A shelf over a fireplace.

Masonry Brick, stone, or similar material installed by a mason.

Mastic A soft or pliable material used to seal small openings.

Meeting rail The horizontal members of window frames that meet or fit together when the window is closed.

Member One part of a unit of a structure.

Mezzanine floor A low secondary floor between two high floors; usually between the ground floor and the next floor above.

Millwork Woodwork furnished and milled in a woodworking shop.

Miter A beveled surface cut on the ends of molding or framing to make them fit together as in a picture frame.

Miter line A line drawn at 45 degrees and sometimes used to transfer dimensions from one view to another view.

Module A standardized unit of measurement in which materials are manufactured.

Monolithic A concrete structure poured in one piece.

Monument A stone marker placed to serve as a point of reference for surveyors.

Mortar A mixture of sand, cement, and water, and sometimes also lime, used for bonding.

Mullion The vertical member separating window sashes in a window.

Muntin The narrow strip which separates the panes of glass in a window sash.

Nave The main or central part of a church auditorium.

Neat Material undiluted or unmixed with other materials.

Newel The principal post at the foot of a stairway or at a secondary landing.

Niche A recess in a wall.

Nominal Approximate, not actual.

Nominal size A size existing in name only and not necessarily agreeing with the actual size, i.e., the size before dressing.

Nonferrous A metal which does not contain iron.

Nosing The rounded projecting edge of stair tread, not included in the tread measurement.

Oblique drawing A form of pictorial representation using the parallel planes to depict an object.

Octagon A plane-geometric figure with eight equal sides.

Ogee A reverse curve.

One-point (single-point) perspective A perspective drawing using only one vanishing point. Also called oblique perspective drawing.

Open web bar joist A joist made up of light metal members and bars.

Orientation The placing of a structure on the property.

Orthographic projection A drawing in which the projections from the object are perpendicular to the plane of projection.

Outlet Electricity—the socket to which connection can be made for a lamp or extension plug.

Piping—the end or side of a pipe, valve, fitting, etc., from which the contents are discharged.

Panel A flat wood or metal surface framed in other wood or metal. Also a flat metal surface for mounting electric equipment and instruments.

Parallel Referring to lines or surfaces that are equal distances apart at every point.

Parapet The part of a wall which projects above the roof.

Parting strip The strip at the sides of a double-hung window to separate the upper and lower sash.

Partition An interior wall separating two rooms or areas.

Party wall A common wall between two buildings.

Penny A term used to denote the length of a nail. As sixpenny or eightpenny.

Perimeter The outer boundary of a figure or area.

Perpendicular A line or plane at 90°, right angle, to another line or plane.

Perspective drawing The drawing of an object in three-dimensional form as it would appear to the eye.

Picture plane An imaginary plane, used in perspective drawing, which is placed between an object and the eye and to

	which all the points on the object are projected.
Pier	A masonry support either built into a wall or freestanding.
Pilaster	An attached pier, rectangular in plan, part of a column.
Piling	Wood or concrete posts driven down into the earth to provide safe footing for heavy loads.
Pilot light	A very small light which usually burns continuously. May be either gas or electric.
Pitch	The incline of a roof or of a run of pipe. The distance apart of a series of points as in screw threads or gear teeth. A black tarry substance used for roofing purposes.
Plan	A horizontal section cut at eye level.
Plangier	That part of the cornice at right angles to the wall.
Planks	Pieces of timber $1\frac{5}{8}$ in. and more in thickness.
Plate	The horizontal double 2- by 4-in. member on top of a row of studs.
Plumb	Vertical; parallel to a weighted or plumb line.
Poché	To darken or fill in (the solids of a plan). Usually on the reverse side of a drawing.
Pointing	The filling and finishing of joints in a masonry wall.
Porch	A covered shelter on the outside of a building.
Portland cement	Common gray cement. Named "portland" because when it was first manufactured it resembled the gray limestone from the Isle of Portland.
Post and beam building	A method of building in which the crossbeams rest on vertical posts.
Preglazed	A window sash delivered to the job with the glass installed and puttied in place.
Priming coat	The initial or first coat of paint. The priming coat is applied to fill the pores of the surface.
Projection	The horizontal distance from the face of a wall to the end of a rafter.
Protractor	An instrument used to measure angles.
Purlin	Structural members spanning the trusses and used to support the roofing material.
Quadrangle	A plane figure having four angles and four sides.
Quarry	An open excavation for obtaining building stones.
Queen post	One of two vertical posts in a roof or similar framed truss.
Quoins	Large cut stones at the corners of a masonry wall.
Rabbet	A groove or cut in or near the edge of one piece of wood to receive another member.
Rafter	A beam extending from a cornice plate to the ridge of the roof.
Rail	A bar of wood or metal extending from one support to another, as in a handrail or fence.
Reglect	A term applied to a groove made in stone or to a brick joint used to receive flashing or counterflashing.
Reglet	A flat molding used to separate panels, etc.
Rendering	The art of coloring or shading a drawing; also of adding trees, shrubs, or people to give a lifelike appearance.
Return	A molding turned back into a wall on which it is located.
Ribbon	A narrow board set into studs that are cut to support joists. A support for joists.
Ridge	The top edge of a roof where two sloping sides meet.
Ridge board	The wood member to which the rafters are nailed to form the ridge.
Rise	The vertical distance from the center of a roof span up to the ridge line. The distance between floors denoting stair rise.
Riser	One of the vertical parts of a stair.
Rocklath	A flat board used as a plaster base and made of a gypsum composition, perforated to form a good bond.
Rowlocks	Bricks laid with the 3¾-in. edge vertical and the 2¼-in. edge horizontal.
Rubble	Roughly broken quarrystone or weather-worn stone.
Ruling pen	A drawing instrument used to draw ink lines.
Run	The horizontal distance covered, as for stairs or half the roof span.
Saddle	A small sloping roof to carry the water away from the back of a chimney. A section of wood or metal placed on the floor across a doorway, a threshold, or a sill.
Sash	A frame in a door or window that holds the glass.
Scab	A short length of wood nailed to the sides of two other pieces to hold them together.
Scale drawing	A drawing which is made to a size or

	scale that is different from the actual size of the object drawn.
Schedule	A formal list of parts or details, as a window or door schedule.
Scratch coat	The first coat of plaster which is scratched or scored to provide a good bond for the next coat.
Screed	A wood strip fastened in place to help a cement man determine the level and thickness of a cement floor.
Scribe	To mark by cutting or scratching a line.
Scupper	An outlet in the wall of a building for drainage of water overflow from a floor or flat roof.
Sea level	The level continuous with that of the surface of the ocean at mean tide.
Section	A drawing of an object which has been cut apart to show the interior construction or material.
Septic tank	A concrete tank, built in the ground, into which sewage is drained. Used when public sewers are not available.
Sheathing	The first covering of boards on the outside of a house or a roof.
Shed roof	A single-pitch roof, sloping in one direction.
Shingles	Specially cut pieces of wood, slate, or composition material applied over sheathing as a wall or roofcovering.
Shoe	A horizontal wood member used as a base for the vertical studs.
Shoring	Timbers used to brace a wall, usually for a temporary period.
Show rafter	A short rafter extending below the cornice.
Siding	The wood covering on the outside of a house.
Sill	The bottom timber of frame construction, which rests directly on the foundation wall. The member which is located across the bottom of a door or window opening.
Slab	A term used to describe a flat area of concrete.
Sleeper	A wood beam used on or near the ground, to support a structure. A wood member buried in a concrete floor to be used as a nailing strip for the flooring.
Sliding door	A door which slides on a track into the wall or past another sliding door.
Smoke chamber	The part of the chimney flue located directly above the fireplace.
Soap	A cut brick used to level horizontal coursing.
Soffit	The underside of parts of a building, as the underside of a cornice, arch, or roof overhang.

Soil stack	The vertical pipe into which the branch sewage pipes drain.
Soldiers	Brick laid with the 8-in. edge vertical and the 2¼-in. edge horizontal.
Sole	The horizontal member, called a shoe, in the framing upon which the studding rests.
Spackle	To cover the joints of wallboard or cracks in plaster with a specially prepared plaster.
Span	The distance between supports for rafters, trusses, or other members.
Spandrel	The space between two openings which are above one another in a wall.
Specifications	The written description that accompanies a set of drawings and describes the work to be performed.
Splay	To make a beveled surface.
Spline	A flexible ruler used to draw curved lines.
Stack	A pipe extending through the roof which serves to ventilate the plumbing system.
Station point	In a perspective drawing, the spot on which a viewer is presumed to be standing.
Stile	The vertical member of a door, window, or panel.
Stirrup	A U-shaped strap hung on a cross header and used to support framing members.
Stool	The wood shelf across the bottom and inside of a window.
Stoop	A porch, platform, or entrance stairway at a house door.
Stratification	The formation of layers, one over the other, as layers of air or heat.
Stretchers	Bricks laid flat, with the 8- by 2¼-in. face exposed.
Stringer	The side supporting members of a stairway. Sometimes called string or carriage.
Stucco	A coating for walls—consisting of cement, sand, and water.
Studs	The vertical members forming the skeleton framing of a structure, usually spaced 16 in. on centers.
Subflooring	The flooring under the finished floor.
Symbol	A sign selected to represent an object, material, or other item of building construction.
Tail beams	Framing members that are supported by headers or trimmers at one or both ends.
Tangent	A straight line, curve, or surface meeting or touching a curve or surface at only one point and not

	cutting it if produced.
Temperature	Heat or cold registered in degrees on a thermometer.
Termite shields	Sheets of copper placed on top of the foundation to block termite invasion.
Terrace	A raised level or platform of earth.
Terra-cotta	Hard-baked clay and sand usually reddish brown or yellow in color. Often used for chimney flues.
Terrazzo	Floor construction using a mixture of marble chips and cement ground to a smooth finish. Thin metal strips are used to outline a design and prevent cracking.
Thermostat	A device for automatically controlling the supply of heat to a system.
Thimble	A circular sleeve extending through a wall or floor to form an opening; most commonly used in chimney construction.
Threshold	The stone, wood, or metal member which lies under a door.
Throat	The passage directly above the fireplace opening.
Tie	A metal strip used in brick veneer to hold the masonry wall to the frame wall.
Tie beam	A framing member between rafters.
Tier	One, two, or more rows placed one above another.
Timber	Cut or uncut wood. When cut, the width and thickness are much greater than in lumber. (See Lumber.)
Toenailing	Driving nails into wood at an angle.
Tongue	A projection on the edge of a board that fits into a groove which is similarly formed on another board.
Total run	Referring to the sum of all the tread widths in a stair.
Tracing	Duplicating a drawing by copying the lines and lettering as seen through a transparent sheet of paper, vellum, or tracing cloth.
Transcribe	To copy.
Transmission	Sending or transferring something from one part of a structure to another or from one location to another, as vibrations or sounds.
Transom	A small window over a door.
Trap	A device in a plumbing or drain system designed to prevent the passage of gases or odors. A device designed to permit the passage of one substance and to prevent the passage of another.
Transverse	Lying or situated across, crossing from side to side.
Tread	One of the steps or horizontal parts of a stair.

Trellis	A structure or frame of latticework.
Triangle	A plane-geometric three-sided figure.
Trim	The light woodwork in a building, especially around openings.
Trimmers	Single or double joists or rafters around an opening in the floor or roof construction.
Troweled	Spread smooth with a trowel. A small tool used by masons.
Truss	A braced arrangement of metal or wood members designed to span between supports.
T square	A T-shaped instrument of metal or wood used in drafting.
Two-point perspective	A perspective drawing using a right and a left vanishing point.
Underpinning	The construction added for support beneath a wall built previously.
Under soil	Soil beneath the surface; subsoil.
Underwork	To do less work than is proper.
Undressed lumber	Lumber that is not squared or finished smooth.
Uniaxial	Having only one axis.
Uppercase	Describing the capital letters of the alphabet as distinguished from the lowercase letters.
Utilities	Useful services such as gas, electric, water, etc.
Valley	The depression where two slopes of a roof meet.
Valley jacks	Rafters that extend from a ridge board to a valley rafter.
Valley rafter	A rafter used to form the depression where two sloping roof surfaces meet.
Valve	A mechanical device designed to regulate or shut off the flow of fluids or gases in a piping system.
Vandyke	A reproduction of a tracing printed by a process which gives white lines on a brown background or brown lines on a white background.
Vanishing point	A point in perspective drawing toward which the horizontal lines of a drawing recede.
Vapor barrier	Thin nonporous sheets applied to framing to prevent condensed moisture from passing through walls.
Veneer	A comparatively thin layer of wood fastened over other wood, or a layer of masonry over a wood frame or other masonry.
Vent pipe	A vertical pipe in plumbing designed to ventilate the system and relieve the pressure due to flushing. Any pipe which ventilates.
Vent stack	The upper portion of a soil or waste stack above the highest fixture.

Venturi A restriction in a pipe designed to increase the rate of flow of a fluid or gas.

Verge boards The boards running down the slope of a roof from the top of the gable; also called rake boards.

Vertical Perpendicular to a line or a plane that is parallel to the horizon line or horizontal.

Vestibule A passage between outer and inner doors of a building.

Vibrator A shaking device which is immersed in concrete as it is being poured to distribute the mixture evenly and prevent voids.

Vitreous A composition of materials that resembles glass.

Volume The space occupied by something; usually stated in cubical measurements.

Volute A line formed by moving around and outward from a central point spirally, as in a turned handrail.

Wainscot A wood lining of an interior wall, usually paneled.

Wall stringer The side supporting member of a stairway alongside a wall.

Wall ties Usually metal strips placed in brick joints to hold two thin walls together or to secure a brick veneer to the inner wall.

Waste stack A pipe in the plumbing system into which the waste liquids are discharged. Usually a vertical pipe.

Waterproof Material or construction that has been treated to resist the penetration of moisture or water.

Water table The top level of the water in the ground. A stringcourse or similar member below the outside covering of a building designed to deflect water away from the building.

Watt A unit of electric power.

Weather stripping A strip of fabric or metal fastened along the edges of doors and windows to protect the interior against the weather.

Weep hole A small opening at the bottom of a wall or column to allow the drainage of moisture which may collect on the inside.

Well opening The opening in a floor providing access to a stair.

Withe A vertical wall of brick one brick in thickness.

Working drawing A drawing containing dimensions and other information required to guide the workmen in the erection of a structure.

Workmanship The execution or manner of making or doing any portion of the work.

abbreviations

Chapter 10 explained and illustrated the use of symbols and conventions to shorten and condense the work on a drawing. In the same manner many words are shortened by the use of standard abbreviations. It was formerly the custom to end an abbreviation with a period. However, in accord with current usage, the American National Standards Institute has recommended the elimination of the period after abbreviations except for abbreviations that form words, as, in. for inch, no. for number, do. for ditto.

It is a good practice to use standard abbreviations in order that the same meaning may be conveyed to everyone. The use of signs such as # for number or pounds (1b), " for ditto, and one or more asterisks (*) in place of numerals for reference notes is not recommended.

addition	add.
aggregate	aggr
alternating current	ac
aluminum	alum
altitude	alt
American Institute of Architects	AIA
American Institute of Electrical Engineers	AIEE
American Institute of Steel Construction	AISC
American National Standards Institute	ANSI
American Society of Civil Engineers	ASCE
American Society of Heating and Ventilating Engineers	ASHVE
American Society of Mechanical Engineers	ASME
American Society of Refrigerating Engineers	ASRE
American Society for Testing Materials	ASTM
American Water Works Association	AWWA
American Welding Society	AWS
American Wire Gauge	Awg
ampersand	&
ampere	amp
angle	L
apartment	Apt.
approved	app
architectural	arch.
article	Art.
asbestos	asb
asphalt	asph
asphalt tile	AT.
assemble	assem
assembly	assy
Associate	Assoc
Association	Assn
at	@
atmospheric pressure	atmos press.
automatic	auto
Avenue	Ave
average	avg
barrel, barrels	bbl
basement	basmt
bathroom	B
beaded one side	B1s
bedroom	BR
bench mark	BM
better	btr
between	bet.
beveled	bev
blueprint	BP
board measure	bdm
bottom	bot
Boulevard	Blvd
boundary	BDY
bracket	brkt

brass	br	dimension	dim.
brick	BRK	dining room	DR
British thermal unit	Btu	direct current	dc
bronze	bro	distance	dist
Brown & Sharpe	B&S	ditto	do.
building	Bldg	division	div
buzzer	buz	double-hung	d-h
cabinet	CAB.	dowel	dwl
candlepower	CP	down	dn
carpenter	CARP.	downspout	ds
cast iron	CI	dozen	doz
caulk	clk	drain	dr
ceiling	clg	drainboard	dbd
cement	cem	drawing	dwg
center	ctr	drawn	drwn
center-matched	CM	dressed and matched	D&M
center to center	c to c	drinking fountain	df
center line	c or CL	dry well	dw
centimeter, centimeters	cm	duplex	dx
ceramic	cer	duplicate	dup
chamfer	chfr	each	ea
channel	[	east	E
checked	chkd	edge grain	EG
chromium plate	cr pl	elbow	ell.
cinder block	cin bl	electric	elec
circular	cir	elevation	el
circumference	CIRC	elevator	elev
cleanout	c-o	emergency	emer
clear	clr	enclosure	encl
closet	CL	end to end	e to e
column	clo	engineer	ENGR
Commercial Standard	CS	entrance	ent
common	com	equipment	equip.
company	Co	equivalent direct radiation	edr
compartment	comp	escutcheon	esc
concrete	conc	estimate	est
concrete block	conc b	excavate	exc
concrete ceiling	conc clg	executive	exec
concrete floor	conc fl	existing	exist.
conduit	cnd	expansion bolt	exp bt
construction	const	expansion joint	exp jt
contract	cont	extension	EXT
copper	cop	exterior	ext
corner guards	cg	extra heavy	xh
cover	cov	extrude	extr
cubic	cu	fabricate	fab
cubic feet per minute	cfm	face to face	f to f
cubic foot, feet	cu ft	facing tile	ft
cubic inch, inches	cu in.	factory	fct
cubic yard, yards	cu yd	Fahrenheit	F
current	cur.	federal	FED.
cycle	CY	feeder	fdr
cylinder	cyl	feed water	fw
dampproofing	DP	feet per minute	fpm
decibel	db	feet per second	fps
degree	° or deg	Fellow, American Institute	
department	dept	of Architects	FAIA
detail	det	Fellow, Royal Institute	
diagram	diag	British Architects	FRIBA
diameter	dia	figure	fig.

fillet	fil	hot rolled steel	HRS
finish	fin.	hot water	hw
finish all over	FAO	hour	hr
firebrick	frbk	house	hse
fire door	fdr	hundred	C
fire extinguisher	f ext	I beam	I
fire hose	fh	Illuminating Engineering Society	IES
fire-hose cabinet	fhc	inch, inches	" or in.
fire-hose rack	fhr	include	incl
fire hydrant	fhy	Incorporated	Inc
fire main	fm	information	info
fireplace	fp	inlet	in.
fireproof	fprf	inside diameter	ID
fireproof self-closing	fpsc	instantaneous	inst
fire standpipe	fps	instrument	instr
flange	flge	insulation	insul
floor	flr	interior	int
flooring	flg	intermediate	inter
fluorescent	fluor	internal	int
flush	fl	invert	inv
foot, feet	' or ft	iron	I
footing	ftg	iron-pipe size	ips
foot-pound	ft-lb	janitor's closet	J cl
foundation	fdn	joint	jt
frame	fr	junction	j
free on board	FOB	junction box	jb
frequency	freq	kalamein	kal
fresh air inlet	FAI	kalamein door	KD
fuel oil	FO	kalamein frame	KF
full size	FS	kalsomine	k
furnish	furn	keyed alike	ka
furred ceiling	FC	kickplate	kp
gallery	gall.	kilocycle	kc
galvanized iron	Gal. or GI	kilogram	kg
gauge	Ga	kilometer	km
general contractor	Gen Cont	kilowatt, or kilowatts	kw
generator	gen	kilowatt-hour	kwhr
glass	gl	kip (1,000 lb)	k
government	govt	kitchen	K
grade	gr	kitchen sink	ks
granite	g	knocked down	kd
grating	grtg	laboratory	LAB
gravity	g	ladder	lad.
grease trap	gt	landing	ldg
guard	gd	lateral	lat
gypsum	gyp	lath	lth
handhole	HH	latitude	lat
hardware	hdw	laundry	Lau
hardwood	hdwd	laundry tray	LT
head	hd	lavatory	lav
heater	htr	leader	L
height	hgt	leader drain	LD
hexagonal	hex	left-hand	LH
hollow metal	hm	length	lgth
horizon	H	level	lev
horizontal	hor	Library	Lib
horsepower	hp	light	lt
hose bibb	HB	lightweight concrete	lwc
hospital	hosp	limestone	ls

linear feet	lin ft	ornament	Orn
linen closet	L Cl	ounce, ounces	oz
linoleum	lino	out to out	o to o
live load	LL	outlet	out.
living room	LR	outside diameter	OD
locker	lkr	overall	oa
long	lg	overflow	ovfl
louver	lvr	overhead	ovhd
low pressure	lp	overload	ov ld
lumber	lbr	painted	ptd
lumen	l	pair	pr
machine	mach	panel	pnl
machine room	MR	pantry	pan.
mail chute	MC	parallel to	‖
main	mn	Parkway	Pkwy
malleable iron	MI	part	pt
malleable iron pipe	mip	partition	ptn
manhole	mh	parts per million	ppm
manufacture	mfr	passage	pass.
masonry opening	MO	pedestal	ped
material	matl	penny	d
maximum	max	per	/
measurement	mst	percent	% or pc
mechanical	Mech	perforate	perf
medicine cabinet	MC	perpendicular	perp
medium	med	pet cock	PC
membrane	memb	phase	ph
men's room	MR	pi	π
metal	met.	piece	pc
mezzanine	mezz	pint	pt
millimeter, millimeters	mm	place	PL
minimum	min	plaster	plas
minute (time)	min	plate	pl
minute (angular measure)	(′)	plate glass	Pl Gl
miscellaneous	misc	platform	plat.
model	mod	plumbing	plum.
molding	mldg	point	pt
monitor	mon	point of tangency	PT
motor generator	MG	polish	pol
mounting	mtg	porch	P
national	natl	position	pos
National Board of Fire Underwriters	NBFU	pound, pounds	lb
National Bureau of Standards	NBS	pounds per square inch	psi
National Electrical Code	NEC	poured concrete	P/C
National Fire Protection Association	NFPA	power	pwr
National Forest Products Association	NFPA	precast	prect
nickel	ni	prefabricated	prefab
nipple	nip.	property	prop.
nominal	nom	pull chain	PC
normal	nor.	push button	PB
north	N	quantity	qty
northeast	NE	quarry	qry
northwest	NW	quarry tile base	QTB
number	No.	quarry tile floor	QTF
octagon	oct	quarry tile roof	QTR
office	off.	quart, quarts	qt
on center	oc	radial	rad
opening	opg	radiator enclosure	rad encl
opposite	opp	radio	R

radius	r or rad	soil pipe	sp
random	rdm	solder	sld
range	R	south	S
receptacle	recp	southeast	SE
recirculate	recirc	southwest	SW
rectangle	rect	speaker	spkr
reducer	red.	specification	spec
reflector	refl	sprinkler	spr
refrigerator	ref	square	sq
registor	reg	square foot, feet	sq ft
reinforce	reinf	stained	stnd
remove	rem	staggered	stag.
repair	rep	stainless steel	sst
required	reqd	stairs	st
return	ret	stairway	stwy
revision	rev	stanchion	stan
revolutions per minute	rpm	standard	std
right hand	RH	Standard Wire Gauge	SWG
riser	R	standpipe	SP
rivet	riv	steel	stl
road	rd	sterilizer	ster
roof	rf	stiffener	stiff.
room	rm	stirrup	stir.
rough	rgh	stock	stk
round	rnd	stone	stn
Royal Architectural Institute		storage	stg
of Canada	RAIC	storage closet	St Cl
rubber	rub.	storm water	St W
saddle	sad.	street	St
safe working pressure	SWP	structural	str
safety	saf	substitute	sub
scale	sc	sump pit	SP
schedule	sch	superintendent	supt
screw	scr	supersede	supp
screwed	scd	supplement	suppl
scupper	scup	supply	sup
scuttle	S	support	suppt
seamless	smls	surface one side one edge	s1s1e
second (time)	sec	surfaced and matched	S&M
second (angular measure)	(″)	suspend	susp
section	sect	suspended ceiling	susp clg
self-closing	SC	switch	sw
service	serv	switchboard	swbd
setscrew	ss	symbol	sym
sewer	sew.	system	sys
sheathing	shthg	tangent	tan.
sheet	sh	technical	tech
ship lap	shlp	tee	T
shower	sh	telegraph	tlg
shutoff valve	sov	telephone	tel
siding	sdg	temperature	temp
sill cock	sc	template	templ
Simplified Practice		tensile strength	ts
(Recommendations)	SPR	terminal	term
sink	SK	terra-cotta	TC
slate	sl	terrazzo	ter
sleeve	slv	thermometer	therm
slop sink	Ss	thermostat	thermo
socket	soc	thick, thickness	thk

thousand	**M**	volume	**vol**
thousand pounds	**kip**	wall vent	**WV**
thread	**thd**	warehouse	**whse**
toilet	**T**	washing machine	**WM**
tongue and groove	**T&G**	washroom	**WR**
top, bottom, and sides	**TB&S**	water	**w**
transformer	**trans**	water closet	**WC**
transom	**t**	waterproofing	**wp**
tread	**tr**	watertight	**wt**
turnbuckle	**trnbkl**	watt, watts	**w**
two shelves	**2 sh**	watt-hour	**whr**
typewriter	**trpw**	waxed	**wxd**
typical	**typ**	weather stripping	**WS**
ultimate	**ult**	weatherproof	**wp**
Underwriters Laboratories	**UL**	weep hole	**wh**
unfinished	**unfin**	weight	**wt**
United States Standard	**USS**	west	**W**
United States Standard Gauge	**USSG**	wide flange	**WF**
unit heater	**uh**	width	**wth**
urinal	**ur**	window	**wdw**
utility room	**UR**	wire glass	**wgl**
vacuum	**vac**	with	**w/**
valve box	**vb**	without	**w/o**
vanishing point	**vp**	women's rest room	**WRR**
vaporproof	**vap prf**	wood	**wd**
variable	**var**	wood frame	**wf**
varnish	**varn**	working pressure	**wp**
velocity	**vel**	wrought	**wrt**
vent, ventilator	**V**	wrought iron	**WI**
ventilation	**vent.**	yard, yards	**yd**
vertical	**vert**	year	**yr**
vestibule	**vest.**	yellow	**yel**
vitreous	**vit**	zinc	**z**
volt, volts,	**v**	zodiac	**zod**

a final word

When you have studied the preceding chapters and completed to the satisfaction of your instructors all of the exercises as outlined, we believe that you will be qualified to start work as a beginner or junior draftsman. Your next objective is to apply for such a position in an architect's office or in a firm employing architectural draftsmen.

With the aid of your instructor, select samples of the drawings which you made for Chaps. 12 to 15 and 17, and include at least one ink tracing on cloth to show to prospective employers. When applying for a position, present a neat appearance and wear a jacket and tie. If you are required to fill out an application blank, print the answers carefully. This will be an indication of your ability to letter. An application carelessly filled out is liable to be quickly discarded or filed away without further consideration.

Do not be discouraged easily when seeking a position, but be prepared to call at many offices in order to find an opening. Keep in mind that there is always an opportunity somewhere for the beginner.

Before you finished your course of study, no doubt you began to think about what sort of work you would be called upon to do after you started in your first position. In most cases, as a beginner, you will be assigned to work with a more experienced draftsman, who will direct your work and instruct you in the general routine of the office. If you are assigned to a group, the group leader will assign and direct the work. Nearly all projects are carried out by a number of draftsmen working together as a team. Therefore, try to cooperate with your group leader and the other members of the group, and do not be afraid to put forth a little extra effort to help along the work. In offices where the architect has need for only one or two draftsmen, you may receive instructions directly from the architect. In any event, everyone will realize that you are a beginner, and if you are a willing worker, you will receive help and encouragement from the more experienced workers around you.

Each draftsman furnishes his own instruments, triangles, scales, lettering guide, and other small tools. Expendable supplies, such as drawing paper, vellum, tracing cloth, pencils, erasers, and ink, are supplied by the employer. The office equipment will include drafting tables, stools, T squares or parallel straight edges, and in some offices drafting machines. Special curves, splines, ducks, beam compass, erasing machines, and mechanical lettering sets, such as Leroy, Unitech, or Wrico devices, will also be considered as office equipment in nearly all drafting rooms.

bibliography

Blake, Arthur, J. Ralph Dalzell, and Gilbert Townsend: "Architectural and Building Trades Dictionary," American Technical Society, Chicago, 1955.

Goodban, William T., and Jack J. Hayslett: "Architectural Drawing and Planning," McGraw-Hill Book Company, New York, 1964.

Graham, Frank D: "Mason and Builders Guides," Theo. Audel & Co., New York, 1963.

———:"Carpenter and Builders Guides," Theo. Audel & Co., New York, 1965.

Halse, Albert O.: "Architectural Rendering," McGraw-Hill Book Company, New York, 1960.

Harris, Norman C.: "Modern Air Conditioning Practice," McGraw-Hill Book Company, New York, 1959.

Helper, Donald E., and Paul I. Wallach: "Architecture Drafting and Design," McGraw-Hill Book Company, New York, 1965.

Kidder, Frank E., and Harry Parker: "Architects and Builders Handbook," John Wiley & Sons, Inc., New York, 1954.

Merritt, Frederick S. (ed.): "Building Construction Handbook," 2d ed., McGraw-Hill Book Company, New York, 1965.

National Electric Code, National Fire Protection Association, Boston, 1962.

Norling, Ernest: "Perspective Made Easy," The Macmillan Company, New York, 1939.

Ramsey, Charles G., and Harold R. Sleeper: "Architectural Graphic Standards," 5th ed., John Wiley & Sons, Inc., New York, 1956.

Steel Construction Manual, American Institute of Steel Construction, New York, 1956.

Uniform Plumbing Code, Western Plumbing Officials Association, Los Angeles, 1958.

index